Servants of the Grail

The real-life characters of the Grail legend identified

First published by O-Books, 2009
O-Books is an imprint of John Hunt Publishing Ltd., Laurel House, Station Approach,
Alresford, Hants, SO24 9JH, UK
office1@o-books.net
www.o-books.com

For distributor details and how to order please visit the 'Ordering' section on our website.

ISBN: 978 1 84694 155 9

A CIP catalogue record for this book is available from the British Library.

Design: Stuart Davies

Printed and bound by CPI Group (UK) Ltd, Croydon, CR0 4YY

Servants of the Grail

The real-life characters of the Grail legend identified

Philip Coppens

Winchester, UK
Washington, USA

CONTENTS

To Daan,
who began to write his own story,
when this story ended.

Acknowledgements

Not a single person lives in isolation, and no human effort is ever done by just one single individual. This book is no exception to this rule. Special thanks are in order to André Douzet. His research, in other areas, laid the foundation of a gigantic puzzle, into which this piece of research slots perfectly.

I would like to thank Geoff Potts for his valuable initial feedback, which greatly helped me in distilling the essence of the story. A researcher's mission is to make sense of the facts, and Geoff's down to earth "no-nonsense please" approach forced me to do just that.

A small group of dedicated researchers have helped along the way. Amongst these, special mention needs to go to Jérôme Landgräfe. I hope that in the years to come, we will see much work from his own pen in the many fields of his interest. Special mention also goes to "Isaac ben Jacob and team" – a veritable team with no name, but with a lot of wisdom and knowledge.

Herman Hegge and I have worked together for more than a decade on various projects. So far, it has been an absolute joy and I hope it will continue for many more years. Specifically, he was an excellent travel companion to, in and from San Juan de la Peña and Jaca – despite the billions of roundabouts we had to negotiate to get there, and which in the end got on both our nerves.

Others that need to be thanked include: Samantha Frye; Andrew Gough; Corjan de Raaf; Odile Martinez; Daniel Libotte; Nathalie Dal Zovo; Shawnna Connelly; Ira Einhorn; Mark Pilkington; Jonothon Boulter; Guy Patton; Jacob Slavenburg; Klaas Van Urk; Sol "Aris" Volkov; Stan Hall; Jack Sarfatti; John & Joy Millar; Chris "Rat" Millar; John Ritchie; Duncan Roads; David & Jennifer Hatcher-Childress; Andrew & Sue Collins; Philippe Canal; Cris Winter; Marcus Allen; James & Lucinda Stokes; Ian Richardson; Mark Oxbrow; Willem & Hendrine Zitman; Iris Douzet; Maurice Monnot; René Mayer; René Abet; Jean-Luc

Chaumeil; Jean-Louis and Jeanine Monere; Alan Scott; Chantal Raillère; Dominique Dartigue-Peyron; Patrice Chaplin; Simon Cox; Colin Geddes; Tom, Kathleen & Daan Coppens; my parents and family. If I have left anyone out, my sincerest apologies.

> "I am a writer of histories. Sooner or later I will have to set myself to putting down the record [...] [Being told to therefore alter certain key aspects and people from the account, he continues:] It won't cost you much to alter events slightly; you will say you were helped [...]. Yes, I know, it's not the truth, but in a great history little truths can be altered so that the greater truth emerges [...]. And further, would you like to put into the heads of your future readers the notion that a Grasal [Grail] exists, up there amid the snow and ice, and the kingdom of Prester John in the remote lands? Who knows how many lunatics would start wandering endlessly, for centuries and centuries?"
>
> Umberto Eco, *Baudolino,* p. 520-1

Introduction

The Grail. Between 1190 and 1240, it formed the central theme of a series of literary works that spoke of, and appealed to, a new social class, that of the knights and warriors and the adventures they encountered on their travels. In recent decades, it unleashed Indiana Jones on one of his death-defying treasure hunts and was the central ingredient of Dan Brown's *The Da Vinci Code,* one of the biggest bestselling novels ever.[1]

For Richard Barber, in *The Holy Grail: The History of a legend,* "it is, in all its forms, a construct of the creative imagination".[2] However, for dozens of other authors, the Grail is not a literary invention, but a veritable treasure, out there, somewhere. Unfortunately, in general, studies trying to identify and trace the physical Grail have taken on flights of fancy. The Grail has been linked with countries from the Middle East to America, as well as with the persecuted Cathars and even extra-terrestrial beings. It has been labelled a code word for the Ark of the Covenant, after the Templars allegedly transported it from the Middle East to a new hiding place in France. Today, "what is the Grail?" is no longer asked and instead, we are repeatedly told – often by these authors seeking the Grail – that we should speak about "a Grail" – which they of course have found. The Grail, today, can be anything to anyone, and is no longer – if it ever was – a precise object, but a word that should be written in lower case – grail: a precious object, or an ambition that one tries to attain, often with great difficulty.

The first person to write on the Grail was Chrétien de Troyes, in *le Conte du Graal* (The Story of the Grail), between 1180 and 1191. Interestingly, Chrétien refers to his object not as "the Grail", but as "un graal", "a grail", suggesting the word was used, in its earliest literary context, as a common noun – and that there were indeed more than one.

The basic Grail account opens with a young man, Perceval, encountering knights and realising he wants to be one. Despite his mother's objections, the boy trains for the knighthood and begins a series of travels. On one such trip, he comes across the Fisher King, who invites him to stay at his castle. While there, he witnesses a strange procession in which young men and women carry magnificent objects from one chamber to another, passing before him at each course of the meal. First comes a young man carrying a bleeding lance, then two boys carrying candelabras. Finally, a beautiful young girl emerges bearing an elaborately decorated "grail".

For whatever reason, Chrétien de Troyes left us with an incomplete poem, numbering 9000 lines of text; he never explained what "a grail" was. Though this non-definition might be seen as evidence that in his days, everyone knew what "a grail" was, in fact, that was not the case. The appeal of his work came, in part, from the unknown object that had obviously inspired this wandering knight, an object used in a setting that was unlike anything he had ever seen.

In the following years, there were there a series of "continuations", written by four, sometimes anynomous, writers, which took the total length of the "Grail account" to ca. 40,000 lines of texts. Meanwhile, others wrote prequels to the story, such as the *Elucidation Prologue,* which focused on the family and descent of Perceval, emphasing that the relationship between the Grail and certain bloodlines is nothing new to *The Da Vinci Code.*

It was, in short, the start of a literary tradition, in which the Grail was to become the central theme. With a literary existence of more than 800 years, there has thus been ample time to write on the subject – and that time has not been wasted to define and redefine the nature of the Grail.

The most defining work, however, was composed almost immediately after Chrétien had finished his work, was written between 1191 and 1202, and was the work of Robert de Boron, who made "a grail" into the "Holy Grail". In his verse romance *La grant estoire dou Graal,* "The Great History of the Grail", more popularly known as *Joseph d'Arimathie,* the biblical character of Joseph of Arimathea acquires the chalice of the Last Supper to collect Christ's blood upon His removal from the cross. Joseph is later thrown in prison, where Christ visits him and explains the mysteries of the blessed cup. Upon his release, Joseph gathers his in-laws and other followers and travels to the west, and founds a dynasty of Grail keepers that eventually will include Perceval.

De Boron's version has become the standard Grail account, and it is the quest for this dynasty of Grail keepers, and the object they protected, that has become an enduring Quest for the Holy Grail, which allegedly even preoccupied the leaders of Nazi Germany, and Heinrich Himmler in particular.

Though the interest of the Nazis in magical talismans like the Holy Grail and the Ark of the Covenant has almost become as mythical as the objects they chased themselves, it is nevertheless well-documented that in the 1930s, the head of the SS, Heinrich Himmler personally oversaw a series of quests, including that by a young SS officer, Otto Rahn, who went in search of the Grail in Southern France, near the Cathar castle of Montségur. Rahn's two books on the subjects, including *Kreuzzug gegen den Gral*[3], were used by Himmler when he visited – inspected – the region in October 1940, when Himmler was in Barcelona while Hitler was holding a conference with the newly installed Spanish dictator, General Francisco Franco. Hitler believed he could persuade Franco to join the war on Germany's side, but whereas Hitler was talking politics, Himmler specifically took in the various castles and locations Rahn had mentioned.

Montserrat Rico Góngora in *The Desecrated Abbey* states that Himmler visited the famous Montserrat Abbey near Barcelona, where he thought he would find the Grail which Jesus Christ was said to have used to consecrate the Last Supper. According to Góngora, Himmler was also inspired by a folk song from Catalonia, the north-eastern region in which Montserrat lies, which has a cryptic reference to a "mystical font of life" situated in the area.

Hitler's right-hand man thought that if he could lay claim to the Holy Grail, it would help Germany win the war and give him supernatural powers. Of course, the relationship between the King of the Jews and the superiority of the Aryan race seem a cumbersome match, so it might not come as a surprise that Himmler shared the outlandish belief with other leading Nazis that Jesus Christ was actually descended from Aryan stock.[4]

Himmler left Montserrat empty-handed.

Though often linked with the cup of the Last Supper, the precise nature of the Grail is in origin undefined. Even though Chrétien de Troyes spoke of "a grail", there is no definitive answer as to what this grail was. This has meant that the undefined Grail can be used as a deus ex machina to try and give some credibility to an author's otherwise poor line of reasoning when setting out his theory, whether fictional or not. Dare we suggest that this also happened in Dan Brown's *The Da Vinci Code,* where the Grail was imaginatively redefined as the vulva, the "V shape", an original, though not ingenious solution to the author's plot.

It has left us with a forest of grails, in which "the Grail" can no longer be distinguished. Like Himmler on his quest for the Holy Grail, no-one who has gone in search for the true origins of the Grail, has ever been successful; it has proven to be perhaps the most arduous of Grail quests.

Still, one man, in the decades following Chrétien de Troyes' account, took it upon himself to answer what the Grail was. Wolfram von Eschenbach is now known as the author of *Parzival,* the work that inspired Richard Wagner's famous opera *Parsifal,* which in literary circles is often described as "the first extant work in German to have as its subject the Holy Grail", as well as taking up a unique niche within the Grail literature, as it doesn't fit in any of the categories the scholars have created. The reason for its unique position is that Wolfram, unlike many of his contemporaries, did not elaborate on Chrétien's story, but expressed disdain for it, labelling it erroneous in many of its details, and stated that he would rectify these errors in *Parzival*. In short, Wolfram claimed the Grail was real, and he knew more about it. He claimed he knew because he had been in contact with a source, "Kyot", from Provence, who was able to furnish him with "the truth". Wolfram claimed that he was able to identify the real characters of the Grail story, as well as identify the true nature of the Grail: a magical stone.

We can compare Wolfram's situation very much with the modern example of *The Da Vinci Code.* Upon the publication, and especially the success, of Dan Brown's book, dozens of other novels appeared that treaded the same themes, some with more success than others. Brown's book also saw a series of "guides", that enhanced upon the organisations, places and people worked into the book, and debated their historical veracity, or not. Amazingly, this would lead to official statements from the Vatican, as well as a high-profile courtcase in which two non-fiction authors, Michael Baigent and Richard Leigh, co-authors of *Holy Blood, Holy Grail,* sued Brown's publisher for copyright infringement.

A series of non-fictional works, specifically on the Grail and Mary Magdalene, also saw re-editions, often with new titles that included the keyword "code" in it, and some which even used the same font and cover design that had made *The Da Vinci Code* stand out in the bookstalls.

Imagine the task of Wolfram von Eschenbach, who amidst this frenzy is trying to argue that Chrétien got it wrong, but that he knows the truth. It is, of course, not an easy task and it does bear some resemblance to some claims made by authors today that they "knew" the truth about Dan Brown's novel – one of whom then adopted the pen-name of Dan Green!

In retrospect, Wolfram failed miserably; he was unable to persuade Western Europe that he had definitively answered what the Grail was. Today, most scholars even doubt the veracity of his source Kyot, believing instead that Kyot was a literary device invented by Wolfram to explain his deviations from Chrétien's storyline. Joseph Goering, when discussing Wolfram, thus calls his work "the most elaborate and inventive retelling of Chrétien's story", to add later that the book illustrates "the fecundity of imagination" of Wolfram.[5]

Nobody, it seems, believed Wolfram when he was claiming to speak the truth. Instead, he was held to be "just" another writer.

Only centuries later, would he be saved from this doom, by being labelled "an oddity", if only because he did not embrace the Christian setting that had become the standard frame of reference into which one spoke about the Grail – the Holy Grail.

Today, the Grail is largely seen as a literary invention, but this may be a serious mistake. For one, Wolfram on Eschenbach never wrote fiction; he was known for writing family histories – non-fiction. Noting that he stated that when addressing the Grail, he was correcting errors and was writing a factual account, there is an obvious blatant problem that is never addressed by any of the scholars: by all accounts, Wolfram was a non-fiction writer, who set out to write a non-fiction account about the Grail.

Furthermore, Wolfram is very specific, not only identifying his source as Kyot, but stating that Kyot based the origin of the Grail on two documents. Despite such information, the experts state they have been unable to identify who Kyot was (which is, of course, their problem, not Wolfram's), and hence they have treated Kyot as a literary invention by Wolfram, or is mentioned, without any further explanation.

Though this work too has not been able to conclusively identify Kyot (something that alas the test of time might have altogether rendered impossible), this work does show and prove that Wolfram's story is based on two documents, exactly as he said.

In short, Wolfram's Grail story was his rendition of Kyot's historical detective work. One of the documents on which the Grail story is based is a family history, which was the history of Perceval, the leader of the family who came to possess the Grail. The other document is a pagan document, thought to be absent from Christian medieval Europe, containing a pagan doctrine that required an initiation… hence, a brotherhood.

Hence, what the "Grail quest" set forth in this book has

uncovered, is threefold. First, there is no reason to doubt that the Grail was indeed a magical stone. Second, that this stone was in the possession of the Aragon royal family that lived on the southern slopes of the Pyrenees – the general region where Rahn and Himmler explored. That this family had created a series of initiations and rites, linked with the worship of this object, and which we will refer to as the "Grail Brotherhood". That the real Perceval, of French descent, was welcomed into this Brotherhood because of his family ties to the Aragon royal family. Third, that the Aragon royal family initiated a project, in which they hoped to transform Europe into a "Grail Kingdom": unite it, and transform into a theocracy, in which the unifying power – object – would be the Grail itself. That their ambition failed (quite early on too), might have contributed to the problems Wolfram faced in convincing the people of Western Europe that he was nevertheless right. But right, it seems by all accounts, he was… and the Grail was – is – real.

Chapter 1: A Grail Cup?

It may come as a surprise to learn that for the Vatican, the Holy Grail exists, and its location is established. In 1982, Pope John Paul II even kissed the cup during a Mass in which he used it, as did his successor Pope Benedict XVI on 9 July 2006. No, he did not do this in some secret underground vault of Vatican City; the "official Holy Grail" was used in a public ceremony, and despite what one might assume, faced with the hundreds of books on the topic, no secrecy or intrigue surrounds it.

The Grail in question is in the Cathedral of Saint Mary in the Spanish city of Valencia. Here, the former chapterhouse contains an artifact, the Holy Chalice, which is believed to have been the official papal chalice used in the early days of Christianity, when only the pope was allowed to perform Mass in public – and used this chalice.

The chalice disappeared in Rome in the 3rd century AD, but apparently made its reapparition in the 12th century in San Juan de la Peña, north-west of Valencia, in the Spanish region of the Aragon, the "country of the troubadours", which stretched from the Spanish town of Valencia to the French city of Marseilles – the region where Rahn and Himmler, and so many others, came in search of the Holy Grail.

The Valencia Cup

The oldest document about the Holy Chalice, or the Valencia Cup as it is also known, dates from 1399 – recent, both from the perspective of the Grail accounts that date to the latter decades of the 12th century, and even more so if we need to establish a 2000 year history if this cup was used by Jesus at the Last Supper.

The document, dated 26 September 1399, is from King Martin El Human, asking for the cup to be brought to the chapel of the Royal Palace at the Alfajeria in Zaragoza.[6] Some argue that the abbot of San Juan de la Peña was in fact forced to hand the object over, and that the king was supported in this endeavour by none other than Avignon Pope Benedict XIII, born Pedro Martínez de Luna, who was an Aragonese – and well-acquainted with the Aragon kings. A notarial deed records the act: "Cáliz de piedra en el cual Ntro. Sr. Jesucristo consagró su preciosa sangre", or the "Stone Chalice where Our Lord Jesus Christ consecrated his precious blood". The Valencia Cup was exchanged for a gold cup and if this cup was indeed the Holy Chalice, then it is clear that the abbot of San Juan de la Peña got little in return for parting with this precious relic.

The Valencia Cup is a composite of several elements, the central aspect being the "vase", identified as the real and original Grail, which at one moment in time was enlarged into a cup – the Valencia Cup.

The artefact is speculated to be a possible artefact of the Graeco-Roman period from the Near East, later set in 14th century Spanish jewellery mountings. The vase is 9.5 cm of diameter, 7 cm tall, with a 5 cm diameter at the bottom, mounted in a double handled basis, thus making a cup that stands 17 cm tall. There is an Arabic inscription on the basis, perhaps a clue of the Cordobese origin of the reworking of the vase into a cup.[7]

Hans Wilhelm Shaefer[8] transcribed the inscription as ALBST SLJS, which he interpreted as "Al-labsit As-Silis", thus linking this with the name of the Grail as it appears in Wolfram von Eschenbach's *Parzival*, who described his Grail Stone as "lapis exilis". Furthermore, Wolfram located the Grail in the very region where San Juan de la Peña is located.

If the hiatus between 1399 and 1210, when Wolfram wrote his Grail account, could be filled, then it is clear that this cup might indeed be the Grail – and the question needs to be asked why so many books have been written about the mystery of the Grail, when the answer seems to be this straightforward.

The answer, of course, is that things are not as obvious as they seem. Though there are reports from the keepers of the Grail in Valencia that date the relic as far back as 14 December 1134, the quoted documents themselves have not been found. A document of 1135 does mention a chalice being exchanged between San Juan de la Peña for a charter from the king, but this is nothing more than a customary transaction and is not a reference to the Valencia Cup.[9]

Suggestive evidence that San Juan de la Peña did *not* possess the Cup of the Last Supper can be seen earlier in the 14th century, when in 1322, Jaime II of Aragon sent a letter to the sultan of Egypt. In it, he asks the sultan to send him the chalice used by Christ at the Last Supper, which belonged to the sultan. If San Juan de la Peña indeed possessed the Cup of Christ, it meant that Jaime II already had it – and why would he ask the sultan of Egypt for it? It is a difficult to answer question.[10]

Though apparently nothing further seems to have come of this prospective acquisition, however, by 1399, the kings of Aragon apparently did possess the Holy Chalice. It suggests that the acquisition from the Sultan either did not leave traces in historical records, or that the transaction of 1399 is a fake. If, indeed, the kings of Aragon desperately wanted to have the Holy Chalice in their possession, and the sultan did not want to sell it, then perhaps they merely bought or manufactured another artefact, pretended to exchange it from the abbot of San Juan de la Peña, invented a prehistory for it, and the lie could be sold.

Despite its dubious origins, the Valencia Cup todat has its own protectors, the Brotherhood of Valencia, or the Brotherhood of the Holy Grail. Showing that even Grail protectors have entered the modern era, the organisation established an internet presence in early 1999. There, the Brotherhood identifies their cup as the Grail of the Last Supper and downplays the doubts that exist over the artefact.

With Wolfram, they share in common that they argue that the protector of this cup was not Joseph of Arimathea, as many popular Grail accounts claim. Joseph was the wealthy business who allowed Jesus' body to be buried in his tomb, from which the Son of God is believed to have risen on the third day. Specifically in modern times, Joseph of Arimathea has been woven into a travelogue in which the Grail was taken from Jerusalem, onwards to France and England, with the English town of Glastonbury claiming he came to their town, carrying with him the Grail – to deposit it in a well at Glastonbury Tor.

Rather than upgrading a minor biblical category like Joseph of Arimathea, the Brotherhood claims it was St Peter, the founding father of the Christianity himself, who sent it from Jerusalem to Rome, where the cup remained until the middle of the 3rd century. Then it was sent to Spain for safe-keeping, where it began a perilous journey, sojourning in San Juan de la Peña, before ending up in Valencia. Still according to the Brotherhood, the actual cup was carved of agate, in Egypt, between the 4th and 1st century BC – making it the correct framework for this cup to be used by Jesus in Jerusalem in ca. 30-50 AD.

As good and as logical as this "certificate of authenticity" may sound, the story is nevertheless unsupported by historical evidence, something it does share with the Grail tradition that has been built on top of Joseph of Arimathea. As a consequence, the earliest proof for the Valencia Cup remains 1399 AD.

However, the history of the cup of San Juan de la Peña after 1399 is well documented. Upon King Martin's death, in September 1410, it was found in the inventory of his properties in Barcelona. In Valencia, Martin V's successor, Alphonse V el Magnanimo, transferred it to his Royal Palace in Valencia about 1424. His brother, Juan, King of Navarra, then presented it to the Valencia Cathedral on 14 March, 1437.[11] It only left the cathedral on two occasions: during the Independence War (March 1809 to September 1813), when it was moved to Alicante and then to the towns of Ibiza and Palma de Mallorca; the second occasion was during the National Uprising (21 July 1936 to 9 April 1939), when it was hidden both in Valencia and in the village of Carlet. At the end of the Spanish Civil War, the "Santo Caliz" returned to the Cathedral, which had been restored after the devastations it had suffered in the uprisings. When Himmler came to Spain in 1940, he could have seen this Holy Chalice on display in the restored Cathedral. That he did not, suggests he was not interested – or convinced – in this Holy Grail.

The impressive sounding Brotherhood of the Holy Grail itself was created by Marcelino Olaechea in 1951, with Pope John XXIII awarding indulgence to pilgrims that went to Valencia to pray to the Grail in 1959.[12] In 1979, the "Capilla del Santo Caliz" was restored, welcoming Pope John Paul II to Valencia in 1982. Here, he kissed the "Santo Caliz" twice and used it in the mass, as did Pope Benedict XVI in 2006. On the occasion of the 1982 papal visit, the diocese of Valencia Cathedral made an exact replica, created by the goldsmith Francisco Pajaron-Andreu, and donated it to the Vatican. The replica was made with identical materials and the agate gem had been imported from Germany.

Truth... or dare?

For the Vatican, this is the Grail, though it has never gone as far as proclaim this from the Papal balcony in St Peter's Square. With so much controversy about the Grail, the Valencia Cup being recognised as the Holy Grail is something they will neither deny nor confirm – though from the available evidence, it is clear that they definitely embrace the conclusion.

The question is therefore whether they are correct, and whether this is indeed the cup that was used by Jesus two millennia ago. In 1960, Antonio Beltran, head of the Department of Archaeology of the Universidad de Zaragoza, made an exhaustive study of the Santo Caliz.[13] He concluded that "there is no evidence against the possibility this Chalice would have been used by Jesus Christ at the Last Supper". This statement has been used and reworked to suggest that this is indeed the Grail. But it is clear that Beltran merely suggests that it could be the Holy Grail – and there are many other cups in existence about which Beltran could have reached the same conclusion.

Furthermore, the legend of the Valencia Cup sits in the unique position that it claims that the Holy Grail is the cup of the Last Supper, but that it disagrees with Robert de Boron's story, which emphasises the role of Joseph of Arimathea.

From archaeological and literary evidence, it is believed that the Holy Grail was brought to the monastery of San Juan de la Peña on the occasion of the adoption of the Roman Liturgy, the formal public rituals of religious worship as promoted by the Roman Catholic Church. It is this alleged source that identifies the presence of the Grail in the monastery on 14 December 1134.

Penetrating even further back in time, its history becomes even coarser. Even the Brotherhood admits that it "probably" remained at the Jaca Cathedral before. The evidence? A "mark" on the Sixtus capitol of that cathedral. But as to its whereabouts between the 3rd and 8th century, when it is assumed the cup arrived in Huesca, there is only a legend.[14]

This legend states that while it was in Rome, where it was used as the Papal Chalice, where Pope Sixtus II in ca. 251, gave it to St Lawrence, the first deacon of the Roman Church, before being martyred. However, Lawrence too would soon die a martyr; the saint was reputedly burned to death on a gridirion, halfway through his odeal apparently uttering the words "Turn me. I am done on this side".

The legend then argues that before his death Lawrence, who was of Spanish origins, sent the Holy Grail to Huesca, allegedly to his parents' farmhouse on the outskirts of Huesca. A painting in the Basilica of St. Lawrence Outside the Walls in Rome, built on top of the Saint's alleged martyrdom and one of Rome's seven great pilgrimage centres, portrayed how he gives the Grail to a Spanish soldier, but the painting was destroyed in the Allied bombardment of Rome's nearby railyards in July 1943.

For the Grail novice, this evidence might seem, despite some speculation that is always required when tackling ancient accounts, impressive. To a more seasoned reader of Grail mythology, it will be clear that if we take the "evidence" of the cup's history before ca. 1100, it is just one in a long list of contenders for the genuine Grail. It is only post 1399, and specifically during the 20th century, that the Valencia Cup has apparently won the recognition as the official Holy Grail.

But this semi-official recognition by the Vatican is the result of careful manipulation, of the Vatican, by those who have tried to ratify the Valencia Cup as the Holy Grail. Though on all accounts it appears that the Vatican supports the identification of this cup as the Grail, it is equally clear that they are somewhat uncomfortable to put their full support behind this identification.

This is best seen in the Pope's visit to Valencia in 1982. The original plan had the Pope say Mass using the Roman canon, using the Valencia Cup, which uses words that identifies the cup being used in Mass with "the" cup of the Last Supper. For those who had fought for the recognition of the Valencia Cup as the true Grail, this would have been the crowning accolade of their quest. It would also mean that for the first time since the mid 3rd century, a Pope had used the Holy Chalice in the manner that it should be used. For sure, for many it would not even have been noticed, but for this pressure group – the Brotherhood – it would symbolise the complete restitution of the Valencia Cup as the "Papal Chalice", with Pope John Paul II continuing what had been interrupted after Sixtus II. However, in a last minute change to the protocol, the Pope did not use the Roman canon and instead opted for a modern mass – in which the cup is not identified with Jesus' cup.

It is a very minor detail, and would have gone unnoticed, but it seems that the Vatican realised that they might not do themselves any favours by embracing the identity of Valencia Cup as the Grail wholesale, just in case someone would later argue that the Valencia Cup is not the Grail at all – and present evidence for that conclusion. It is the same reasoning behind the Vatican's unwillingness to give definitive answers on Marian apparitions, or the Shroud of Turin, or so many other relics: if they get it wrong, they will be the one to loose face. And like God, the Church very much prefers to be perceived as faultless.

The Vatican should not be blamed for its unwillingness to specifically embrace the cup as the Grail. The evidence pre-1100 AD is simply not there – and remains iffy until 1399. For sure, the Valencia Cup comes with a legendary history that suggests it could be the Grail, but again, there are many other cups with similar claims.

Take for example the 12th century chronicler William of Tyre, who stated that the Grail Cup was in the Italian town of Genoa. The "Sacro Catino" had fallen into the hands of Genoese crusaders after the fall of Caesarea in 638 AD. Not only was this the alleged Cup of the Last Supper, it was also said to be a gift of the Queen of Sheba to King Solomon, and created from one giant emerald. The cup arrived in Genoa in 1102 and was installed in the church of St Lawrence, the same deacon whose name appears in the Spanish Grail account. Twelve knights were appointed to protect it and anyone caught on suspicion of trying to touch it – or worse – played with his life.

The history of this cup is well-documented since 1102, but is legendary before that timeframe. A variation of the legend has it that the crusaders found it in a temple in the Lebanese city of Tyre, not Caesarea.

Unlike the Valencia Cup, the Sacro Catino is no longer intact. Taken by Napoleon for scientific analysis, the cup broke, with all but one piece returned to Genoa in 1816 – the missing piece being held in the Louvre in Paris, where it is of course surrounded by those objects, like the Mona Lisa, the played a role in *The Da Vinci Code*. In those days, this Grail was much more popular than the one in San Juan de la Peña, but when the cup broke, it signalled the demise of its popularity. Though it is believed to have been made of glass – not emerald as the legend suggests – had it survived Napoleon's interest, the Genoese would have had a powerful alternative to contest the Valencia Cup with. Now, its scattered remains sit in a Genoese museum, together with the alleged ashes and head of John the Baptist – though it should be noted that Venice claims to hold the head of John the Baptist also, as do many other towns and churches.

The evidence that this is the Holy Grail is not undeniable, it remains the best contender for the crown. That the evidence is far from conclusive, says more about the evidence that surrounds its fellow competitors than anything else. But when one scans the hundreds of modern books on the Grail, few if any have singled out the Valencia Cup for any specific attention. Worse: scant attention has been paid to this cup by those scholars that have specialised in Grail mythology, and even less attention has been paid to the site where the Valencia Cup made its official appearance: San Juan de la Peña, located in the region where Wolfram von Eschenbach said the Grail was located – and where the SS sent its explorers to locate the objects.

The Grail Kingdom

The Pyrenees are an impressive mountain range. They are named after Pyrene (fire in Greek), who was the daughter of Bebryx and was raped by Herakles. Terrified at giving birth to a serpent, she fled to the mountains and was either buried or eaten by wild animals.

For the most part, the main crest forms a massive frontier, with Andorra sandwiched in between. Catalonia and the Basque Country, which are the only two territories extending on both sides of the mountain range. Even in the 21st century, modern infrastructure planners have understood the challenge to link the roads to the south with those of the north. Few major roads cross them – the "autoroutes" prefer crossings into Spain at their lower extrimities – near Perpignan, on the Mediterrenean coast, and Biarritz, on the Atlantic coast. The French autoroute system does connect these two towns, to the north of the Pyrenees, from Perpignan via Carcassonne, Toulouse, Tarbes, Pau and finally Biarritz. There is a more southern route, via Quillan and Foix, which runs parallel to the autoroute section between Narbonne and Toulouse. Even though Foix sits relatively far from the actual Pyrenees, progress along these routes is still, despite the availability of cars, slow and windy when compared with the speeds one can reach on the autoroutes.

This is the general area of Perceval in his quest to the Grail Castle. Perceval's route takes him over the incredible high mountains in the kingdom Brobarz, which has been identified with Ribagorza, in the Aragon province of Huesca, or Sobrabe, equally in Aragon. The "incredible high mountains" are obviously the Pyrenees. Even Perpignan is listed in the Grail account, identified as Pelrapeire, which was ruled by Condwiramur, the niece of the Duke Kyot of Catalonie, obviously Catalonia.

In my first attempt to reach San Juan de la Peña, I had decided to take the route from Pau, dropping almost straight south to Jaca, the closest town to San Juan de la Peña. Having travelled from Perpignan, the distance on the map suggested a relatively short journey, which I estimated at four hours. But an apparent series of endless roundabouts, an apparently endless tunnel and what was in truth a minor road once having crossed into Spain, despite its rather majestic title of "E 07", still meant that the total journey time was in excess of seven hours. On the return leg, it would take more than ten hours, when I opted for the Foix route.

The Pyrenees do not like cars and many impossible passages have indeed been circumvented by the creation of tunnels. But at the same time, the route from Pau to Jaca shows that in ancient times, the voyage would have been much longer in time, but not necessarily more difficult. When on foot or on horse, the Pyrenees do allow for passages – even though their profile from a distant does not suggest this.

Once south of the mountain range, it is remarkable how quickly the landscape changes. The Pyrenees drop as quickly as they rise… Though Jaca is a winter ski resort, you do actually ask where the giant slopes of the Pyrenees have disappeared to. When climbing from Jaca towards San Juan de la Peña, you can see the Pyrenees once again rising in the distance; you know you are climbing, but though the Dutch might consider the ascent to San Juan de le Peña to be steep, any Pyrenean shepherd would laugh in their face about such a – for him ridiculous – suggestion.

The area that I crossed is now widely considered to be the home of the Grail. It acquired that fame largely due to a troubled and often incomprehensible history. In medieval times, when Chrétien was writing his accounts further north, at the court of Champagne, the region just north of the Pyrenees was the stronghold of the Counts of Foix, powerbrokers if ever there were any. They were the local nobles that played an important role in that other conundrum that has contributed to the mythology of the Holy Grail: the Cathar heresy.

The link between the counts of Foix and Catharism is best illustrated by Esclarmonde de Foix, the daughter of Roger Bernard I, Count of Foix, who became a prominent figure in Catharism in 13th century France.

Esclarmonde was widowed in 1200, which apparently gave her the liberty to turn to the Cathar Church. She was elevated to the ranks of the Perfects – Catharism allowed women to achieve high positions in the Church – by the Cathar bishop Guilhabert de Castres, in Fanjeaux in 1204. The ceremony was conducted in the presence of her brother, Raymond-Roger de Foix, Count of Foix.

She settled in Pamiers, where she took part in the conference that was held there in 1207 and which was the last debate between the Cathars and the Roman Catholic Church, represented by Dominic Guzman. The following year, Pope Innocent III launched the Albigensian Crusade against the Cathars.

It was specifically Otto Rahn who identified the Cathars of Montségur as the last known holders of the Grail – which he apparently linked with a magical emerald – a stone – that had fallen from the sky, and which in some popular accounts was with Lucifer's Third Eye. As Lucifer has fallen from heaven, as Mankind had attained its Original Sin, this eye had solidified into an emerald. Those who possessed it, seem to have had a relic of the Fall, which was also seen as a hope for a better future.

The Cathars are normally described as a "heretical sect" that lived in this region. But in truth, Catharism was not a Christian heresy, but an altogether different religion, which offered a powerful alternative to Christianity. It had the support of the local lords, this at time when the region had just been reconquered from several centuries of Muslim dominance. When the Church saw that Catharism was rapidly spreading from this area across Western Europe, it decided to organise a crusade – the first carried out in Europe, and against Europeans.

Béziers was one of the first towns the crusaders encountered. Details of the Siege of Béziers were written down by William of Tudela. He wrote that after seeing the crusading army settle, which stretched nearly a league around the city, the people of

Béziers remained confident: "The army won't last a fortnight," they said confidently, "They haven't the provisions for such a mob!" It was the height of a summer's day, with vast plumes of dust swirling on the plain beneath the town.

Then, a messenger from the encroaching army carried a list of the 222 Béziers inhabitants that were suspected of being Cathars and which it wanted to see surrendered, to the town wall. In the name of God, these named and known heretics were to be surrendered immediately, or God's mercy would bow to God's wrath. The leaders of the town replied that these written demands carried little more weight "than of a peeled apple": "We would rather drown in a sea of tears than alter our beliefs", is how another chronicler records their reply.

Apparently not willing or unable to carry out any other form of diplomacy, the papal forces decided to burn everyone in the city. When some of the crusaders questioned the validity of this operation, as 15,000 innocent people would die only to arrest 222 people whose sole crime was not to believe in the Christian God, they were informed that even though all were to be killed, heretics and Christians alike, "God would sort out his own".

Various other towns, like Carcassonne and Narbonne, heard about the drama that had befallen Béziers and complied with the demands of the papal troops. As each town capitulated, the Cathar priests, known as Perfects, fled, literally running into the Pyrenees, the chain of hills that had been named after the Greek word for fire, to escape their own certain fate, which would be death by burning. Approximately 200 Cathars eventually had taken refuge in the castle of Montségur, when in 1243, the 10,000 strong papal troops laid siege to the castle.

In March 1244, the Cathars finally surrendered and approximately 220 were burned at the foot of the pog when they refused to renounce their faith. Though often said to be a legend, it is in fact quite well documented that in the days prior to the fall of the fortress, several Cathars descended down the steep slopes of the pog. Of course, it was rumoured that their escape was linked with the removal of a mysterious treasure. Seeing how precarious and dangerous the descent was, this treasure must have had minimal weight and dimensions.

While the nature and fate of the object they may or may not have been carrying with them has never been identified, there has been much speculation as to what it might have consisted of; the Holy Grail is chief amongst them.

It was specifically Otto Rahn who came to Montségur in search of the Grail. Some sources even report that in 1944, on the 700th anniversary of the fall of Montségur, German aircraft were seen in the area directly above Montségur flying in strange formations, either drawing in the sky the sign of the Celtic cross or the swastika.[15]

The southern counterparts of the Counts of Foix, reigning on the southern side of the Pyrenees, were the kings of Aragon, and their powerbase was San Juan de la Peña, which some have seen as the Spanish counterpart of Montségur – and the Grail Castle.

The tourist guidebook makes no qualms about arguing that the monastery of San Juan de la Peña is the "sacred ground where Aragon originated".[16] Around 720, when Spain was invaded by the Muslims, a group of hermits retired to this fabulous location. Perched underneath a rocky overhang, their new home was equipped with a natural shelter against the elements, including an abundant supply of water that trickles or streams from the overhanging rock above.

In 920, count Galindo Aznarez I of Aragon conquered the lands south of the Aragon river and founded a monastery on the land inhabited by the hermits. The Monastery was dedicated to San Julian and Santa Basilisa. Today, the feastday of husband and wife St. Julian and St. Basilissa is celebrated on January 9; they are remembered for their love for their faith that led them to do something heroic: they turned their home into a hospital. This way, they could take care of the sick and the poor who had no one to help them. No doubt, this dedication underlines some of the amibitions of these early monks and their monastery.

The Monastery of San Juan de la Peña itself was created by Sancho el Mayor de Navarra, when he incorporated the existing monastery into a larger series of buildings, and began with the construction of the High Church. Major additions have been, and continue to be, added to the complex.

The oldest part of the construction that remains intact is the "Lower Church", on the ground floor. It was constructed in 920 and was the original church of the complex. On the first floor stands its successor, the High Church of San Juan – the High Church of St John – dedicated in 1094 and built by King Sancho Ramirez, the second king to be buried here. In the middle of three chapels at the end of his High Church stands the Holy Grail – an exact copy of the Valencia Cup as we know it today. It is here, at the time of the building of the Lower and High Church, that the Valencia Cup was said to be: first hidden from Muslim invaders, then held by the Aragonese nobility, until its removal to Zaragoza in 1399.

Next to the High Church is the Pantheon of Nobles, a mausoleum containing the tombs of the Aragon and Navarra nobility. These men followed the example of King Ramiro I of Aragon, the first king to be buried here in the 11th century – hoping that their bodily presence resting in the vicinity of the Valencia Cup would give their soul everlasting peace.

John the Baptist

San Juan de la Peña means Saint John of the Rock. Whenever there is talk of the Grail, there is often a reference to John the Baptist. Some authors, such as Lynn Picknett & Clive Prince in *The Templar Revelation*, the book that Dan Brown identified as being a major inspiration for his *The Da Vinci Code*, have gone as far as to suggest that the Baptist was the real focus of devotion of many of those whom we would label as "Grail seekers".

Picknett & Prince claim that a genuine understanding of the events around Jesus and his Resurrection – or not – survived throughout the ages, untouched by the agendas of the Vatican and other Christian powerbrokers. This, they believe, centred on the knowledge that John the Baptist had been a powerful and popular preacher in the Palestine, whose movement was violently taken over by Jesus, who corrupted John's doctrine, but which was nevertheless able to survive in its original format amongst small groups of adherents, such as the Mandaeans. When contact between the West and the Middle East was re-established at the time of the Crusades, this knowledge made its way to Western Europe, where – they claim – it was implanted as a secret doctrine that ran parallel to (if it was not identical with) the Grail mythology.

The Mandaeans, often called the Christians of Saint John, because they followed John the Baptist, seemed to have followed an ancient form of Gnosticism. They practiced initiation and rituals that were resembled Freemasonry more than it does Christianity as we know it.

They have no Sabbaths, and do not practice circumcision. When they pray they do not turn towards Jerusalem, but towards the north. In their homeland, north is also the direction of the great mountains from which the rivers Tigris and Euphrates flow. The source of these rivers is the World of Light, where God lives and reigns. They believe that through immersions in the "waters of light", they receive a renewal of life from the God. They not only despised Jesus, but also despise the Christian baptismal ceremony because they say that it is performed in dead – still – water.

According to the Mandaeans, the cosmos is made up of two

forces. One is the world of light, located to the north, the other the world of darkness, located to the south. This cosmology reveals their dualist theology, which they shared with other Gnostics and the Cathars. The standard dualistic religious theme speaks of two forces that are in opposition and battle against each other. It is in the fights between the two that the world was created, but without the consent of the ruler of light. Man was created by the forces of darkness, but in every man, there is a "hidden Adam", the soul, which has its origin in the world of light.

Death was the day of deliverance, when the soul left the body, and started on a dangerous journey to the realms of light. It were – of course – only the Mandaeans and other non-sinners that would manage to complete the whole journey — everyone else would end in hell, which was nevertheless not everlasting. At the end of the world, a judgment would be made on who would be wiped out, and who would rise to the realms of light in extremis.

Perhaps the presence of a head of the Baptist and a Grail in the same museum in Genoa is nothing but coincidence. But the same connection between the Grail and John the Baptist exists in San Juan de la Peña, where the Baptist does indeed reign supreme.

Still, it seems his presence is not directly related to the Grail. The local legend states that a young nobleman from Zaragoza was hunting on the slopes of Mount Pano for deer. Chasing the deer, the deer jumped over an edge, with the hunter quick to pray to John the Baptist to save his life. His horse miraculously survived the jump, landing on his feet. Safe at the bottom of the ravine, he saw a small cave, containing a small church dedicated to John the Baptist, containing the body of a hermit, identified as Juan de Atares. This remarkable coincidence – so much so that it seems more legendary than factual – made him choose to embark on a hermetic life of his own, in which he was joined by his brother. The cave, of course, was the site of San Juan de la Peña.

John the Baptist's characteristic is baptism – by water – to wash away the original sin Mankind was said to have acquired at the time of the Fall.[17] In San Juan de la Peña, the presence of an ingenious system of hydraulic engineering is one of the most intriguing aspects of the Monastery that stares the visitor in its face – yet will go unnoticed to most. Even in the middle of summer, water trickles from the rocky overhang down into the cloister, into what has aptly been named "The Fountain". From here, it trickles into a pond, to its left, running behind the wall of the High Church, behind its chapels – and the Grail that was held inside the central one. It then appears on the Lower floor to the left of the Lower Church, as something that could be described as a waterfall. It is a site where coins are thrown into, a tradition similar to the lighting of a candle in a church – to seek a favour of God.

It is a remarkable piece of engineering, with a specific goal: the water descending from the rocky overhang was used to stream through the two churches. The water baptised this site, which is no doubt why its patron saint is John the Baptist.

The cliff itself, high above the Monastery, reveals that this site has had this connotation for a very long time. Rocky overhangs are known to have been favoured by man since times immemorial as sites of religious importance. The cliff face, however, also was – and can still be at times of rain – the site of a waterfall. The water from above tried to escape from the hill, downwards… it is the Aragon river in the valley below that carries away this and so much more water. Through the ages, the water trying to escape the cliff face has resulted in a gaping "wound" in the rock, an opening through which the water can stream – and fall in front of the Monastery. It would have been a majestic sight, and would have accentuated the religious importance of this site. It is clear why Christians would remodel this no doubt pagan site into a Christian centre dedicated to John the Baptist: the site was continuously washed by the water.

It is this feature of a continuous stream or trickle of water that was without a doubt the main raison why the Aragon kings wanted to be buried here. The mausoleum itself might not reveal it, but the section of the museum display next to it shows the site of the tombs of the kings. These kings were buried right into the wall of the rock, but also right next to the irrigation system, where it drops from the upper to the lower level.

Symbolically, it means that the bodies of the Aragon kings were "washed" – their sins removed – in the water that streamed by their side. It is universal symbolism that was retained by the Church. For example, for centuries, the bodies of children that had died before receiving baptism were not allowed to be buried in the cemetery. However, a special, non-consecrated section of the graveyard was often set apart for them, whereby these children were buried next to a wall from where the rainwater was made to drop on their tombs – which was interpreted as the rainwater baptising the souls of these innocents.

The symbolism in San Juan de la Peña was even more profound, when we note the presence of the Holy Grail. The Holy Grail, the cup of Christ, had transformed a normal fluid into the mythical Blood of Christ. The Valencia Cup sat literally on top of the water, before it reached the bodies of the Aragon kings. The bodies of the Aragon kings were thus continuously "washed" by water that had been transformed by the Grail. Who would not want to be buried in such a manner?

This aquatic aspect of the Grail transformation and the "underground stream" that runs through the layout of the site are not explained in any of the literature available on San Juan de la Peña. It is an "open secret", there to see for anyone who wants to see it. But once you understand the method in which a natural phenomenon was re-engineered to become a highly symbolic mausoleum, it becomes apparent why the Aragon kings held the site in such devotion. It is clear that this devotion equally involved a mixture of a cup, "the Grail", the relationship with water, and the role of John the Baptist. The theory that the Baptist and the Grail go hand in hand, equally works in San Juan de la Peña.

But perhaps the role of John the Baptist has got more to do with the baptising aspect, rather than with the figure of John itself, as Picknett & Prince would have it. Furthermore, we have lived with the assumption that the Grail is indeed a cup, and that it is the cup used at the Last Supper... is it?

Chapter 2: The Quest for the Grail book

What is the Grail? Not only are there several contenders for "the Cup of Christ", there is general confusion as to whether the Grail is a cup at all. For Frederick Locke, the identification of the Grail as a Cup was "a succession of attempts to force the Grail to yield a monolithic meaning, to determine for it a precise synonym. To some it is the chalice of the Eucharist, to others a misinterpretation of the horn of plenty of Celtic mythology, and to still others a phallic symbol when taken in conjunction with the Lance."[18]

Some have seen detached the Holy from the Grail and have not seen it within a Christian context; instead, they have defined it as the cauldron of the Tuatha de Danann, "peoples of the goddess Danu", one of the legendary races of Irish mythology. The Tuatha Dé Danann had four treasures, gifts from the goddess and brought to the people by the sun god Lugh, which would give them a chance in defeating their enemies, the Fomorians. The magical gifts came from four great magical cities: Falias, Gorias, Findias and Murias. From the Falias, the Danann received the talking stone of truth, the Lia Fail, which would reveal who was the rightful king of Ireland. The second treasure was the great magical sword, called Freagarthach (the "Answerer"), from the city Findias. The third treasure, the invincible spear, came from Gorias. The last treasure, from Murias (which translates as the seas), was the Cauldron of Dagda, which could feed everyone in Ireland without emptying. It was also said to restore the strength and energy of those who ate the food. Some even suggest it had healing powers.

As a sacred treasure, the "Magic Cauldron" is an essential theme throughout Celtic mythology, especially in Wales and Ireland. The Spoils of Annwn related a quest for the cauldron, which some have regarded as the archetype for the quest for the Holy Grail. For sure, there are certain correspondences between the cauldron and the Grail. But the problem of the Grail is not to point out parallels – the problem is to show its precise origins.

Thus a cauldron – whose shape and size is described as a tub – cannot be carried with ease by a single maiden, as the Grail is carried in the Grail accounts. Whereas the cauldron contained food, the Grail did not; it is the appearance of the Grail that creates the mysterious appearance of food, but there is never any hint that the food comes from the Grail – merely that the presence of the Grail is the cause of the food's appearance. And in most Grail accounts, this has a very simple explanation: once the Grail has been carried inside the hall, the participants are ready to start their meal – a feast. This might seem like going down into pedantic detail, but it is this type of sloppy thinking that has failed to successfully identify the Grail.

At the beginning of the 20th century, Grail researcher Jessie Weston confirmed that the debate about the Grail's origins is terribly complex: one group of scholars could maintain, by solely using Christian elements, that the Grail legend was a Christian legend. Others could use the folkloric elements to argue a Celtic provenance. Weston wrote in 1919 and since, the two camps have not come to a mutual conclusion.

Today, the entire Grail debate remains a collection of contradictory arguments, whereby any conclusions seem impossible. If the Grail is indeed a Christian relic, if it is indeed the central aspect of the Eucharist, why is it borne by a maiden, at a time when women were not allowed to be part of the Church's rituals? Placing a woman – a maiden at that – central immediately identifies its unconventional – non Christian – nature. And though women were treated more equally in original Christianity, the equality of both genders is typically pagan.

Why is it that there is such difficulty to identify what the Grail is? The problem lies with the original Grail accounts themselves, which either not mention what the Grail actually is, or when they do, it is seemingly so general or esoteric, that its description does not allow for an identification. No wonder then that many have concluded, perhaps to salvage their mental sanity, that the Grail is just that: it can be anything you want it to be.

By extension, some authors have argued that the Grail was just that for the first person to speak of it, Chrétien de Troyes: a literary device to capture the imagination of the reader, who felt it would be best to leave it open, so the reader could define it individually, but which was not based on any actual object. "Keep your readers guessing..."

It is true that the initially undefined Grail created a spate of publications, which either tried to complete the unfinished account, or were spin-offs of the original account. Richard Barber has noted that this sequence of publications led to the invention of a new art form, the prose romance, which would later become the modern novel.[19] It underlines the appeal of the Grail as a centrepiece in the history of literature. But the problem of such literary approaches is that they have described the plethora of books that tackled the Grail, but have failed to analyse the original account by Chrétien de Troyes himself.

The origins of the Grail

Chrétien de Troyes has been attributed with being the person who introduced the concept of the Grail. His date of birth is unknown, but suspected to be ca. 1135, in the city of Troyes, in the Champagne region, east of Paris. Trained in Latin to enter the priesthood, he became a translator of Ovid, specifically working on *The Art of Love* and *Metamorphoses*. He was also a poet in his own right, composing four romances for Marie, Countess of Champagne and daughter of the French King Louis VII. Marie would later marry the English king Henry II. It is believed that Chrétien lived at her court and that he was thus writing specifically for her interest and entertainment.

Chrétien's romances form the most complete expression from

a single author of the ideals of French chivalry. All are written in eight-syllable rhyming couplets and are respectively *Erec and Enide, Cligés, Yvain* and *Lancelot*. All of Chrétien's works are set at the court of Arthur, with the notable exception of *Cligés*. Nevertheless, there is still an interlude at Arthur's court. *Erec and Enide* is a tale about Camelot; *Cligés* dealt with Tristan, *Yvain* praised noble love and marriage, whereas the adultery of Guinevere formed the basis of *Lancelot*.

However, it would not be these poems, but *Le Roman de Perceval ou le Conte du Graal*, for which Chrétien would be remembered. It was composed ca. 1175 for Philip, Count of Flanders, Chrétien's employer in later life. It was left unfinished at Chrétien's death (ca. 1185), after he had written ca. 9000 lines – 25 of which mention the Grail. Chrétien had already mentioned its main character, Perceval, on two previous occasions, before making him the main character of his Grail story; he featured in a list of knights in *Erec and Enide*, and he makes a brief appearance in *Cligés*.

Chrétien's Grail story was a departure from his customary rendition of love stories, which might have been the result from a change in employer. *Le Conte du Graal* is the account of a boy who becomes a knight, but who soon learns that his life of slaughter and fighting is void, or at least incomplete: fighting is not a purpose onto itself, but needs to be interpreted within the framework of a divine task, whereby the knight has a spiritual duty – symbolized by the principles that the knights of the Grail brotherhood live by. Rather than put love at the centre of a man's life, this story was about making a divine task the goal of your life. To a large extent, the Grail tradition would contain a certain dislike for love, which became to be seen as a weakness and a hindrance to fulfil one's destiny.

Few have focused on this move away from love. This is a shame, as it reveals one key ingredient that was a sign of

Chrétien's time: the Cathar preachings similarly saw love and sex as traps of the materialistic world, allowing Mankind not to grow towards its divine destiny, which was to throw off the bonds of this earthly realm and all its trappings (in particular fame, possessions and love), and endorse a spiritual life-style, directed towards a union with God upon dead.

That no author writes within a void, was made clear in 2006, when Michael Baigent and Richard Leigh took Dan Brown to court, claiming he had used their *Holy Blood, Holy Grail* as primary source for *The Da Vinci Code*. Baigent and Leigh apparently wanted part of the revenue of the novel, though the judgment ruled Brown had not used that book as his primary source – nor, should it be said, was there anything specifically original about *Holy Blood, Holy Grail*.

The courtcase brought to light the debate of sources. Where did Chrétien get his information from? Was it a totally fictious account? If not, who was his inspiration? They are, once again, questions that are seldom posed, because of the reigning paradigm that the Grail was a literary device.

Little is known about the life of Chrétien, but much is known about the life of his masters. Marie of Champagne's husband, King Henry, had gone to the Holy Land, but died in 1181, a week after his return. She refused to marry the widowed Philip of Alsace, the Count of Flanders, for unknown reasons, but Chrétien did enter his service. In 1190, Philip took the cross for a second time, but when he arrived at the Siege of Acre, he was stricken by the epidemic passing through the crusader camp, and died on August 1, 1191.

It is in the circle of Philip of Alsace that we find a direct reference to what might be "the Grail": Philip's father, Thierry of Alsace, had been bequeathed a Chapel of the Holy Blood of Christ. It was his reward from Baldwin III, the King of Jerusalem, for his bravery during the Second Crusade. Thierry went four times to the Holy Land, the second time in 1147 during the Second Crusade. He led the crossing of the Maeander River in Anatolia and fought at the Battla of Attalya in 1148, and after arriving in the crusader Kingdom, he participated in the Council of Acre, where the ill-fated decision to attack Damascus was made. He participated in the Siege of Damascus, led by his wife's half-brother Baldwin III of Jerusalem, and with the support of Baldwin, Louis VII of France, and Conrad III of Germany, he lay claim to Damascus; however, the native crusader barons preferred one of their own nobles, Guy Brisebarre, lord of Beirut, but in any case the siege was a failure and all parties returned home.

Despite such failure, Baldwin III apparently gave him this precious relic, which he apparently donated to the Flemish city of Bruges in 1150, a town where he had found sanctuary during a previous military campaign, where it remains to this day.[20] However, there is no evidence for its presence in the town as early as 1150. It is now believed that the relic was recovered during the Fourth Crusade (ca. 1204) and its origin is believed to have been Byzantium. Some have even argued that the Crusade was diverted to Byzantium to sack the city and retrieve its horde of precious relics, who could then be shipped en masse to Western Europe.[21]

Whenever the city came in the possession of the Holy Blood, for eight centuries, the Procession of the Holy Blood through the streets of Bruges was held on Ascension Day, at 3pm. It was one of the most sumptuous processions in the world. For the other 364 days of the year, the Holy Blood sits in the Basilica of the Holy Blood, tucked into a corner of one of Bruges' most prominent squares. In a side chapel, behind a silver sanctuary, the Precious Blood is hidden, only taken out for veneration at specific times.

Is this Holy Blood of Christ the source of Chrétien's Grail? Chrétien's account postdates the legendary arrival of the Holy Blood by approximately 25 years (1150 to 1175); Chrétien lists a knightly and royal tradition surrounding a precious relic, carried in a procession. Did his master desire a romance that displayed his relationship to the Holy Blood? Perhaps.

Though it may seem that the mystery has been solved, when it comes to the Grail, nothing is ever that straightforward. Identifying Chrétien's sources is difficult, and because one scenario fits, it does not mean it explains all. Where, for example, does the tradition of King Arthur fit into this Flemish account?

Chrétien lived at a court where many new English traditions were being introduced. Thus, it is often accepted that Chrétien based his story on Celtic material, such as the story of Peredur, a Welsh legend that contains many Grail-like overtones. *Peredur son of Efrawg* is one of the three Welsh romances associated with the Mabinogion. It is likely that Peredur was a Brythonic prince ruling over a region in Northern England. He has a father, Efrawg, who was believed to be etymologically linked to York.

Efrawg died when Peredur is young, and his mother raised him in isolation in the woods. As he came of age, he met a group of knights, and went with them to the court of King Arthur. At the court, he suffered the ridicule of the knight Cei and set off, promising to reclaim his honour. On his travels, he met two of his uncles. The first showed him how to bear arms, and instructed him not to question the significance of what he saw. The second uncle revealed a severed head on a platter.

Peredur continued on his journeys, staying with the nine witches of Gloucester and falling in love with Angharad Golden-Hand. He eventually returned to Arthur's court, and learned that the severed head was that of his cousin, who had been killed by the witches of Gloucester. Aggrieved, Peredur avenged his family members, and returned home a hero.

The account shows obvious parallels with Chrétien's, and it might explain Chrétien's identification as "Perceval the Welshman". It might also explain why most of Chrétien's stories were set at the court of King Arthur, a typically English export of its time. Of course, in *Peredur,* the Grail would thus be a severed head on a platter, and it is here that some have hence speculated there is another link with John the Baptist. The Bible reveals all we need to point out: "When the daughter of Herodias came in and danced, she pleased Herod and his guests; and the king said to the girl, 'Ask me for whatever you wish, and I will give it.' And he solemnly swore to her, 'Whatever you ask me, I will give you, even half of my kingdom.' She went out and said to her mother, 'What should I ask for?' She replied, 'The head of John the baptizer.' Immediately she rushed back to the king and requested, I want you to give me at once the head of John the Baptist on a platter.' The king was deeply grieved; yet out of regard for his oaths and for the guests, he did not want to refuse her. Immediately the king sent a soldier of the guard with orders to bring John's head. He went and beheaded him in the prison, brought his head on a platter, and gave it to the girl. Then the girl gave it to her mother. When his disciples heard about it, they came and took his body, and laid it in a tomb."[22]

Hence, we need to ask what came first: the Grail, Peredur, or the account of John's beheading? Furthermore, some of have pointed out that though the story of Peredur is older than Chretien's story of the Grail, the telling of it might have been influenced by Chrétien. Nothing, indeed, is ever simple when it comes to the Grail.

At the same time, not only was there an English influence, there was also a famous revival of the Jewish Cabbala at Troyes, led by Rashi. Rashi de Troyes (1040-1105) made the astonishing statement that the Biblical Genesis narrative was written to justify genocide. Rashi's precise words were that God gave the creation story and included it in the Torah "to tell his people that they can answer those who claim that the Jews stole the land from its original inhabitants. The reply should be; God made it and gave it to them but then took it and gave it to us. As he made it and it's his, he can give it to whoever he chooses". Rashi is nevertheless best remembered for his prophecy that Godfrey of Bouillon, with whom he may have had a close friendship, that "Thou wilt take the Holy City [Jerusalem] and thou wilt reign over Jerusalem three days, but on the fourth day the Muslim will put thee to flight, and when thou returnest only three horses will be left to thee."[23] It might be this prophecy that explains why Godfrey declined to be crowned king of Jerusalem.

As *Holy Blood, Holy Grail* points out: "Like its Eastern equivalents, Cabalistic training entails a series of rituals a structured sequence of successive initiatory experiences leading the practitioner to ever more radical modifications of consciousness and cognition. [...] Of the "stages' of Cabalistic initiation, one of the most important is the stage known as Tiferet. [...] For medieval Cabalists the initiation into Tiferet was associated with certain specific symbols. These included a hermit or guide or wise old man, a majestic king, a child, a sacrificed god. In time other symbols were added as well a truncated pyramid, for example, a cube and a rose cross."[24]

The authors point out that "The relation of these symbols to the Grail romances is sufficiently apparent. In every Grail narrative there is a wise old hermit Perceval's or Parzival's uncle frequently who acts as a spiritual guide. In Wolfram's poem the Grail as 'stone' may possibly correspond to the cube. And in the Perlesvaus [a continuation of Chrétien's account] the various manifestations of the Grail correspond almost precisely to the symbols of Tiferet. Indeed, the Perlesvaus in itself establishes a crucial link between the Tiferet experience and the Grail."[25]

Thus, Jewish mystical elements might also have contributed to the Grail story – and definitely its continuations. But one vital question has so far not been posed: what did Chrétien say about his sources?

Contrary to what scholars sometimes want us to believe, Chrétien is very specific about his sources. He claimed that he had put into verse a book that his patron, Philip of Flanders, had loaned to him. However, the identification of a book as the source of the Grail account does not really help. In principle, it makes the quest for the "Grail origin" even more difficult, as we have a multitude of possibilities: stories from England (which could incorporate English, Welsh and Scottish material), original French material, Jewish material, documents from the Holy Land – or documents recovered en route to Jerusalem, etc. The origin of the Grail could therefore be said to be from the furthest Western regions of Europe, to the Middle East. But at the same time, it does offer one important clue: the story of the Grail was already written down and was passed down in this format to Philip of Flanders, who asked Chrétien to put it to verse – and/or translation. And this might explain why Chrétien was chosen for the task.

As a translator, Chrétien de Troyes must have been exposed to many documents that required translation. Many of these books captured the imagination of the nobility, who used people like Chrétien to translate what they most cherished. It is clear that Philip of Flanders therefore had found such a "lost book", but it also seems that he was able to read it, or at least roughly knew what it was about, suggesting it was perhaps written in a language he knew, or at one point had already been translated. Furthermore, it seems that the "lost book" was written in prose, with Chrétien receiving the commission to put it to verse. This suggests that the original account of the Grail was either factual – historical – or a novel – but not a poem.

The Grail - act two

With Chrétien's death, the Grail story was left unfinished. At best, it was incomplete. At worst, it was erroneous – and that was exactly the charge of Wolfram von Eschenbach. As previously mentioned, Wolfram's account is best known for its influence on the German composer Wagner's opera *Parsifal.* Some authors have argued that Wagner based his account on Wolfram – or even adopted it wholesale. Wagner himself stated that Wolfram's version was "irrelevant", though there were certain elements that he did use in his opera.

Whereas Chrétien's circle of influence was French-English, Wolfram himself was a Bavarian by birth, from the town of Eschenbach, a little southeast of Ansbach, in Franconian territory. Though of noble birth, he was poor, possibly because he was a younger son. All that he owned was the small estate of Wildenberg (now Wehlenberg), near Ansbach. In *Parzival,* he speaks of the Count of Wertheim as "Min Herre", "My Lord", but that may simply be an honorary title and not an indication that he worked for the count. It is known that Wolfram led a wandering life-style, and that after 1203, he repeatedly stayed at the Court of the landgrave Hermann of Thuringia at Eisenach. Parts of his *Parzival* were composed there.

Like Chrétien, Wolfram had written earlier works, *Willehaim* and *Titurel,* before tackling the Grail in ca. 1210. After the landgrave's death in 1217, Wolfram returned to his native home. The date of his own death is uncertain, though he certainly survived the landgrave, whose death he alludes to in his poem *Willehaim.* He was buried in the Frauenkirche of Eschenbach, where his tomb was still to be seen in the 17th century, but at the time, the year of his death was no longer legible.

Among the numerous medieval versions of the Quest for the Holy Grail, the Romanian historian of religion, fiction writer, philosopher, and professor at the University of Chicago, Mircea Eliade considers Wolfram von Eschenbach's *Parzival* "the most complete story and coherent mythology of the Grail".[26] Eliade was particularly struck by the fact that Wolfram deliberately included numerous Oriental motifs, and did so with respect. Eliade notes that "whatever one makes of the works of Wolfram and his successors, it is evident that the symbolism of the Grail and the scenarios it inspires represent a new spiritual synthesis that draws upon the contributions of diverse traditions. Behind this passionate interest in the Orient, one detects a profound disillusionment aroused by the Crusades, the aspiration for a religious tolerance that would have encouraged a rapprochement with Islam, and a nostalgia for a 'spiritual chivalry'."[27]

In essence, Wolfram's Parzival was the "retelling and ending [...] of the unfinished romance [...] of Chrétien de Troyes."[28] Wolfram had taken from Chrétien the long account of the adventures of Gawain, which comprise most of the latter part of the French poem. To this, he added a prologue and a conclusion, which have, however, very little to do with the Grail quest as such. But by doing so, *Parzival* was the first complete Grail romance. Even though it is not the chronological successor to *Le Conte du Graal*, it is deemed to be of more interest and importance than the continuations, such as the story of Robert de Boron, who works the story of the Grail into the legend of Joseph of Arimathea. Goering has argued that "one can say, without much oversimplification, that Robert simply adopted the plot of the *Gospel of Nicodemus*, and then inserted the Holy Grail into this story wherever appropriate."[29]

Twenty years separated Wolfram from Chrétien. Topical references in his work allow it to be dated to ca. 1200-1210, which is also the richest period in the history of medieval German poetry.[30]

The all-important question is whether Wolfram merely had a literary ambition to complete Chrétien's work. It might be, but as we shall soon see, there is much more to it than that. First, Wolfram gives names to some previously nameless characters, including Titurel, Anfortas, Sigune, Condwiramurs and Condrie.

He adds some further details about the latter, including her knowledge of herbal medicines that she used to bring relief to the stricken King Anfortas. These names might all be literary inventions to make the story easier to follow – but perhaps not.

Another addition that is specific to Wolfram is a long prologue about the double marriage of Gahmuret, Parzival's father. Again, this might be a literary invention, but it is unclear how this account could contribute to the "flow" of the story. If anything, it seems that Wolfram had certain material at his disposal about the people mentioned in the account, which he added to the basic framework that Chrétien had written. For, in style, this preliminary information adds nothing to the narrative, and, if anything, pushes the real action further into the story. Wolfram thus has much in common with the Italian writer Umberto Eco, who equally has an interest in medieval history and a passion for the Grail, and is known to have said that he often used the first fifty-one hundred pages as a test for the reader, hoping that most will abandon the book, with the real narrative only beginning later, for those that have endured the initiation.

From Wolfram, we hear of Perceval's childhood in the wilderness, his meetings with the knights, his departure for Arthur's court, his killing of the Red Knight, his education by Gurnemans, the rescue of Conduir-amour (called Blancheflur by Chrétien) and his subsequent marriage to her, and his unsuccessful visit to the Grail castle.

Wolfram's scope is thus much wider than Chrétien's. And that is not all: there is the introduction of Belacane, the heathen queen by whom Gahmuret has a son (Fairefis). The two brothers, Gawain and Feirefiz (Fairefis), will eventually meet and Feirefiz will marry one of the virgin attendants to the Grail, before returning to his homeland – which seems to be in either Africa or the Middle East – with the Grail.

Whereas Chrétien shows us a humble and repentant Perceval visiting the hermit's cave and taking part in a normal church service there, Wolfram's rendition of this account is nine times as long and describes in detail how Parzival, still proud and unrepentant even though he knows he is in a state of sin, is told by the brother of the Fisher King Anfortas of the dangers of pride and the need for humility and submission to God's will.

Some scenes are closely modelled on those in Chrétien's poem, though he still makes significant changes: he portrays the first meeting with Conduir-amour free of any sexual elements, whereas the corresponding French scene is quite the reverse. The role of Sigune, Perceval's cousin, whose lover has been killed and who mourns him throughout the work, is given more significance in *Parzival* than in *Le Conte du Graal*, and she, like many other characters, is named by Wolfram, but left anonymous by Chrétien.

The alterations and additions of Wolfram are largely seen as literary fabrications of Wolfram. It is possible, but it is the same type of speculation that often surrounds Chrétien's account. Specifically, it is idle speculation, not taking into account of what the author himself said. Afraid to break the mould in which academics have placed the "Grail romances", accepting Wolfram's statements about his work as fact is an approach that few have taken.

Indeed, why would Wolfram lie when he is stating that he is not lying at all, but faithfully reporting on information he has received? Everyone who has claimed that Wolfram's story contains fictionalised accounts, has never addressed the question why Wolfram would lie. If we take Wolfram's word for it, then he used specific knowledge that had come into his possession and which had allowed him to add names and details to previously anonymous characters in Chrétien's story. He also argued that this information had allowed him to correctly identify the nature of the Grail.

What is the Grail?

Chrétien's "Graal" is assumed to be a vessel. In Medieval Latin, these were named "gradalis", which is believed to have become "gradal", or "graal", in Medieval French. *The Oxford Dictionary* lists vessel as: "(1) a ship or large boat; (2) a hollow container used to hold liquid; (3) a tube or duct conveying a fluid within an animal body or plant structure; (4) (in or alluding to biblical use) a person regarded as embodying a particular quality: giving honour unto the wife, as unto the weaker vessel." The word is also linked with a blood vessel, showing a connotation with blood – which possibly could have led to the many interpretations as the vessel of the blood of Christ – and hence the Cup of the Last Supper. For the moment, let us suggest a vessel is "a hollow container used to hold something" – for, after all, why should hollow containers only ever hold a liquid?

Unlike Chrétien, Wolfram identified his "Grâl" as a stone. It is assumed by many scholars that this is proof of the fact that the nature of the Grail in those early days was very open, each author picking an object as he pleased, in an effort to distinguish himself from his fellow writers. Some scholars however argue that Wolfram's understanding of French was poor, and hence that he was unable to comprehend the true meaning of "gra(d)al" – vessel.

Wolfram had the passing of time and the presence of fellow writers on the subject against him. The academics are right that some that followed in Chrétien's tradition invented subplots and identified the Grail to their own liking. It was Robert de Boron in *Joseph d'Arimathie* who transformed the Grail into the Chalice of the Last Supper, filling it with the Blood from the Cross, the Blood of Christ. It thus became the "San Greal", the "Holy Grail", but also the "Sang Real", the "True Blood" or "Kingly Blood".

But because Robert de Boron did so, does not automatically mean Wolfram did as well; and, again, Wolfram said he did not.

We need to note that Wolfram clearly stated that Chrétien's story contained "errors", which Wolfram felt he had to put right. And he claimed he was able to do so, because he had been given precise information, apparently not available to any of the other authors writing on the Grail around the turn of the 13th century.

At the same time, Wolfram no doubt realised that with Robert de Boron's version, he had just witnessed the first in a series of romances that would take Chrétien's unfinished story as the introduction to a series of personal interpretations of various authors – whereby the factual basis of the account would become lost. In retrospect, it is clear that Wolfram indeed tried to set the record straight, but that no-one has since given him his due credit. At best, his critics have argued that Wolfram's account does not fit the standard Grail account and many have therefore taken his account in isolation. Though it should be seen as a stand-alone account, he should be accorded this position for he alone was trying to reveal the historical, factual nature of the account.

The Kyot problem

For Wolfram, Chrétien had made serious errors when he had made the "lost book" that he had received from Philip of Flanders into a poem. Wolfram wanted to be remembered as the person who went back to the original source, the "lost book", and retold the story – with a sense of German efficiency that he felt had been lacking in Chrétien's work: more facts, less romance; more fact, less fiction – more boring, less exciting.

Whereas Chrétien claimed that he had worked from a book given to him by Philip of Flanders, Wolfram stated that he had been in contact with a Grail expert: "Kyot of Provence." Kyot of Provence most likely retold a story that he had heard in Spain, where there were both Muslim and Jewish philosophers, or the Languedoc region of southern France, a region that at the time was caught up in the religious turmoil of Catharism; when Wolfram wrote in 1203-1210, the Cathar Crusade was brewing –

the military campaign commencing in 1209.

Who was "Kyot of Provence"? In short, no-one knows… for sure. Hence, Hatto in his translation of *Parzival* labels him a "pseudo-source" – a literary fabrication, implying that Wolfram used this imaginary person to "mask his own creative activity".[31] Indeed, the single problem that Wolfram has faced in being considered a historian, rather than a novelist, is that "we" have been unable to identify who his source was. And "our" failure, has thus meant that "we" have labelled Wolfram as someone who must have invented his source.

Still, several authors have tried to map "Kyot of Provence" with a real person. San Marte made a translation of Wolfram's *Parzival* in 1842. He believed Kyot was a genuine source and that the account originated in Provence and was linked with the rise of the Knights Templars, the famous organisation of crusading warrior monks. Specifically, San Marte considered that the Lapis Exilis was the Stone of the Lord, which at the beginning of all things was with God; that the passage of the Graal to the Kingdom of Prester John was a reference to the Middle Eastern sects of followers of John the Baptist and that the Graal was not a Christian relic. He argued that Wolfram's Provençal Kyot may have been Guiot de Provins.[32]

The next translator, Karl Simrock, denied Kyot's historicity and centred the cult of the Grail around the cult of St John the Baptist.[33] He argued that the head was used to maintain the life of a dying emperor in the eleventh century, that the Templeisen were the Knights of San Salvador de Mont Réal and that the Graal and its veneration was indeed the bailiwick of the Christians of St. John.

Still other scholars have observed that Wolfram's methodology of writing actually suggested that he indeed acquired his wealth of information on the Grail topic by listening, rather than reading (or imagining) – which would argue for the likelihood that Kyot was a real person. Indeed, even those who argue Wolfram invented the story, tend to agree that his writing betrays an oral origin. So *someone* told him this story. Why couldn't this be Kyot, as Wolfram says?

If Kyot has since not been identified – is this Wolfram's fault, or evidence of the failure of scholars to identify one person? For sure, these scholars are faced with a formidable task, but surely their failure in no way would allow a rushed judgment that he therefore does not exist? Unfortunately, the corridors of science often work in a way where the impossibility of resolving a problem results in ridiculing the premise on which the problem is based. Thus, we once again see how the Grail has suffered from a long series of "editorialisation": various interpreters have built upon the interpretations of their predecessors, whereby in the end, it is no wonder that other scholars conclude that the Grail can mean anything to anyone.

To truly understand the nature of the Grail, we need to return to Chrétien and Wolfram, respectively the first person to mention the Grail, and the person who stated he had to correct Chrétien's account. Though no-one will doubt the assertion that they are the most authentic Grail material, what would happen if we would treat that authentic material as possibly genuine? Might it reveal that the Grail account is indeed a historical account – and the Grail and its Brotherhood real people?

Chapter 3: The Hermetic Grail

The story of the Grail itself, as Jessie Weston has pointed out, "must be sought elsewhere than in ecclesiastical legend, or popular tale."[34] Weston believed that "whether it were not possible that in this mysterious legend [...] we might not have the confused record of a ritual, once popular, later surviving under conditions of strict secrecy?" [35] This would place the Grail legend noth within the framework of the Church and its rituals, but within the so-called "mystery religions". These mystery cults were Hellenised-Romanised renditions of Egyptian and other Middle Eastern religions, whereby the public – "popular" – nature of these festivals became substituted by a series of initiations, with each grade of initiation bringing more awareness – similar to the various years one passes in school, each year accumulating more knowledge.[36] The "student body" was known as a brotherhood, and they were quite on par with some of the college fraternities that exist today, specifically in the United States, where some, like the popular Skull & Bones, are seen as modern equivalents of ancient secret societies.

Weston's insightful suggestion is one of a small list of studies on the Grail that take into account what is obvious: that the Grail legend is pagan in nature and that the Grail was guarded by a brotherhood that required initiation and secrecy. It should of course not come as a surprise that this message is also at the core of the Grail story as expressed by Wolfram von Eschenbach. Alas, it is also the most often overlooked element in practically all discussions on the Grail. In its efforts to divine the nature of the Grail, all the details about those who serve it, have been left out of any critical study.

Weston wrote at the start of the 20th century, when many volumes of ancient knowledge were either difficult to access or available in only certain languages. Nevertheless, with limited material available, Weston was already able to point out that the mystery cults were the most likely origins of the Grail legend, even though the argument was based on some oral traditions – which have always been frowned upon by "real scholars". But since 1919, large volumes of written material have surfaced that have confirmed those oral traditions and which have allowed a re-evaluation of Weston's conclusions, this time using material that is accepted by researchers: written sources.

The Grail in the sky

That Wolfram's story fits in this pagan tradition is seldom noticed, largely because the Grail is studied by experts in Christian symbolism, not pagan mythology. Still, even in Wolfram's days, the pagan nature was noticed by some of his contemporaries. Gottfried von Strassburg is considered to be one of the great Arthurian writers of Germany. At one point, Gottfried attacks an unnamed poet whom he calls "friend of the hare", and it is commonly assumed this poet was Wolfram.[37] Gottfried accused Wolfram of inventing "wild tales", but of specific interest is his accusation that Wolfram had apparently gotten these stories from books of the black arts – a catch-all term for pagan material: "Inventors of wild tales, hired hunters after stories, who cheat with chains and dupe dull minds, who turn rubbish into gold for children, and from magic boxes pour pearls of dust... These same story hunters have to send commentaries with their tales: one cannot understand them as one hears and sees them. But we for our part have not the leisure to seek the gloss in books of the black art."[38]

Throughout Wolfram's account, there are repeated references to magic, geomancy, astrology and other pagan practices that have no presence in Christian mythology. The presence of astrology in the Grail legends may seem normal, but within its historical context, it is odd.

Astrology was popular in Graeco-Roman times, but the fame of horoscopes declined at the end of the 4th century AD. Astrology only enjoyed a new upswing and a wide dissemination in Europe until the translation of Arabic texts into Latin in the 12th century, after flourishing at the Abbassid court in Baghdad. Interestingly, it is Wolfram who claims that Perceval's father, Gahmuret, had fought for this court. It places both Wolfram's story – and those of his characters – away from a Western Christian background, and into a larger, religiously diverse context.

One specific detail about the Grail is often pointed out, but seldom explained. Wolfram states that Kyot's source Flegetanis "said there was a thing called the Grail, whose name he had read clearly in the constellations."[39] This stellar connection is twice-present, as Kahane and Kahane suggest that "Flegetanis" might be derived from the Arabic al-Falakiyatu or falakiyatun, meaning Astronomy/Astronomer, which is the title of an Arabic Hermetic treatise on astrology, *al-Falakiyatu 'l kubra,* "The Great Astronomy".[40] Others have pointed out that Flegetanis translates as "familiar with stars" in Persian, and that "Felek Thâni" means guardian of the planet Mercury in Arabic.

In almost all pagan traditions, symbolism is depicted on the night's sky. Some Christian saints, like Saint Saturnin, are both in name and symbolism linked with the planet Saturn, underlining that part of the Christian cult borrowed from the pagan tradition. One excellent example within the pagan tradition is the story of Arthur and the Round Table, a tale that is often incorporated into the Grail mythos. Arthur is linked with the Great Bear, with the Round Table being the zodiac, the belt-shaped region in the heavens on either side of the ecliptic. It has been divided into twelve constellations or signs, which form the basis for the "houses" of astrology. Interestingly, these houses also represent the degrees of advancement – the grades – on the scale of initiation.

Though Arthur and the Round Table have stellar counterparts, there has been a lot of speculation as to what the reference of "the Grail in the sky" might be, so far without a definitive outcome. Some have linked it with the Great Bear, because of its Arthurian connection, whereby the trapezoid section is interpreted as a "cup". Others have linked it with stellar alignments, or planetary conjunctions, specifically those of Jupiter and Saturn – a well-known and important event in astrology.

None of those interpretations have however been successful in unlocking the enigma of the "Grail in the sky". Nevertheless, when we use the Corpus Hermetica as the key, its identification is straightforward. The Hermetica is a collection of eighteen texts, which are codifications of the Egyptian religion for a Greek audience. They were written in the 3rd century BC by the Egyptian priest Manetho, in the form of dialogues, between the god Hermes (the Greek equivalent of the Egyptian god Thoth, the God of Wisdom) and the initiate/student, named Tat (another reference to Thoth).

The fourth treatise of the Hermetica is titled the "Cup", or "Monad" – which in Greek is known as the "krater". It is the cup that is filled with intellect and which is placed amongst us as a prize to be won. It is an astral vessel, which descended from Heaven to Earth. It is this Crater, this Cup, which is not the Cup of the Last Supper, but the true Grail: the knowledge of God that had been placed within the reach of Mankind, and whose quest – Grail Quest – it was to acquire this.

The treatise itself provides further insights into the nature of the true Grail.Hermes is asked why He (God) set up the Cup. His response: "He filled a mighty Cup with it [nous - intellect], and sent it down, joining a Herald [to it], to whom He gave command to make this proclamation to the hearts of men: 'Baptize thyself with this Cup's baptism, what heart can do so, you that has faith can ascend to him that has sent down the Cup, you that knows why you came into being!'" It is here, with the reference to baptism, that the role of John the Baptist and his link with the Grail tradition becomes apparent too. One scholar, R. Van den Broek, is nevertheless quick to point out that this initiation is not specifically a baptism by water – it is a "baptism with knowledge". Still, it can be a baptism by water, as in the Eleusian Mysteries, initiation was symbolised by the drinking of a cup. However, Van den Broek argues, "references are not specific, which might have been on purpose."[41]

Hermes goes on to state that many understood the Herald's tidings and doused themselves in Mind (nous), thus becoming partakers in the Gnosis; when they had "received the Mind" they were made "perfect men", an interesting name to use, for the Cathar priests were known as "perfects".

A connection between this Cup – the Hermetic vessel – and the Grail was hinted at as early as Romanticism, by Joseph Görres, in *Einleuting zum Lohengrin,* written in 1813. G.R.S. Mead, one of the best known translators of the *Corpus Hermeticum,* also believed that the imagery of the Cup might have a connection with the legends of the Holy Grail.

But above all, this passage explains the "Grail in the sky", as the "krater" of the Hermetica is linked with the constellation Crater (the Cup), a constellation between Cancer and Leo. It is one of the 88 modern constellations and was also one of the 48 listed by Ptolemy. It is visible in both hemispheres, until 60º of North latitude (the latitude of St Petersburgh) and is observed from January to July, culminating in the meridian at the end of March. This is of interest, for Easter – linked with Christ's crucifixion – is defined by astrological means: it is first Sunday (Day of the Sun) after the first full moon on or after the Sprinx Equinox – meaning Easter occurs when the Grail "shines" in the sky. As such, the constellation Crater would be the true "Cup of the Last Supper" too!

Crater may today not be as well known as other constellations, such as Orion, or stars, such as Sirius, but in Antiquity, it was a well-known and important star. As with all other stars and constellations, Crater is linked with mythology; it is said to represent the goblet of Apollo, which is a story that is very similar to the story of the Grail. One day, the Sun-god, Apollo, sent his pet raven down to Earth to bring the thirsty god a cup of fresh water. But Apollo's sacred raven was not a very dependable bird. On arriving at the Spring Equinox, the raven saw that a fig tree was just beginning to bear fruit. "What matter if I wait only a few days until the fruit ripens?" the raven asked itself. And it waited. When the fruit ripened the raven then stayed several more days eating the fruit until it was all gone. He then filled the cup with fresh spring water, but realized that his master would be angry for the long delay. Then he noticed a water-serpent nearby and grasped it in his claws. So with cup in mouth and serpent dangling from his claws, the raven flew up to Heaven. He explained to Apollo that the serpent had attacked him and that this had caused the delay. Apollo was not taken in by the lie. He was so angry with the bird that he flung him, cup and serpent out of Heaven. The Greeks depicted the myth in the sky as Crater – the Cup – and Corvus –the Raven –, perched on the serpent's back.

The Greek philosopher Plato mentioned Crater in his *Timaeus*, saying "it is one and in it mingle all souls". According to the 4th century author Macrobius, the unembodied souls drank oblivion from the constellation Crater, after which they became embodied on Earth. Humans were unaware of their true origin, or their purpose in life. We would wander aimlessly, were it not for the mystery traditions, which spoke of the existence of God and the need to follow a stringent doctrine, which would bring enlightenment to the soul – purify it – whereby it attained the knowledge.

This re-acquisition of the forgotten knowledge of the existene of our soul – and of God – was symbolised by drinking for the second time from this Cup, annihilating our amnesia.

The drinking of the Cup therefore has a dual symbolism: it is the source of oblivion, but it is also the road to enlightenment. This is the core message of the Hermetic doctrine, but also of the Grail Quest. Furthermore, this enlightenment resulted in immortality – not physical immortality, as George Lucas and co. depicted it in *Indiana Jones and the Last Crusade,* but spiritual immortality. It matches the role of the Grail, which equally grants immortality for those who serve it.

In his *Commentary on the Dream of Scipio,* Macrobius provided more detail as to what the ancient Greeks believed occurred in the process of the incarnating soul: "Pythagoras thought that the empire of Pluto began downwards from the Milky Way, because souls falling from thence appear to have already receded from the Gods. Hence he [Pythagoras] asserts that the nutriment of milk is first offered to infants because their first motion commences from the galaxy, when they begin to fall into terrene bodies. [...] From the confine, therefore, in which the zodiac and galaxy reach each other, the soul, descending from a round figure, which is the only divine form, [...] which is a monad, passes into the duad, which is the first extension. And this is the essence which Plato, in the *Timaeus,* calls impartible, and at the same time partible, when he speaks of the nature of the mundane soul."

In this text, Macrobius therefore clearly identifies the Hermetic doctrine, which includes the fall of the soul, from the monad into the "human soul". The monad is literally the One – God – at the centre of the universe, from which souls flake off, drifting along the Milky Way, until the fall from that road onto Earth. When it incarnates, having drunk from the Cup, the soul has forgotten its divine origin, whereby its mission in life is to go and retrieve that knowledge, which will then equip it with the mechanism to return to the Monad. The mechanism of this division and reunification is the Cup – the Grail.

This is no just interpretation: Macrobius specifically identifies the process of incarnation with drinking from the Cup: "As soon, therefore, as the soul gravitates towards body in this first production of herself, she begins to experience a material tumult, that is, matter flowing into her essence. And this is what Plato remarks in the *Phaedo*, but the soul is drawn into body staggering with recent intoxication; signifying by this, the new drink of matter's impetuous flood, through which the soul, becoming defiled and heavy, is drawn into a torrent situation."

Next, he writes about "the Grail in the sky": "But the starry cup placed between Cancer and Leo is a symbol of this mystic truth, signifying that descending souls first experience intoxication in that part of the heavens through the influx of matter. Hence oblivion, the companion of intoxication, there begins silently to creep into the recesses of the soul. For if souls retained in their descent to bodies the memory of divine concerns, of which they were conscious in the heavens, there would be no dissention among men about divinity."

Thus, pagan mythology is able to answer, simple and straightforwardly, that which Christian mythology has struggled with for eight centuries: What is the Grail?

The central message of the Grail is therefore that some souls are called forth to it. Some humans are more advanced on the path to re-assimilation into Oneness than others; they are less intoxicated by the Cup's contents. In the story of the Grail, it is the Grail itself that will call these people to serve it.

That some are "selected" is also present in the story of Macrobius: "But all [souls] in descending, drink of oblivion; though some more and others less. On this account, though truth is not apparent to all men on the earth, yet all exercise their opinions about it; because a defect of memory is the origin of opinion. But those discover most, who have drank least of oblivion, because they easily remember what they had known before in the heavens."[42]

Oblivion, intoxication and forgetfulness are all descriptions of the soul that has incarnated, without knowledge. To achieve understanding, it is important to drink again, which will restore intellect – for which the Greeks used the word "nous".

Interestingly, this pagan doctrine was present in early Christianity, in specifically those strands that were later labelled heretical. The *Pistis Sophia,* a Gnostic text from the 3rd century AD, also describes two vessels, one of forgetfulness, one of wisdom, which is presented to the soul. It is in this rendition that both cups were linked with Hermes, who is often the deity who asks the soul to drink from both.[43] And whereas the original drink led to forgetfullness, the second time, it led to understanding and immortality. As a consequence, the Grail is thus Hermes' Cup, the key to immortality.

Though in Greek tradition Hermes is the messenger of the gods, in Hermetic tradition, Hermes was identified with Thoth, the God of Wisdom – whose counterpart in Greek tradition is Apollo – closing the circle when it comes to the identification with the "drinking cup" and the constellation Crater.

Tobias Churton states that "had von Eschenbach's 'Flegetanis' […] seen Libellus IV.25 of our present Corpus Hermeticum, he would have read there the story of a dish or bowl sent down to earth by God."[44] The question, of course, is whether or not Flegetanis had indeed seen the Corpus Hermeticum – a question which will be answered later on. But based on the evidence, the answer seems to be positive.

The Stone and Bird of Immortality

The story of the soul's voyage through Life and the Beyond was depicted on the night's sky, used as the ultimate blackboard. But what is the "other Grail", this "thing" left on Earth by a troop of angels who then returned to the stars?

The Hermetist seeks to attain eternal life and many have concluded that the Grail provides physical immortality: "And let the man that has intellect in him recognize that he is immortal."[45] Indeed, though the Quest is the quest for the soul's reunion with the One, there does appear to a more "down to earth" aspect to the Grail, one that perhaps does give physical immortality, but at least physical longevity.

Wolfram writes that "there never was a human being so ill but that, if he one day sees that stone, he cannot die within the week that follows. And in looks he will not fade. His appearance will stay the same, whether maid or man, as on the day he saw the stone, the same as when the best years of his life began, and though he should see the stone for two hundred years, there will never be a change, save that his hair might perhaps turn grey. Such power does the stone give a man that flesh and bones are at once made young again."[46]

This brings about a duality: the Grail and the Grail Quest is a spiritual quest, for those souls, united in a brotherhood, that have drunk the Water of Memory from the Cup and are trying to return to the One. This is the "spiritual Grail" – an ambition. But Wolfram adds that the Grail is also a physical object, something on Earth, that is apparently in the possession of this brotherhood, something that apparently aides the initiates in their spiritual quest, and something that is apparently of a rather unconventional nature, for proximity to it results in physical longevity – the inability to age, as if time has stopped, or at least has slowed down tremendously.

The presence of the stone that was placed on Earth and which allowed Mankind to return to God does not allow physical death, if the servant has been or remains in its proximity. Still, Wolfram states that "when life dies for them [the members of the brotherhood] here, they are given perfection there [in heaven]",[47] suggesting the purpose of the brotherhood was physical proximity to the Grail Stone, but indeed the pursuit of a spiritual ambition. This one sentence clearly shows that the Grail Brotherhood is not an organisation of immortals, but of human beings, whose service to the Grail will have proven their worthiness to enter Heaven.

In the end, spiritual immortality was the ultimate aim of the initiate, in which eternal life was reserved in heaven; the soul would turn to heaven for its real life, where it will enter into God – the reunification with the divine Monad. The Corpus Hermeticum argues that to become one with God is the happy end for those who possess gnosis – knowledge – nous.[48]

Antiquity knew many "brotherhoods" that preserved this "Body of Hermes", this knowledge. One of them was the previously mentioned cult at Eleusis. The Eleusinian Mysteries were initiation ceremonies held every year for the cult of Demeter and Persephone. Of all the mysteries celebrated, these were held to be the ones of greatest importance. They are also typical, as the rites were kept secret, and initiation was believed to unite the worshipper with the gods and included promises of divine power and rewards in the afterlife.

There were four categories of people who participated in the Eleusinian Mysteries: 1) the riests, priestesses and hierophants; 2) initiates, undergoing the ceremony for the first time; 3) others who had already participated at least once, who were also eligible for 4) those who had attained epopteia, who had learned the secrets of the greatest mysteries of Demeter.

This already explains a system of four grades, to which those responsible for the Mysteries added two further distinctions: the

Greater and Lesser Mysteries. Plato's spiritual framework was in perfect alignment with this, when he noted that "the ultimate design of the Mysteries [...] was to lead us back to the principles from which we descended."[49] Interestingly, the Lesser Mysteries were held in March, though the exact time was not always fixed and changed occasionally, unlike the Greater Mysteries. The Greater Mysteries took place in late Summer and lasted ten days.

Interestingly, Wolfram identified the Grail Brotherhood with a group of people, the "templeis", who are normally identified as the Knights Templar, a group of Christian warrior monks whose organisation was officially recognised by the Pope in 1128 AD. Wolfram makes a specific link between these knights and the Grail – and what it is: "I will tell you how they [the templeis] are nourished. They live from a Stone whose essence is most pure. If you have never heard of it I shall name it for you here. It is called 'Lapsit exilis'. By virtue of this Stone the Phoenix is burned to ashes, in which he is reborn – Thus does the Phoenix moult its feathers!'"

The Grail is hence also linked with the phoenix, a mystical bird who was said to burn to death only to be reborn. The symbolism of the phoenix is specifically Egyptian, and was later adopted by the Greeks, who identified it with Venus, the Morning Star – which Christianity later identified with Lucifer, as well as Mary Magdalene. And hence, the confabulated story of how the Grail grew into the vulva of Mary Magdalene and the Third Eye that fell from Heaven, was born.

Wolfram's connection between a phoenix and a stone is once again difficult within a Christian context. There is no such Christian imagery and as a consequence, it poses a major problem for those that try to interpret the Grail as a Christian relic. If there is not a single reference to a phoenix and a stone, then indeed, we would have to conclude that the story of the phoenix and the stone was baffling – a figment of Wolfram's imagination, bordering on madness. But the "Christian apologetics" seem unaware – or do not mention – that the connection between a phoenix and a stone is well known within pagan literature, specifically the Egyptian creation myth of Heliopolis, where the phoenix sits on top of a sacred stone and heralds a new cycle by rising from his own ashes. The myth of the phoenix is also told by the Roman author Ovid in his *Metamorphoses*, the works Chrétien de Troyes translated.[50]

Stories of "the Bennu" – the Egyptian name for the phoenix – were known in Greek times, in evidence in references by Herodotus, the 6th century BC Greek historian who travelled in Egypt: "Another sacred bird is the phoenix; I have not seen a phoenix myself, except in paintings, for it is very rare and only visits the country (so they say at Heliopolis) only at intervals of five hundred years, on the occasion of the death of the parent bird." The Greeks identified the word "bennu" with their own word "phoenix", meaning the colour purple-red or crimson. They and the Romans subsequently pictured the bird more like a peacock or an eagle. But in Egypt, the Bennu bird was a large imaginary bird, resembling a heron: it was a male bird with beautiful gold and red plumage. At the end of its life, the phoenix built itself a nest of cinnamon twigs that it then ignited.

Some have suggested that the phoenix is based on a type of bird species of East Africa. This bird nests on salt flats that are too hot for its eggs or chicks to survive; it therefore builds a mound several inches tall and large enough to support its egg, which it lays in that marginally cooler location. The hot air rising around these mounds resembles the turbulence of a flame, which may have inspired the imagery of the bird being born from its ashes.

The story of the Bennu bird is also identical to the story of Apollo's raven. The Bennu was associated with the sun and represented the ba or soul of the Egyptian sun god Ra. In Greece, it was

Apollo, the god of art and wisdom, who carried the sun across the sky every day. It is his raven who decides to sojourn on Earth for a period of time. In Egypt, the Bennu was specifically linked with a period of time. Ancient Greek historians such as Herodotus and Diodorus reported that the Egyptians priests attempted to mathematically calculate the time of the return of the Bennu. He was thus said to live for 500 or for 1461 years, the later coinciding with the Egyptian Great Year, in which all the stars of the firmament had returned in their proper place – once again highlighting a stellar component of the Grail mythos.

The Book of Enoch

The Grail Stone that extends human life is now clearly not the Christian relic. Wolfram goes as far as stating that the Grail was capable of extending physical life. Such symbolism is far removed from anything Christian; physical immortality is nowhere mentioned in the Bible, nor is it specifically important. If anything, it is rather frowned upon. Furthermore, no-one connected with the Cup of the Last Supper, such as the apostles, are never linked with a tradition that this cup would give them immortality or long life.

But it is only one of a number of pagan aspects (which are seldom highlighted) that can be found in Wolfram's account. We already noted that Jessie Weston, first in the paper *The Grail and the Rites of Adonis* and later in the book *From Ritual to Romance,* drew attention to connections between the Grail legend and elements of middle-eastern vegetation rituals. Weston noted that in the Adonis cults, women were given the option of either cutting off their hair, in mourning for the annual death of the god, or prostituting themselves to a stranger for money that would be offered to the goddess. In the Grail tradition, the Grail maiden Sigune is a woman who cuts off her hair, for apparently no specific reason – only those who understand the Hermetic context of the story will be able to read its true context. It is thus possible to see the baldness of Sigune, mourning for the death of her lover, as a relic of the tradition of cutting off hair in mourning for Adonis.

Still, Wolfram's account is not void of Christian symbolism. Identifying that the Grail resides on Earth and why this is the case, Wolfram writes: "When Lucifer and the Trinity began to war with each other, those who did not take sides, worthy, noble angels, had to descend to Earth to that Stone which is forever incorruptible." And: "I do not know whether God forgave them or damned them in the end: for if it was His due He took them back, since that time the Stone has been in the care of those whom God appointed to it and to whom he sent his angel. This, sir, is how matters stand regarding the Grail."

The mention of Lucifer seems to identify this story as Christian in nature. Still, for many Christians, the rest of the account will be largely unfamiliar territory. Nowhere in the Bible does it state that in the battle against Lucifer, a stone was placed on Earth, to which angels had to descend, and that the Stone was cared for by a group appointed by God – the Grail brotherhood.

However, there are some references to the importance of stones in books that are not included in the official bible, but which are nevertheless part of the Jewish-Christian tradition. One of these apocryphal accounts is the Book of Enoch. Enoch was the grandfather of Noah, the patriarch who was able to survive the Deluge. In chapter 68:1, Noah is quoted as saying that "my grandfather Enoch gave me all the secrets in the book and in the parables which had been given to him, and he put them together for me in the words of the book of the parables."

The earliest literature of the so-called "Church Fathers" is filled with references to this Book of Enoch. Justin Martyr, Irenaeus, Origen and Clement of Alexandria all make use of the Book of Enoch. But even though it was widely known and read during the first three centuries after Christ, it became (together with many other books) discredited after the Council of Laodicea in 364 AD. It was then officially "lost", though by the late 1400s, rumours began to circulate that a copy of the Book of Enoch was still extant somewhere. It was the Scottish explorer James Bruce who in 1773 returned from six years in Abyssinia (Ethiopia) with three Ethiopic copies of the lost book. The Ethiopian Church had never taken the same approach towards this book as its Western counterparts, thus safeguarding it for more than 14 centuries. In 1821, Richard Laurence published the first English translation.

Officially, Wolfram therefore had no access to this account, yet it is in chapter 18 of the Book of Enoch that we see a story that closely resembles the story of the Grail: Enoch "surveyed the stone which supports the corners of the earth" and "saw the path of the angels".[51]

The story of Enoch was also told by the Jewish historian Josephus. He brings it in line with the Corpus Hermeticum, when he stated that Enoch had concealed his Wisdom – nous – written down on precious rolls or books, under the pillars of Mercury. He added that these books were the same as those of Hermes, the "Father of Wisdom", who had similarly concealed his books of Wisdom under a pillar. What at first thus seems to be a Christian source of inspiration, in the end turns out to redirect us towards the Hermetica.

Wolfram's sources

Could von Eschenbach have had access to Hermetic material? Could Flegetanis, his source, have possessed such documents? At a superficial level, the *Corpus Hermeticum* was apparently unavailable to Wolfram. It was only rediscovered and translated in the 15th century, by the Florentine instigator of the Renaissance, Cosimo de Medici. As Wolfram lived 200 years earlier, it seems that he therefore had no possible access to the contents of the Hermetica.

But that is theory, and theory should never come in opposition of evidence. In chapter 13 of *Parzival,* Wolfram mentions one "Thabit ibn Qurra" and identifies him as a philosopher. Not many scholars have taken note of this apparently unimportant reference. Rather than an obscure name, or a literary invention, Thabit is a real person, who lived from 835 to 901 AD. He was expelled from the Middle Eastern town of Harran and went to live with the Caliph of Baghdad, Muthahid. Many learned people from his home town followed him to Baghdad, where he was officially recognised as a scientist. Wolfram opens his *Parzival* with the exploits of Gahmuret, Perceval's father, and states that he served in the service of the caliph of Baghdad – as we shall see, approximately 150 years after the death of Thabit.

It should not come as a surprise to learn that at the core of Thabit's belief was the Hermetica. He wrote a total of 166 books, many of which were commentaries on Greek texts, such as those of Plato, Pythagoras, Proclus, Aristotle and the Hermetica. All of these works would later become the cornerstone of the Renaissance, the movement itself inspired by the Europe's rediscovery of the Corpus Hermeticum.

Furthermore, as we know that Wolfram spoke about seeing the Grail in the stars, it should be noted that Thabit was also an astronomer, who did observations in Baghdad to determine the attitude of the sun and the length of the solar year. Finally, it should be noted that the names for the planets in *Parzival* are listed with their Arab names, suggesting an Arab origin for Wolfram's source. Years before the accepted exposure of the Western world to the Hermetica, Wolfram may thus have had access to it, via Arab channels. It is, no doubt, this anomaly that has blinded many researchers for seeing the true Grail. In this case, it is not the Water of Memory that needed to be drunk, but letting go of theoretical frameworks that disabled the intellectual ability to let the evidence speak for itself.

We know that Wolfram identifies his source as one "Flegetanis", who had heard the story of the Grail in Toledo. Of specific interest is that Flegetanis is indeed labelled a heathen, a pagan. It is in correspondence with Thabit, stating in one of his books: "We are the heirs and propagators of Paganism."[52]

As Wolfram was writing in ca. 1200 AD, it is clear that Flegetanis must have heard the story of the Grail in the previous decades. Hence, the 12th century and Toledo is the timeframe and the location where we need to look for Wolfram's historical source. It is no doubt not a surprise that at the time, Toledo was the site where there was a renewed interest in the work of Thabit.

It was Gerard of Cremona (1114-1187) who went to Toledo specifically to find Thabit's work on Euclid, the *Almagest*. Cremona himself translated other texts of Thabit, which eventually give him the title of "father of Arabism in Europe" – a title he earned as he translated no less than 76 books from Arabic into Latin.

Many of Thabit's text reached the West in Latin translations, made by a school founded by the Archbishop of Toledo, Raymond, under the directorship of Archdeacon Dominico Gundisalvi. It brought the world of Arabian learning within the reach of the scholars of Latin Christendom. Was "Flegetanis" one of the members of this school, or perhaps "merely" a person who had heard one of the translated texts, and passed its contents on to Wolfram? Was one of these translated documents one of the documents in Philip of Alsace's possession, who passed it on to Chrétien de Troyes? It is at present impossible to answer these questions affirmatively, but as a framework, I would suggest that it is the most logical historical framework proposed so far: the introduction of the Grail in Western literature chronologically coincided with, and was done by those historians that were exposed by a revival of pagan writings, specifically in Spain, focusing on the Hermetic tradition, which spoke of a divine "Cup" – the Grail Cup, the symbol of Man's divine Quest to reunite itself with the One.

Many Grail authorities have argued that the Grail is new to the late 12th century and that it was introduced by Chrétien de Troyes. This has allowed them to work with a clean slate and endlessly speculate on what the Grail may or may not be. So far, we have seen that the Grail has a clear Egyptian and Greek component and that its nature is therefore pagan, and predates Christianity.

Wolfram von Eschenbach himself stated that his story was old, but had been repackaged: "Hear now age-old tales as if they were new, that they may teach you to speak true."[53] He also notes that it was written in Arabic, but contains a message that was found in Greek religious philosophy.[54] The story retold by Wolfram "as if it were a new tale" was the retelling of the story of Hermes Trismegistus, written down in the Corpus Hermeticum.

Chapter 4: The Grail Initiation

The various texts that make up the Hermetica have been described by the Dutch Hermetic scholar Jacob Slavenburg as a "code".[55] Slavenburg thus posits that the Hermetica are texts that require a decodation. Slavenburg identifies the following specific characteristics of this code that are present in the Hermetic accounts:

1. the use of nicknames;
2. the use of codes – signs, ciphers, etc.;
3. magical writing, i.e. allegories, words with double meanings, etc.

The Hermetica not only gave us the expression of "hermetically sealed", underlining the Hermetica was a text that needed to be decoded, the word Hermes also gave us the word "hermeneutics", for the art of interpreting hidden meaning.

These are the same techniques used by Wolfram in his *Parzival*. Wolfram wanted to re-tell the story of the Hermetic texts, placed in a modern, i.e. medieval setting, but he would nevertheless use the same literary techniques the authors of the Hermetic texts had employed.

This is precisely what Wolfram said: "Hear now age-old tales as if they were new, that they may teach you to speak true."[56] For such endeavours, new terms are often coined, to rejuvenate tired or controversial words; and this is where the role of Chrétien de Troyes, when he coined the term "Grail" to describe the cup – the Crater – comes into its proper perspective.

There are further parallels between Wolfram's *Parzival* and the *Corpus Hermeticum*. In *Parzival*, we read: "This grace is His Who penetrates our thoughts. Thoughts are darkness without light. Only the Deity can be so pure and bright that He pierces that wall of darkness, like a rider running to the attack, but soundless and noiseless."[57] The fifth treatise of the *Corpus Hermeticum* reads: "so that one of His rays, at least one, may flash into your mind. For thought alone can see that which is hidden, inasmuch as thought itself is hidden from sight."[58] Both texts speak of how thought can be penetrated by divine grace – which brings illumination.

It is not the only parallel. In *Parzival,* we read: "God is man and His Father's Word."[59] In the Hermetic treatises, we read: "The shining Word coming forth from Nous is the son of God."[60] God can only be comprehended by insight and intuition – the reason which is so dear to our modern Era is of no use for the servant; nothing within the realm of reason will reveal the presence of God; insight and intuition will.

It is in the fourth treatise that we specifically learn that it is Intellect that is the substance of God – Nous. The soul needs to be filled by that intellect. The Grail cup is thus filled with insight. It is in this cup that we leave this knowledge behind when we incarnate; to remember what we have forgotten, we need to drink from it again. Drinking from it, will gives us knowledge.

The water of the cup is thus a baptism of intellect. The call for baptism is clearly present in the Hermetica: "Dip yourself in this Krater, you who are able."[61] The role of baptism is also important in Wolfram's account. In *Parzival,* the baptismal water also comes from the Grail: "The baptismal font was tilted slightly in the direction of the Grail, and immediately it was full of water, neither too warm nor too cold."[62] Baptism therefore takes the form of drinking from the water, but also from being baptised in it: to become submerged in knowledge.

One vital aspect of the Hermetic code is that the central object of worship is left undefined, as this was reserved knowledge for the initiate. This approach echoes Chrétien's, who left the nature of the Grail undefined too. It is important to note that for all of Wolfram's criticism of Chrétien, he never once argued Chrétien should have identified the Grail. That Wolfram himself did as much, is no doubt due to the fact that by then, the Grail was already being transformed in a Christian relic: the Cup of the Last Supper. Furthermore, with Chrétien and Wolfram, we see that the nature of the Grail remained unidentified; even Wolfram only go as far as to say that it is a stone. But what the purpose of this object is, is never specified. Instead, we only get to hear about what the object is able to perform.

When we delve into the Hermetic texts, we do see the true nature of what the Grail truly is, and what it contains. At first sight, this may seem a contradiction: that Wolfram and Chrétien do not give details, and the Hermetica does. But the difference is that the Grail story was written for the general public, which, according to the Hermetic principle, should not be told about the secret of the mysteries; only the initiates, the Grail Brotherhood, were allowed to know.

The secret nature of the brotherhood is hinted at in a discussion between Trevrizent and Perceval, when the former states: "Whoever asked me about this before and squabbled with me for not telling him about it has won infamy by it. It was Kyot who asked me to conceal it."[63] Therefore, just like the Hermetic brotherhood was fortunate enough to learn the contents of the Corpus Hermeticum, so the Grail Brotherhood was able to learn about the Grail upon initiation.

The contents of the Grail

The Cup or Monad, the fourth treatise of the Hermetica, is a discussion between master and pupil on the nature of Mankind's nature. It argues that some people "understand" and others do not: "They who do not understand the tidings, these, since they possess the aid of Reason [only] and not Mind, are ignorant wherefore they have come into being and whereby."

Man is thus described as being made up of a mortal body, with an immortal soul. It stresses that there is a "divine spark" in all of us. Each of us has a "part of God", but only some are aware of it.

Those who are, are blessed with "Mind". Those who understand, will live on Earth to contemplate God's work. Those who do not understand, will pursue physical pursuits and earthly pleasures.

It thus separates Mankind into two categories, whereby it is this knowledge what divides the candidates for the Grail Brotherhood from the non-candidates. At the same time, the explanation of this division and the true nature of Man, is the first major revelation members are privileged to receive.

The Hermetica makes an important distinction between the minds of men: it argues that all Mankind has received Reason (logos), but not all have Mind. "Mind" has been placed on Earth as if it were a trophy individual beings can win: the Grail Quest. But what is Mind? Modern psychology would label this "self-awareness". In the Bible, this seems limited to knowing that Adam and Eve, after eating from the Tree of Knowledge, are naked. But it is clear that in the Hermetica, this is not what is hinted at. Though Mankind might be different from all other species on Earth in the possibility that we alone possess self-awareness, the "Mind" in the Hermetica seems to be of an even higher order. It hints at the possibility that somehow, within each of us, is not only a divine spark, but also divine knowledge, which possessed as a discarnate soul, but which the soul has apparently chosen to forget while incarnated on Earth – as otherwise there would not be a distinction between Mankind and the gods. The Hermetica states that those without Wisdom are like irrational creatures, who act upon their feelings and impulses, give in to the pleasures of the body and its appetites, in the belief that for its sake, man had come into being.

Those who had received "Mind", had been released from death's bonds. To understand what this specifically means, we need to enter into the core belief of the Hermetica. Ancient Egyptians – and Hermeticists – believed that Mankind was subject to a cycle of incarnations, in which whether or not a person would reincarnate depended largely on whether he had lived correctly. Only when that person understood how to live, and lived accordingly, was he free from this cycle: he would return to the Creator, the One, no longer subject to the cycles of continued incarnations on Earth. In the Hermetica, this is written down as to "how many are the bodies through which we have to pass" before we can find "The One".

Perceval's Initiation

These are lofty principles, but the Hermetic text is also very practical. It states that most of Mankind is in inner turmoil: one cannot give himself to the body, and yet have divine gnosis. To attain the latter, all pleasures of the body need to be despised: food, drink, sex, women, etc. It argues that it is indeed hard "to leave the things we have grown used to, which meet our gaze on every side, and turn ourselves back to the Old Old Path". That which we can see, is easy to believe, "whereas things that appear not are hard to believe".

The "Old Old Path" is the Grail Quest, and that what Perceval set off on when he left his mother, in search of adventure, a voyage that would lead to his initiation into the Grail Brotherhood.

The path to God came in two distinct possibilities. One is direct, whereby the seeker is guided to his destiny. It is as if an unseen hand guides a person along a series of synchronicities, which in retrospect will be shown to be a series of carefully designed events that to the uninitiated mind will be understood as coincidences – rather than the divine path that they are. For the person following this path, it requires a trust in God: "if you are in the right mind, you ought to put your trust in God. He will help you, for He Must. His help has never failed."[64]

The other path is through a mediator, whereby guides – physical guides rather than a series of synchronicities – bring a person to the required level of understanding that for someone who is trying to return to God, God must help, and has "never failed" to do so.

As to Perceval's quest, that is one that is largely constructed through mediators, though it is God himself who directs Perceval to find his first mediator, Sigune: "The dauntless young warrior was riding in search of adventure. Then God too thought for his guidance, and Parzival found a hermitess."[65]

Perceval then goes on to meet a knight pilgrim, who advises him to seek out his third teacher, Trevrizent. But Perceval leaves it to God's intervention whether or not his path will cross that of the hermit. In the end, his horse decides to lead the knight to his destiny.

Later, Perceval reflects that "only now do I perceive how long I have ridden unguided."[66] And when he finally arrives at the Grail Castle, the abode of the Grail Brotherhood, it seems that God had already announced his future arrival. Trevirzent explains that "we fell on our knees in prayer before the Grail. All at once we saw written upon it that a knight should come, and if from him a question came, our sorrow would be ended."[67]

When he has finally arrived at the Grail Castle, Perceval seeks admittance to the Brotherhood. His initiation occurs in two stages: twice, he will appear before the Grail, but the first time, he will fail the challenge.

The failure comes about when Gurnemanz advises Parzival not to ask too many questions when is in front of the Grail court. But when he heeds that warning, it is actually the cause of his first failure: he remains a fool as he does not pose the proper question.[68]

Later, Perceval reflects: "I will allow myself no joy until I have seen the Grail [...] My thoughts drive me toward that goal, and never will I serve from it as long as I shall live. If I am to hear the scorn of the world because I obeyed the law of courtesy, then his counsel may not have been wholly wise. It was the novel Gurnemanz who advised me to refrain from impertinent questions and resist all unseemly behaviour."[69]

However, it is clear that an improper understanding of courtesy is not the only aspect of Perceval that is not yet ready. For one, he assumes that Gurnemanz himself was not the cleverest of men, not fully versed in the proper behaviour; but Perceval never ponders the question whether Gurnemanz may have said exactly what he was supposed to say, to see whether Perceval would rise to the challenge. It should thus not come as a surprise that one knight even goes as far as say outright that Perceval does not possess intelligence – that he is unlikely to become a member of the Brotherhood.[70]

Years later, a somewhat wiser Perceval reaches a refuge where the hermit Trivrezent (or Trevrezent) lived. It is here that the second stage of his admittance to the Grail Brotherhood will commence.

At first sight, the name of this hermit seems meaningless. But it follows the Hermetic code, whereby those with eyes, will see. Trevrezent is in fact a transliterated version of "Trismegistus," "Thrice-Great," the title given Thoth-Hermes, the supreme Initiator in the Hermetica. The name is most likely derived from "Triplex scientia" which in French becomes "Treble Escient", threefold wisdom, or Trevrezent, or Trevrizent.

As such, the story of Perceval and his meeting with Trevrezent is identical to the meeting of Tat, the pupil, with the master, Hermes. It underlines the fact that Perceval is indeed in search of initiation… into the Hermetica.

Trevrizent is described as a saint, truthful, an ascetic who does not eat meat and who leads a holy life and frequently fasts. Perceval is welcomed, cleansed and anointed in the ritual fashion, and refreshed with "herbs". This might seem quite innocent, but it is also a procedure common to all initiation rituals. In preparation for initiation into the Eleusian Mysteries, there was a day of fasting in commemoration of Demeter's fasting while searching for Persephone. The fast was broken while drinking a special drink of barley and pennyroyal, called kykeon.

In the Eleusian Mystery, the next step involved the initiates entering a great hall called the Telesterion. In the center stood the Anaktoron (the palace), which only the hierophantes could enter, andwhere sacred objects were stored. Here, the initiates were shown the sacred relics of Demeter. This was the most secretive part of the Mysteries and those who had been initiated were forbidden to ever speak of the events that took place in the Telesterion. The penalty was death.

This has a direct parallel in the Grail initiation, as Trevrezent then escorted Perceval into a cavern. Caves were used as sites of initiations for millennia, representing the return of the candidate into the womb of Mother Earth, to be reborn. Inside the cave, Perceval was instructed about the descent of Lucifer and his companion angels, accompanied by "neutral" spiritual beings. Trevrezent tells Perceval of the Holy Grail, and that only those who serve it may know it, forming a brotherhood of dedicated knights: those who have received "Mind".

Though Trevrezent at first states that the Grail is connected with Lucifer and the rebellion in heaven, whereby the Grail was placed on Earth and that the neutral angels could use it, later, Trevrizent apologises to Perceval, stating that he had lied to him as a means of distracting him, adding that the neutral angels are damned also, for they had not sided with God.

Some have seen this change in doctrine as a literary problem: thhat Wolfram had created one mystery too many and had to now retract. But why he could not have done this by removing or reworking the original passage is never explained. Instead, it seems apparent that Trevrezent knew that certain knowledge could only be imparted on a piecemeal basis, whereby each new ingredient slightly modifies – distils – the previous premise.

The Fall of Mankind is therefore explained as the decision of the "angels" to begin a series of incarnations on Earth, which is linked with the drinking of the cup that brings forgetfulness. Wolfram seems to be suggesting that the neutral souls had to incarnate, though they are served by the Grail – is the Grail Brotherhood therefore the collective of the incarnated souls of the neutral angels, who use the Grail as the mechanism to return to God? Of those incarnated souls, surely the neutral souls must find it easier to throw of the pleasures of the Earth than Lucifer's minions, who specifically desired to come and live on Earth and partake of its earthly pleasures?

If this interpretation is correct, then this is actually one aspect where Wolfram excelled above Manetho who left us the Hermetic treatises. Of course, even if this interpretation is correct, the question is whether Wolfram's conclusion was correct or not.

But back to Perceval. Though somewhat wiser, Perceval nevertheless still boasts about all he had done and of his desire to serve the Grail. But the hermit warns him against pride, upholding instead the virtue of humility. He tells Perceval of the Fisher King's fate, and that no one could know where the Grail was to be found unless it summoned him. But there had been one, years before, a "witless fool," who had left the castle sin-laden because he had failed to ask his host the reason for his suffering. Perceval then admits to the hermit that he had been that "fool" – a perfect name for someone without "Intellect", but only using "Reason". And it is here that semantics, that other "code" used by the Hermetica, once again comes to the surface, as Perceval is actually a play of words of "fol parfait", the "perfect fool".

Perceval's admittance of being this fool, is of course another prerequisite for his initiation. And Trevrezent builds upon this admission, revealing the opportunities and misdemeanours Perceval had in the past and how to still become endowed with Mind, despite previous failures. Though Perceval may not be the wisest, one of his greatest accomplishments is that he has been able to turn away from the passions of the body: "A life so concluded that God is not robbed of the soul through fault of the body, and which can obtain the world's favour with dignity, that is a worthy work."[71]

Though Perceval has many faults, no-one is perfect. If anything, the Grail Initiates all seem to have more faults than virtues; the only difference, it seems, is that the initiates are aware of, and have accepted them. The Fisher King Anfortas' fault was agnosy, which Hermetism considers to be the greatest of evils. It is therefore clear that Anfortas was unable to adequately serve his office as Grail King. He constantly suffered from his wound, whereby on occasion his wails seemed to echo around the Grail castle that made the hair stand up on people's neck. Worst of all, his shortcomings have resulted in his inability to continue to further the cause of the brotherhood – his pierced testicles have made it impossible for him to procure an heir who would be the rightful Grail King.

As a consequence, a new heir needed to be sought, within the small group of noble men that the Grail finds worthy. Though it is never specifically stated as such, it seems that Perceval, a nephew of the king, is selected, who then has to embark on a series of adventures that will eventually bring him face to face with the Grail, before he is tested one final time, to see whether he will be able to take the office of Grail King: the Grand Master of the Grail Brotherhood. Even though he will initially fail the test, he is given a second try and the Grail's need for a "noble heir" may be another reason why Perceval was given a second chance.

The story of Perceval is therefore very human; he is not born as a Greek superhero that will one day do great things. Instead, we are confronted with a boy who is capable of extraordinary anger. Once he has conquered that vice, he needs to work through various other "character deficits" before he is finally allowed to become a member of the brotherhood – and even then, he is warned to take special care of his lust for pride – humility should be of paramount importance to him.

The Hermetic Initiation

As already mentioned in passing, the story of the Grail and Perceval follows the classic sequence of the ancient initiation methodology. Firstly, someone will prepare the myst. Next, the myst will be baptised, the first confirmation that the myst is willing to continue; the information received so far has been understood and he makes a commitment to further his learning. Once baptised, the mystagogue will inform the myst of the total doctrine that is at the core of the "secret school". Thus, Trevrizent explains to Perceval the mysteries of the Grail.[72]

Apart from using the same structure, the Hermetic treatises and the Grail initiation also reveal their oral nature: the instructions consist of either formal lectures or informal conversations, conducted by the master in a private conversation with the student. In *Parzival,* the secrets of the Grail brotherhood are explained in four discourses: on God (461, 28-467, 10), on the Grail (468, 23-471, 29); on Anfortas (476, 24-484, 30) and finally on himself (495, 7-499, 30), mimicking the treatise-like approach of the Hermetica, with each treatise focusing on specific subsections of the Hermetic doctrine.[73]

Like the Hermetic doctrine, Perceval's lessons are more than merely the secrets of the brotherhood or the nature of the Grail. Trevrizent also teaches Perceval knowledge of herbs,[74] but especially of astrology. Hermeticism also explains the basic premises of astrology, but at the same time argues that its power is limited to the bodily world and does not encompass the perfect soul. For a soul that has received Nous, that soul rules the planet, rather than the planets rule him. This message is echoed in *Parzival*, where it is stated that "Destiny no longer has any power over it; he has achieved the soul's peace."[75] He has become liberated from the bonds of the material world, for he has full understanding.

That Perceval's initiation is into the Hermetic tradition, is substantiated by Wolfram's inclusion of herbal lore in Perceval's learning. The Hermetica is not only a body of religious material, it is also a body of medicine. Hermes' symbol to this day remains used as the traditional symbol of healing – the doctor.

In the second century AD, Clement of Alexandria mentioned "Books" of Hermes, adding that there were 42 suck books, "all worth knowing".[76] Thirty-six contained the total philosophy of the Egyptians, which the prophets should know by heart. The other six dealt with aspects of medicine.

The important role of medicine is also stressed when Trevrizent reveals that dragonwort is one of the herbs that might cure Anfortas' wounds: "With a poisoned spear he was wounded so in the jousting [...] pierced through his testicles."[77] In Antiquity, the poison from a snake or from plants springing form the blood of a snake was an ancient recipe from making such potions. A Hermetic treatise states that Dracontea is "the plant of Aquarius. If you wash yourself with the juice of this plant, you will not get stung by any reptile." The text then goes on to provide further details. It shows that the nature of the wound was known, and its natural antidote was written down in ancient Hermetic medicinal doctrine – dragonwort – which was identified as a possible cure.

Once equipped with this body of knowledge, the myst is admitted into the brotherhood, where he will see the Grail and understand life's true purpose. It is Cundrie, the messenger of the Grail, who announces to the myst that he has reached the stage of spiritual peace.[78] Perceval is now spiritually reborn; he is a "New Man". In the *Corpus Hermeticum,* it states: "I am not now the man I was, but I have been born in Intellect."[79] In *Parzival,* Perceval's rebirth is the topic of the 15th and 16th book, which have no counterpart in Chrétien's *Le Conte du Graal,* which underlines once again the Hermetic nature of Wolfram's account.

Now that he is aware of the secrets of the doctrine, the initiate is asked to keep the mystery a secret – just like the initiate into the Mysteries of Eleusis was told to keep silent, on pain of death. In the Hermetica, Hermes tells Tat that this is so as "in order not to divulge all to the many but only to those whom God himself selects."[80]

In case there remains some doubt about the initiatory nature of the Grail, it should be noted that what Perceval learns is specifically referred to as the "Mysteries of the Grail".[81] Furthermore, as the student has now become an initiate himself, he will be asked to become a teacher, to continue the perpetual mission of the Grail: later, Perceval will teach Feirefiz and prepare him for his initiation; he, in his turn, will return to his country, to teach the message of the Grail there. And it is here that we see the missionary zeal of the Grail Brotherhood: not so much to convert, but to inform, the people of the world of the true spiritual doctrine.

The Grail procession

One of the most enduring images of the Grail legends is that of the procession of the Grail, leading up to a meal in which the Grail gives nourishment to those around the table – witnessed by Perceval on his first visit to the Grail Castle, when he was still a young knight who did not yet understand what he sees.

The Dutch Hermetic scholar Gilles Quispel argues that a

sacred meal was the normal extension of the initiation rites into the mystery tradition. Sacred meals are known in the cults of Mithras, Isis, Serapis and other traditions in which the Hermetic literature sits.[82] In the Eleusian Mysteries, the Pannychis was one of its including highlights; it was an all-night feast accompanied by dancing and merriment. The dancing was done in the Rharian Field, which was, according to legend, the first location where grain grew. A bull sacrifice also took place late that night or early the next morning. That day, the initiates also honoured the dead by pouring libations from special vessels – perhaps a further parallel to the Grail Cup?

One of the former Grail maidens is Sigune, who is Perceval's cousin and who acts as one of his guides on his road to enlightenment. She was a childhood companion of both Perceval and his future bride, Condwiramurs, presumably at different times. She tells him how she had formerly been the Grail Bearer, like her mother Schoysiane before her.

The role of the Grail Bearer was apparently reserved for teenage women, maidens, before they married. This again is in direct parallel with the mystery religions, where centres were operated by a group of young women, often led by an older widow. Indeed, Wolfram notes that Sigune became an anchorite after her fiancé died: "This engagement-ring I wear for the sake of a man, whose love I never knew by any human action; yet my maidenly heart is compelled to love him. He is here within, the man whose jewel I have worn since Orilus slew him in joust. […] I am a virgin and unwed yet before God he is my husband."

As a consequence, she is no longer able to carry the divine Grail, deciding to live entirely alone in a cell with no door. On Perceval's third encounter with Sigune, she tells him that though she lives in the wilderness, she is nourished by the Grail: "Cundrie the sorceress brings my food punctually every Saturday evening. So I have no concerns about food of which

I always get enough."[83]

The role of the Grail Bearer was specifically important, as the procession of the Grail is that of a procession of maidens, in which one is specifically selected to carry the Grail. She who carried the Grail, had to "preserve her purity".[84] The account also suggests that it is the Grail itself who selects its bearer – just like it selects those whom it deems opportune to return to serve him.

At the time of Perceval's visit, the Grail Maiden is Repanse de Schoye: "Last of all came the lovely maiden, Repanse de Schoye. The Grail permitted, I was told, only her to carry it, no one else. In her heart there was much virtue, and her skin had the luster of flowers."[85] In Wolfram's account, which is seen as one of the most detailed renditions of this procession, she is wearing an Arabian pall,[86] which once again underlines the Arab – pagan – context of his story.

The Grail procession comprises the knights and the 24 maidens attending the Grail entering the hall, but it is only Repanse de Schoie who is permitted by the sacred object to be its bearer; she comes last. This gives a total of 25 maidens. Furthermore the attendants were grouped in numbers: first four, then eight, then twelve divided into two sixes. Each group carries corresponding numbers of lights.

This composition and the detail given to it in the account has baffled many commentators and for the unattentive reader, it might just be deemed a fruit of Wolfram's imagination. But two authors, Henry and Renee Kahane, were amongst those who pointed out the marked similarity of this line-up with the *Hermetica,* where the groups, in the same order, "represent the twenty-four stations of the journey of the soul: 4 elements plus 8 spheres plus 12 signs of the zodiac plus 1, the Monad." [87] Thus, both the Grail and the Monad – the Cup – come last and the Grail procession once again reflects its Hermetic origins.

The first group of four maidens, dressed in brown wool, reflects the four elements. The second group of eight maidens, dressed in green samite, reflects the celestial spheres. The third group of twelve maidens, wearing silk dresses of two fabrics interwoven with gold, reflects the twelve signs of the zodiac. Finally, one woman dressed in Arabian pall stands for the One-and-Only, God.

That the number is important is later enforced, when Perceval mentions to Trevrizent that he saw 25 maidens.[88] Every Grail procession always contains 25 maidens, suggesting that the number is indeed important.[89]

After Repanse de Schoye has carried the Grail inside, she is then placed at the centre of the group, with twelve maidens on either side.[90] Kahane & Kahane conclude that "the Grail procession, in other words, is a representation of the mystic journey of the soul toward the Monad, itself symbolized by the Grail."[91]

The Isian Initiation

The Grail procession was only reserved for the eyes of the initiates. But in ancient times, these Mysteries also had more public processions that were witnessed by hundreds if not thousands of ordinary people. And should it come as a surprise to learn that it is in the account of one such procession that lies the source of Chrétien de Troyes' story?

Though we have focused on Wolfram's account, Chrétien's basic plot can also be read as the story of a Hermetic conversion. *Le Conte du Graal* is the "Story of the Grail" and could be a direct reference to the story of the krater. From this perspective, Chrétien would have focused on the Grail – the Cup – itself, whereas Wolfram's *Parzival* is more focused towards the path of the initiate and the mission of the brotherhood.

If the fourth Hermetic treatise is at the foundation of Chrétien's story, then Wolfram is indeed allowed to criticise *Le*

Conte du Graal as a subversion of the story. However, it is more likely that the eleventh book of Apuleius's *Metamorphoses* (also known as *The Golden Ass*) was the real inspiration for Chrétien's story.

The Golden Ass is the only complete Latin novel to survive. Chrétien, or his master, may have been involved with the schools of Paris, which were rapidly rediscovering the classical literature and philosophy. The extent of his exposure to this new wave of thinking has so far not been conclusively proven – or disproved.[92] But the textual correspondences between Apuleuis' *Metamorphoses* and Chrétien's account would suggest he was aware of these – perhaps via the Count of Champagne, his sponsor.

Apuleius lived in the 2nd century AD. Born at Madaura in North Africa, he was educated at Carthage and Athens. He travelled extensively in the East in order to become an initiate of various religious mysteries, and then practised for some time as an advocate in Rome. Returning to Africa, he married a rich widow, Aemilia Pudentilla, whose family charged him with having won her by magic. His defence survives as *Apologia* or *De Magia.* He was subsequently acquitted and devoted the remainder of his life to philosophy and literature.

The first ten books of *Metamorphoses* detail the transformation of Lucius, a frivolous young man, into an ass. This unfortunate transformation occurs as the result of Lucius' desire to use magic – without having received the proper training for it. Like Perceval, Lucius is a fool, bedazzled by items he does not understand and hence should steer away from.

The story then speaks of his ensuing tribulations. The 11th book tackles Lucius' repentance, when he becomes a disciple of Isis and finally seems to have understood – he has received knowledge. His restoration to human shape occurs by the mercy of Isis; his initiation into her rites form the climax of the work and are regarded as being based on direct acquaintance with the Isis mysteries.

The book can thus be seen to correspond with Apuleius' personal life – a somewhat fictionalised autobiography, in which the ass as an animal portrays the stupidity of the myst. The novel is filled with information on mythology and mystery religions and thus became the source of much borrowing by later writers, such as Boccaccio and Cervantes. Did Chrétien also borrow from it? If so, it is clear that his Grail procession has been borrowed from the Procession of Isis and that the Grail is the aureum poculum of Apuleius – the Golden Cup.

Even though one interpreter, Richard Barber, stated that Chrétien's account has no "hidden meanings [...], no agenda of ritual or symbol or allegory"[93], Barber follows this with the statement that "The Story of the Grail differs from [Chrétien's earlier documents] in that Chrétien is dealing with the psychology of growing up rather than the psychology of love."[94] The story of Lucius is just that: the story of a man growing up.

Lucius' salvation doesn't come from a teacher's wisdom; his comes through divine revelation. Isis reveals herself in a vision to Lucius, who witnesses "the parade which precedes the Great Procession". After a group of men and women in fancy dress and other worshippers, there "came on the groups of those who had been initiated in the sacred mysteries, men and women, of all ranks and ages, shining in the pure radiance of their linen dress. The women had their damp hair wrapped round with a transparent veil and the heads of the men, completely shaven, gleamed brightly. A shrill tinkling sound spread around from the bronze, silver and even golden sistra which they were shaking."

This group was followed by the "noble priests of the sacred cult, the earth-bound stars of the great religion, in their white linen vestments bound around their chests and reaching to their feet. These carried the spectacular symbols of the greatest gods.

The first carried a lantern giving out a clear light, not at all like those used to illumine our evening banquets but a golden cup giving out a flame broader than its central opening. A second priest, dressed in the same manner, carried the altar, that is, the auxilia, named because of the protective providence shown by the Goddess. A third walked carrying a palm-branch skilfully gilded and a staff of Mercury. A fourth displayed the symbol of justice, a deformed left hand with an open palm: this seemed more suitable than the right hand because of its natural sluggishness and its lack of cunning and versatility. The same man carried a small rounded vessel in the shape of a female breast from which he poured milk. A fifth carried a golden basket full of laurel twigs and a sixth an amphora." We note the presence of a "golden cup" as one of the symbols of Isis that are carried by the priests. Still, it is not the climax of the procession…

"Without delay the gods then came forward, condescending to walk on human feet." This is most likely a reference to the statues of the gods being carried around by the priests. First is Anubis, whereby priests carry his sacred symbols and utensils. One priest "carried a chest containing secret objects and concealing within itself the operta of the glorious religion."

It is another priest that reveals the re-appearance of the Grail as a cup, depicted as a sign on the breast of a priest: "Another bore on his happy breast the adored image of the highest Deity. This was not like an ox nor a bird nor a wild beast nor even of a human being but it aroused awe by its artful inventiveness and uniqueness. It was an inexplicable statement of the higher religion which must be covered by a great silence. It […] was a small cup most skilfully hollowed out with a round base, decorated on the outside with marvellous Egyptian images. Its mouth was not very high but rose up to a channel ending in a long spout. The handle on the other side was twisted far back and joined to the cup by a long curve. On it was an asp which in a contorted knot held itself up with its scaly neck in a streaked puff." Here, we have the definition of the Grail Cup, as no doubt Chrétien de Troyes saw it. With the presence of the asp, we have returned to the story of Apollo's raven and how he was delayed in filling the cup by a serpent.

Once he has seen this procession, Lucius states that he "reached the edge of death and crossed the threshold of Prosperina. I was driven through all the elements and I returned. In the middle of the night I saw the sun blazing with a clear light. I came close to the gods below and to the gods above and worshipped them in their presence." Finally, he ends with the message: "behold I have told you things which you must not understand, even though you have heard them." Like Perceval, the initiated Lucius is asked not to repeat what he has now experienced and knows.

The doctrine of the Hermetica and the Mysteries of Isis are largely identical. Thoth, the precursor of Hermes Trismegistus, was the Egyptian deity who expounded and put down in writing the initiation mysteries of Osiris, Isis and Horus. It were the mysteries that initiated people into the doctrine of the Hermetica; the Mysteries were the preparation, whereby the mysts worked together as a brotherhood to study the Hermetica, so that they would become familiar with and have direct experience of the Monad.

It is intriguing that so many have not seen the initiatic nature of the Grail story, whereby the treasure hunt for the Grail and the possibility of the "Cup of Christ" drew a veil across the Grail that seemed to squelch its call for a spiritual quest. Indeed, many have been told things they did not understand, even though they had heard them.

But is the story of Perceval and the Grail merely the retelling of the meeting of Tat with Hermes, i.e. "The Cup" tract of the Corpus Hermeticum? Or is it, like the story of Lucius, inspired on real events? Does "the code" go beyond this, and does the account actually relate to real people? If so, then perhaps the names that Wolfram used in his account may be able to reveal the names of these actual characters. If so, it would mean that real historical characters once possessed the Grail?

Chapter 5: The Spanish origins of the Grail

Wolfram von Eschenbach claimed that the account on which he had based *Parzival* came from Kyot the Provencal, who himself had to learn Arabic to translate his own, much older source, itself a restatement from an even more ancient version.

In the study of the Christian Gospels, such a source document has been labelled the Q document, or Q (from the German Quelle, "source"), which is a lost textual source for the Gospel of Matthew and Gospel of Luke. Though now widely accepted, the same cannot be said for the Grail, even though it is now clear that the Grail was not an invention, but a reworking of a known, more ancient, account – exactly like Wolfram had said.

In the 12th century, people with knowledge of Arabic were able to put their hands on Hermetic documents, including "chapter 4", detailing the story of the Grail – or the Cup. That document itself was indeed a restatement of an older belief, based on the ancient Greek and Egyptian religions.

But the story of Wolfram is more than just the rendition of that document; it is also the story of a quest, by the likes of Perceval, meeting characters like Anfortas and Trevrezent. When we once again consult the work of Jacob Slavenburg, we note that one of the specific characteristics of the code present in the Hermetic accounts was the use of nicknames. And the question should be asked whether these are real people, or fabricated characters, invented by Wolfram so that he could drive home the message of the Hermetica?

Wolfram himself writes: "he [Kyot the Provencal] searched in old books of Latin for the name of the people, who God accounted worthy of keeping the wonderful Grail." Wolfram himself thus suggests that the characters are indeed real, underlining the dual sources on which his account was based: one is about the Grail (the Hermetic treatises, specifically the Cup), the other are Latin, historical texts about the people who kept the Grail. But before we try to identify these people, first we need to try to identify his "Deep Throat": Kyot the Provencal.

Kyot the Provencal

Ulrich Ernst described Kyot as a key element to Wolfram's account: "Since the beginning, the Wolfram-research is loaded with the heavy mortgage of the Kyot problem, which on the way to an adequate interpretation of 'Parzival' has created a dividing barrier, which has even placed the great poet himself in a dubious light."[95] Karl Simrock was one of those who argued that Kyot was a literary invention, to make Wolfram's story seem more genuine. The controversy is as follows: if Wolfram invented Kyot, then Wolfram did not base his account on a story in existence; if Kyot existed, then Wolfram did not at all invent the story of the Grail, which would mean his Grail account sits within an older tradition.

Whether or not Kyot was invented, Wolfram does provide detail to this character. He stated that "Kyot, the well-known master, found in Tudela, discarded, set down in heathen writing, the first source of this adventure."[96] Wolfram at one point refers to "Kyot the singer".[97] At the time, singing was the normal method of how these texts would be rendered, echoing the tradition of the troubadours – the medieval versions of the opera or the modern musical. From this description, Kahane and Kahane pinpoint Kyot as "a man of the 12th century Renaissance. He represents the culture of the Catalan-Provencal Raum. His training must have taken place in the atmosphere of the Arabic-Jewish-Spanish cultural symbiosis which marked the group of translators and geomancers of Tarazona."[98]

Despite such detail, many have argued that Kyot must have been a fictional character, as Wolfram described him as a "famous author". Yet, as he remains "officially" unidentified, by default the scholars argue that he cannot have been famous. Alas, this is circular reasoning and none of those claiming Kyot is a fictional character have not been taken to task for it. If anything, Wolfram is aiding us, by stating that Kyot is actually a famous author, and hence we should seek his identity within the small group of famous chroniclers of his time.

Several candidates have been put forward for who Kyot the Provencal might be. The most often fingered possibility is Guyot de Provins. The name, orally, is very close to "Kyot from Province". He lived from 1145 until 1208, travelled widely and retired to become a monk, first at Clairvaux, then at Cluny. His patron was Philippe of Alsace, Chrétien de Troyes' patron.

However, critics argue that despite an apparent similarity in name, he was not of Provence, but of Provins, a Northern French town in the Champagne region, between Troyes and Paris. Furthermore, it has been argued that none of his writings deal with Grail material, which is true, but this in itself should not be held against him, as he might merely have given such material to others, unwilling to write about it himself.

At the beginning of the 13th century, already old, Guyot de Provins compiled his "Bible", a satire on the different feudal estates of his time. In it, he listed his several protectors, which included Emperor Frederick Barbarossa, Henry II of England, Richard the Lionheart and Alfonso II of Aragon.

It is possible that Wolfram and Guyot met on the occasion of the festivities organised by Frederick Barbarossa in Maguncia or on the Wartburg in the court of the Landgrave Hermann of Thuringa. The Wartburg was the German court most frequented by such poets, and Wolfram was there in 1203.

Another candidate for "Kyot" is one Guillelmus Narbonensis, William of Narbonne. His name is found at the bottom of acts from Toledo, dating from ca. 1160 – the correct timeframe, and the correct location.[99] Like Toledo, Narbonne was a centre of Latin-

Hebrew translations and a great centre where alchemy flourished – alchemy itself being based on the *Corpus Hermeticum.*

Wolfram himself specifically refers to Tudela, a town in Navarre, close to the Aragonese borders. It belonged to the bishopric of Tarazona, which became one of the great centres of the transmission of Arabic culture to the west. The work was done under the direction of Bishop Michael of Tarazona (1119-1151), with Hugh of Santalla being one of its best known translators. Hugh frequently dealt with Hermetic materials, particularly those on science. He translated the *Book of Causes,* which ends with a famous alchemical text, known as the *Tabula Smaragdina.* The book was an Arabic treatise from the 9th century, attributed to Apollonius of Tyana, who is known to have been a Hermetist.

Tudela is the location from which the next candidate comes from, as Kahane & Kahane have identified Kyot as William of Tudela, "Kyot" being Wolfram's transliteration of the Catalan "Guillot", a diminutive of "Guillem" – William.

Guillem de Tudela was the author of the first part of the *Guerre contre les Albigeois.*[100] He stated that this story was inspired by the *Chanson d'Antioch,* which contains a well-known legend of the Swan Knight, in which an unknown knight arrives in a boat pulled by a swan, in order to protect a princess. The story of the Swan King is similar to an episode in the story of Lohengrin, Perceval's son.

He is however best remembered for *Guerre contre les Albigeois,* or the *Song of the Cathar Wars,* which is the recounting of the events of the years 1204-1218 in Southern France. In an effort to extirpate the Cathar heresy, Pope Innocent III launched what became known as the Albigensian Crusade.

The 'song' was written in two parts, the first by William of Tudela, the second by an anonymous author. William has often been identified as a supporter of the Crusade, whereas the author of the second part is wholeheartedly in sympathy with the southerners, although not with the heretics themselves. The Song stands as a historical source of great importance, not least because it depicts the side that lost – and whom are often left out of the accounts. The poem is also a skilful, dramatic and often impassioned composition, evoking the brilliant world of landed knights and the glories and bloody realities of battle.

William of Tudela was a Southerner, as well as a contemporary of Wolfram – which is what Wolfram argued.[101] We know that he was a clerk brought up in Tudela, in Navarre, then moved to the French town of Montauban, where he stayed for eleven years. Wolfram also described Kyot as a jongleur and William of Tudela described himself as such.

Three primary candidates, but who is it? Perhaps an injection of further details about Kyot might bring the shortlist down to a winner.

It is stated that Kyot had to learn the "abc", "but without the art of black magic" before he was able to understand the "heathen language" in which the Grail story was written down in: "It helped him that he was baptized, else this story would still be unknown. No heathen art could be of use in revealing the nature of the Grail and how its mysteries were discovered."[102]

Many students have found it intriguing that Wolfram stresses the Christian side of Kyot. After all, we are confronted with a book here and it is clear that Kyot is not the most likely person to discover its secrets: he finds it discarded, does not understand its language and once he has learned it, is able to understand the story of the Grail. Kahane and Kahane agree that the reason for stressing Kyot's Christian nature is bizarre, but "a cautious guess is that that William of Tudela was a marrano, a converted Jew."[103]

The "abc" itself is a reference to geomancy – and not a reference to the possibility that Kyot was illiterate, as some less well-versed critics have read into this statement. It is known that William of Tudela was a geomancer, as he stated that he used it to foresee the devastation of the Albigensian Crusade. It is a method of astrological divination based on 16 patterns, based on the mansions of the moon and the zodiac, which result when points marked at random in four consecutive rows are reduced to one or two points per row by marking each pair of points with a row until only one or two points are left. The "art" was allegedly invented by Idris, i.e. Enoch or Hermes. Geomancy was known by the Sabians and was introduced in Western Europe by Hugh of Santalla in the second quarter of the 12th century… in Tudela.

Wolfram was aware of the Cathar movement and Kahane & Kahane argue that Wolfram shows a certain interest in and sympathy for Catharism.[104] William of Tudela was of course aware of them, having written one of the most authoritative accounts on their strife. But William has been labelled an opponent of Catharism. Still, in the opening lines of his Song, William clearly does not condemn all the Languedocians outright and makes an effort to be impartial, including praying for the massacred people of Béziers.

Still, though William of Tudela seems to be an ideal candidate, no-one has been able to provide complete proof of who Kyot de Provencal was. Nevertheless, there is now abundant evidence to show that Toledo was an important town for the introduction of such Hermetic documents in Western Europe.

Toledo (Toletta) was the residence of the Spanish king, Alfonso VII. Wolfram writes that Toledo is the residence of king Kaylet, allowing for a possible identification of Kaylet with Alfonso VII.

Toledo had previously been the capital of the Visigothic kingdom of Spain, which fell to the Muslims in 711. The city was reconquered by Alfonso VI of Castile-Leon in 1085. Alfonso VII was born on March 1, 1105 and was the son Raymond of Burgundy and Urraca, the widowed daughter and heir of Alfonso VI. After the death of her husband, she married Alfonso el

Batallador (the battler), the king of Aragon and Navarre, in 1108. When Alfonso VII came of age in 1127, Alfonso of Aragon and the young Alfonso VII made the peace of Tameras, in which Alfonso VII gained the lands of Alfonso VI. Alfonso VII died on August 21, 1157 and was buried in the Cathedral of Toledo.

As a royal residence, Toledo was also a great centre for learning. The School of Toledo came about in 1135, partly thanks to funding of Queen Urraca. It was in that year that Gerardo da Cremona (1114-1187) installed himself in Toledo, specifically to find Thabit's work on Euclid, the *Almagest*. Cremona himself translated other texts of Thabit, which eventually gave him the title of "father of Arabism in Europe". It is certain that Wolfram was inspired by this body of documents, as there are references in *Parcival* to Thebit and Kancor.[105]

Richard Barber sums up the status of Kyot, and the fact that his existence can only be proven based on circumstancial evidence: "Is this all Wolfram's imagination, or did Kyot really exist? If we answer the latter question in the affirmative, we accept the existence of a lost Grail tradition of great importance."[106] In the end, Barber prefers not to accept the possibility of such a "Q Grail document", or the "UrParzival" as it is commonly referred to, even though no detailed analysis of this possibility is ever performed in his work. Instead, he prefers the option that the entire account was the fruit of Wolfram's imagination – and then goes on to suggest that the Grail is, in fact, all part of our imagination.

Like others, he assumes that Kyot is a fictitious source, even though he admits that Wolfram gives more detail than most about his "fictitious source" than all others.[107] Wolfram actually gives so much information that for those within his lifetime, it would have been able to identify Kyot. But it is not his fault that out of a handful of strong candidates, historians have been unable to discover every detail of their life, which would thus have allowed us to identify who precisely Kyot was. The non-identification of Kyot is not Wolfram's problem; it is ours...

The Grail Code

There are over 600 names in *Parzival* and its sequel *Titurel* combined, resulting in one of the longest identification parades ever. As most believe we are faced with a literary invention by Wolfram, any identification with historical characters seems futile. On the other hand, we have Wolfram's statement that the characters of those who possessed the Grail were genuine people, whose names and histories his sources had investigated in Latin documents. Furthermore, Wolfram's literature should be described as "historical" – he did not write fiction, and stating that *Parzival* is nothing but a work of fiction therefore needs an explanation why Wolfram departed from his non-fictional writings to meddle in the fictional literature.

Still, some have tried to identify the story's characters with real people. Dr. Sebastian Evans in *In Quest of the Holy Graal*, published in 1898, identified Innocent III with the Rich Fisherman, the Emperor with the King of Castle Mortal, Saint Dominic, the founder of the Dominicans, with Perceval, the Interdict of 1208 with the languishment and enchantments of Britain, and the question which should have been asked, but was not, with an omission of Saint Dominic to secure the exemption of the Cistercians from certain effects of the Interdict.

He continues: Lancelot is the elder Simon de Montfort; Gawain is Fulke of Marseilles; Alain le Gros is Alanus de Insulis, the universal Doctor; Yglais, the mother of Perceval, is Holy Church. The Graal is, of course, the Eucharist, which is denied to Logres. However applaudable to try and match the account with history, Evans' effort is tentative at best, and does little to help the cause.

Interestingly, most of those who have attempted this match, have tried to find correspondences with the kings and nobles of

Aragon. This is interesting, for Guyot de Provins, one of the primary candidates for the role of Kyot of Provence, had strong ties with Aragon. Guyot wrote about the kings of Aragon, who were his magnanimous protectors: his patron was Alfonso the Chaste, Alfonso II, the son of Alfonso I (1104-1134), who freed Saragossa from Moorish domination in 1118. Living in France, he faced the same challenge I faced so many centuries later, when trying to reach San Juan de la Peña. Guyot followed the procession of troubadours to Toulouse, from where there were two ways to reach the residence of his Maecenas, Alfonso of Aragon: one was by Foix, crossing the border through the pass at Puymorens; the other, easier route was by passing through Carcassonne, Perpignan, hugging the coastline until Barcelona, and from there onwards proceed to Saragossa.

Joseph Görres in *Lohengrin, ein alt Deutsche Gedicht, &c.*, was published in 1813 and argues that Mont Salvatch stands in Salvatierra, in Arragonia, at the entrance into Spain, close to the Valley of Ronceval.

In *Crusade against the Grail,* published in 1933, Otto Rahn considered that the characters appearing in *Parzival* were modelled on actual medieval personalities too. For example, he believed that Perceval was le Vicomte de Carcassonne Trencavel; Repanse de Schoye was Esclarmonde de Foix; and the hermit Trevrizent, Parsival's uncle, was the Cathar Bishop Guilhabert de Castres. He identified Alfonso II as Wolfram's Castis, who was promised to Herzeloyde. The latter was Perceval's mother, and was identified with Viscountess Adélaide de Carcassonne.

Rahn identified the Grail characters with major figures of the Cathar movement, and posited that the Grail Castle was none other than Montségur. Indeed, there are linguistic similarities as in *Parzival,* the Grail Castle is called Monsalvat, similar to Montségur and with the same meaning: "safe mountain, secure mountain". Furthermore, the name of Raymond de Péreille, the actual historic seigneur of Montségur, has a slight similarity to the protagonist of Eschenbach's epic, the knight Perceval. And in *Titurel*, the first king of the Holy Grail is actually named Perilla.

Alas, these historical events took place in the years following 1200 – which is indeed the time when Wolfram wrote, likely between 1203 and 1210. But what might thus seem to be a perfect match, is alas, a total mismatch, for Wolfram claims that the history he writes about, is older.

Wolfram, in 1210, writes that "The famous master Kyot found the prime version of this tale in heathenish script lying all neglected." This means that Kyot, some time before, had found a manuscript, which had some age to it already. We would thus assume that the document is between fifty and one hundred years old, making the events related in *Parzival* roughly one hundred years old, or ca. 1100.

Using this as his starting point, Swiss scholar, André de Mandach, began his research, resulting in the first publication of his work in 1992, arguing for the existence of an "UrParzival".[108] De Mandach felt that Wolfram's account might not only be based on real events, he also wondered whether the legend was perhaps written in a code.[109] We have already argued that this is the case when we come to the account of Perceval and his meeting with Treverzent, which copies the account between Hermes and Tat in the *Corpus Hermeticum*.

The key to unlock this code, de Mandach felt, lay in the history of the Northern Spanish kingdoms, in the period of 1104 to 1137. Kahane & Kahane had already identified the Catalan-Aragonese Mischkultur, in which Orient met Occident, as a vital channel for the transmission of the Grail myth.[110] And is it not a nice coincidence that Flegetanis, our enigmatic "first source", is a family name in the Empordà, the northern Catalonian region of Spain?

The period of 1104-1137 is roughly 50 to 100 years before respectively Chrétien and Wolfram's accounts. It is also the timeframe in which Toledo had become Christian territory, under a Christian ruler, with – from 1135 onwards – a "School of Toledo", which became a centre of learning and translation of Arab texts.

Eventually, de Mandach realised that the key to breaking the code was the "honorary surnames", nicknames, which not only was a key characteristic of the Hermetica, as referenced by Slavenburg, but the giving of nicknames itself was a popular tradition in Spain and specifically in Islam since the 7th century AD. These names were often used to distinguish between people with identical names – a problem which becomes specifically bad when confronted with a series of kings that all share the same name, and are only distinguishable by the numbers historians have added to these – or the nicknames they had taken. Indeed, the practice became so popular that it was exported to other parts of Western Europe, with kings being labelled "the Good", "the Seemly", "the Just", etc.

De Mandach argued that Anfortas, identified as a king, was thus King "something" Anfortas – "something" requiring to be substituted with a name like Alfonso, Raymond, or another popular name of the time. This approach is much more direct than most researchers' attempts, when trying to explain that Anfortas might come from the ancient French "enferté(z)", itself derived from the Latin "infirmitate(m)". Such reasoning is indirect at best.

De Mandach's approach led enabled him to identify this person as King Alfonso I of Aragon, who was nicknamed "Anfortius". Indeed, it is that simple: Anfortas was Anfortius. He is identified as such numerous times, including in his will, and in Flamenca, where he is known as "Anfors".[111] Coins minted under his reign identify him as "ANFUS REX", some of these coins having Toletta (Toledo) on the reverse side. Just on this basis alone, it is clear that de Mandach had just cracked the code. The question is why it lasted until 1992 until someone did so.

Though sceptics might argue that Anfortius is not totally identical with Anfortas, it should be remembered that Anfortius was his Latin nickname, with Anfortas having an Occitan appearance – as Kyot the Provencal, as an Occitan speaker himself, would do.

But the key to a successful decodation is not finding the key, but whether or not all subsequent decodations are then made easy, straightforward, before all pieces fall into place. That is indeed the case...

For if Anfortas/Alfonso I is the key, then it is his cousin, Rotrou II de Perche, who confirmed that the code was broken. Rotrou II de Perche was the lord of "Val Perche": Perche-val... hence Perceval. And like Rotrou was Alfonso's cousin, so was Perceval Anfortas' uncle.

With Anfortas and Perceval being the nicknames of two historical figures, whose family relationship was identical to the relationship described in Wolfram's document between the Fisher King and Perceval, de Grail code had been broken.

The Fisher King

Anfortas, known to us as Alfonso I, the Battler, was born in 1074, the king of Aragon and Navarre, from 1104 until his death on 6 or 7 September 1134. In life, he must have been a formidable figure: research of his remains by Antonio Duran Gudiol has revealed that he measured an impressive 192 cm (6ft 3.5'). He was a formidable fighter, known for a series of victories known as the "Reconquista", the recovery of Spain from the Moors for the Christians. He married Queen Urraca in 1107, at which time a union between the two kingdoms of Aragon and Castille was on the cards. The marriage had been arranged by Alfonso VI of Castille in 1106, to unite the two chief Christian states against the Almoravides, and to supply them with a capable military leader: Alfonso I.

However, the alliance between the two kingdoms was never realised. Husband and wife quarrelled with the brutality of the age and it resulted in open warfare. Alfonso had the support of one section of her nobles, but they were not numerous enough to maintain the alliance. The marriage of Alfonso and Urraca was finally declared null by the pope, on the grounds that they were third cousins.

Though the union had not succeeded, another route for peace occurred during his lifetime: the creation of several chivalric orders. Before his death, Alfonso I made a will, leaving his kingdom to the Knights Templar, the Hospitallers and the Knights of the Sepulchre. It were of course the Knights Templar who had been identified as the protectors of the Grail by Wolfram – as was Anfortas. Therefore, in Alfonso I, we have a king – the Fisher King who owns the Grail in Wolfram's story – passing one third of his estates to the Knights Templar – the protectors of the Grail.

That was not all. When deadly injured in battle, he ordered that he was transported to San Juan de la Peña, a voyage of two days and 115 km. He died there.[112] San Juan de la Peña has of course a strong Grail tradition, as we saw in chapter 1. We also note that there is a tradition that those who are in the presence of the Grail, will not die during the following seven days. Was this the purpose behind his return to San Juan de la Peña? Perhaps.

But in spite of his will to leave all of his territories to the crusading monks, his younger brother and successor, Ramiro II refused to carry it out. Alfonso I was furthermore buried in the abbey of Montearagon, near Huesca,[113] even though his request had been to be buried in San Juan de la Peña.

Munsalvæsche

"For thirty miles around has been hewn neither timber nor stone to build any dwelling but one, rich in earthly splendours. If anyone sets out to find it alas he will not do so; although there are many who try. It must happen unwittingly if one should see the castle. I presume, Sir, that you know of it; Munsalvæsche it is called. This castle controls a realm named Terre de Salvæsche. It was bequeathed by old Titurel to his son, King Frimutel."

Some, like Rudolf Steiner, have claimed that the Grail Castle cannot be found in the physical realm. Nevertheless, when he was asked to pinpoint its "earthly presence", he stated that this spiritual temple floated over Northern Spain. Steiner's identification as Northern Spain seems to come very close to the truth. There is every possibility that San Juan de la Peña was indeed the renowned Munsalvæsche, the residence of the Grail king and the location where the Grail was held.

It is indeed, as the Catholic Church seems to accept, the site where the "Holy Chalice" was once held, before it ended up in Valencia. But whereas San Juan de la Peña is often referred to as a Monastery, it was much more special than that: it was also the residence of the Aragon kings.

In 1071, Pope Alejandro II provided special protection to the monastery, which remained under papal authority and thus outside the bailiwick of the Bishop of Jaca – a privileged position for any religious site to find itself in. It meant that San Juan de la Peña could not be interfered with by the normal church hierarchies – only by the Pope himself.

This special status was reaffirmed in 1095.[114] Throughout this period, the Aragon kings, such as Sancho el Mayor, Ramiro I, Sancho Ramirez and Pedro I, continued to favour the monastery. The last three spent Lent there every year and chose it as the burial place for themselves and their families. San Juan de la Peña thus became a royal mausoleum. And if Anfortas was the Fisher King, then San Juan de la Peña, his capital, was Munsalvæsche.

The High Church, where today a copy of the Holy Chalice is on display in the middle of three chapels, was started under Sancho

Ramirez and was consecrated on 4 December 1094, by Bishop Pedro of Jaca, in the presence of King Pedro I.[115] Over the following decades, the link between the Aragon kings – specifically Alfonso I and Ramiro II – and the monastery remained close. After 1137, when de Mandach argues the Grail story had ended, the relationship between the kings and the monastery weakened. The reason for this was that the conquests, made by Alfonso I, had displaced the centre of political power towards the Ebro valley, further south. Ramiro II's successor, Ramon Berenguer IV, was a member of the Barcelonese aristocracy, which ended the close relationship between the House of Aragon and San Juan de la Peña, and moved the capital elsewhere. It meant that by the beginning of the 13th century, when Wolfram wrote his account, the political situation had already changed, making a historical identification already more difficult than one might expect.

Still, the Fisher King, Alfonso I of Aragon, made large donations to San Juan de la Peña. He thanked his victory near Tauste to the relics of San Juan de la Peña. He, like his predecessors and successors, stayed in San Juan de la Peña, specifically during the week before Easter. It is known that Alfonso I also stayed in San Juan de la Peña at other times, such as in May 1108, showing that it could definitely be seen as his residence, and the Grail Castle.

Anfortas was labelled "Le Roi Pescheor", the Fisher King, a nickname that was the result of him spending his time in what according to Chrétien was a "plan d'eau", a river, or what was known as a "see", a lake, according to Wolfram. The river Aragon flows in the valley beneath San Juan de la Peña. But just 200 metres from the new monastery of San Juan de la Peña used to be a lake that was renowned for its many fish. This reputation lasted well into the 20th century, though the lake was dried out from the 1970s onwards (it sits close to the modern car park). As Wolfram locates the lake close to Munsalvæsche, San Juan de la Peña once again conforms perfectly to Wolfram's narrative. Wolfram also locates Munsalvæsche in a forest[116] and San Juan de la Peña sits in a forest – any visitor arriving by car will immediately recognize this, as the car park is set at the beginning of this forest itself.

However, Wolfram situates Munsalvæsche in "Katelangen", Catalonia, whereas San Juan de la Peña sits in Aragon. This apparent contradiction can be smoothed out, as when Wolfram was writing his account, San Juan de la Peña was indeed part of Catalonia, after Ramiro II of Aragon had abandoned the Aragon and San Juan de la Peña to Ramon Berenguer IV, the count of Catalonia.

Furthermore, even Chrétien's voyage of how Perceval reaches the Grail castle coincides with how one reaches San Juan de la Peña: there is a river to cross, then a journey through a forest, before you reach a tower – a "square" tower, as Chrétien states. The square tower of the Old Monastery is indeed what gives San Juan de la Peña its billboard characteristic. De Mandach has also identified other details of Chrétien's account with those of San Juan de la Peña, as it existed in his days.[117] It has led de Mandach to the conclusion that Munsalvæsche, the residence of the Grail king, was most definitely San Juan de la Peña, the residence of the kings of Aragon, and of Anfortas – Alfonso I.

Such a hard identification might seem to go against the more popular accounts, which try to derive the meaning and location of Munsalvæsche from various literary methods: "soft science". For the "soft scholars", Munsalvæsche is Mont Sauvage: the Wild, or Savage, Mountain. But others have argued that it might be Mont Salvaige, Mont du Salut, or Mont du Sauveur: the Mountain of the Saviour. In Spanish, this would be Mont Salvador. Still, within this soft science, is it a coincidence that an impressive peak near San Juan de la Peña, reaching 1546 metres in height, is called San Salvador? The mountain peak is officially called "Cristo Salvador del Mundo y del Hombre".

With its immense rocks and dense forests, it is a formidable sight. On the top of this peak is a hermitage, which is called "San Salvador". Salvador in Occitan is Salvadou or San Salvat, which is close to Salvaesche. To the east of San Juan de la Peña, there are even families with names such as Montsalvatje.

However, there is an even stronger connection: inside San Juan de la Peña, the church on the top floor of the monastery is dedicated to San Salvator. The church was dedicated on 4 December 1094, by King Peter I, for the memory of Sancho Ramirez, in the presence of Anfortas and Bishop Pedro de Jaca. It is in this chapel that the Grail – a replica of the "Valencia Cup" – still stands and greets the modern tourists.

It shows that though de Mandach's work is truly remarkable, in the end, it is so logical and straightforward, that one can only wonder why it took so long before anyone was able to put all these pieces together.

The Grail dynasty

These initial findings led de Mandach to identify the other characters of the Grail story. The Grail dynasty is a series of three male successors: Titurel – Frimutel – Anfortas. This overlaps with Ramiro I (1035-1069), Sancho Ramirez I (1063-1094) and finally Alfonso I, all kings of Aragon.

Wolfram starts the Grail tradition with Titurel. He is the key person who brings the Grail from the East. It is Titurel, i.e. Ramiro I, who transformed San Juan de la Peña and made it his main residence. Coincidence? It is clear that Ramiro must have had a good reason for transforming the site of San Juan de la Peña; and is it not interesting to note that "a good reason" is lacking from the official accounts as to why Ramiro decided to invest so heavily in this site? But with the successful identification of Ramiro I as Titurel, the Grail accounts could actually shed light on a historical enigma. Was San Juan de la Peña transformed as it was the residence of the Grail?

Alfonso I's brother was Ramiro II, who in the Grail account is listed as Trevrezent, the hermit who explains the story of the Grail to Perceval. At first sight, there seems to be a major problem with this identification: Ramiro II married Agnes of Poitiers. It is Agnes of Poitiers who was also the niece of Philip of Alsace and Flanders – the noble to whom Chrétien de Troyes dedicated his story to – and who was also the man who gave Chrétien the document which he then turned into the first Grail account. The link between Aragon and Chrétien's Grail has thus been made...

But Trevrezent is identified as a hermit. This may seem to be a contradiction with Ramiro II, as he was married to Agnes de Poitiers. But this conclusion would be bad historical research. Ramiro II's nickname was, in fact, "the Monk", as he was one. Ramiro was bishop of Barbastro-Roda and was given papal dispensation to abdicate his monastic vows in order to secure the succession to the throne when his brother had died heirless. Indeed, once again history and the Grail account overlap and each provides further information about an auspicious situation: Anfortas, who is known to have suffered from a debilitating illness that prevented him from creating offspring, had invested in Perceval, making him his successor as Grail King, as he knew that he would die heirless. However, though Perceval would be the leader of the protectors of the Grail, and carry out its mission, on a totally mundane level, everyone knew that Rotrou II de Perche would never inherit the physical kingdom of Aragon, and hence, Alfonso I had created a will in which it would be divided between the three monastic orders, which Wolfram had identified as the protectors of the Grail.

However, as Anfortius' will was contested, his brother Ramiro II was told to annul his marriage to God, and instead marry a woman, so that a legal heir for the kingdom of Aragon could be created. This, he did.

Crowned king, Ramiro II almost immediately had to fight off Alfonso VII of Castille, who was one of those trying to lay claim to the Aragonese crown. His kingship lasted exactly three years: he married Agnes of Poitiers in 1134, had a child with her, Peroniella or Petronila in Latin, and then gave her hand away to Ramon Berenguer IV of Barcelona, known as Kyot of Katelangen in the Grail account. His nickname was indeed "the little Guillaume" or "Guiot" or Kyot in Occitan: Kyot of Katelangen, little William of Catalonia. Ramiro II then abdicated in her favour and returned to his monastic life.

Petronila would marry Ramon Berenguer IV in 1150, each ruling their country separately, though he had the final say. When Ramon Berenguer IV died in 1164, Petronila renounced the crown of Aragon in favour of her eldest son Ramon, who, in compliment to the Aragonese, changed his name to Alfonso II of Aragon and Barcelona, the first person to rule both Aragon and Catalonia. This dynastic union remained in place for more than 500 years.

However, with her marriage and succession, we have left the timeframe of the Grail account. Therefore, let us return to the Fisher king himself. We note that the Fisher King had a serious wound on his leg, which ails him greatly. Peter L. Hays in *The Limping Hero*[118] states how the wound, in *Parzival*, is a lance point through the testicles, a divine punishment for the king's neglect of his sacred trust, The Holy Grail.

A lot has been written about this symbolism, identifying the Fisher King with fertility gods and arguing how his wounds were symbols of how his land had turned into a "Waste Land". But amidst dozens of layers of symbolic interpretation, it seems no-one thought about wondering whether it might actually have been a genuine, historical account. Indeed, Alfonso I as a king did not reproduce – he was heirless. This caused the country great concern, as there was no successor to the throne – and in the end, we note that it was his brother who had to break his vow of chastity to guarantee an heir to the throne. It were definitely testing times for Aragon, the "Grail country".

Alfonso I was a fighter, and a wound in battle that would inflict infertility would certainly have been a possibility – though whether it would have been made public knowledge, is another matter. One of a king's primary roles is the creation of offspring. Rumours or knowledge that the king is unable to reproduce, could be perilous: the people would loose trust and other claimants to the throne may not have been able to contain their excitement, rallying troops to invade Aragon. This is exactly what happened when the king died and one claimant to the throne felt that he had more rights to the throne than the king's brother.

Though we do not know the precise cause of Alfonso I's impossibility to procreate, we do know that eh was married to Queen Urraca in 1107; it is often said that the marriage was void of love; Alfonso I is described as a soldier, unable to give love, even depicted as beating his wife. But unless Urraca herself was adamant she did not want to have a son with this man, it is clear that the marriage was created for one specific purpose: the creation of an heir. The possibility that no heir was ever conceived – and that Alfonso was apparently not all that interested in women – might have to do with the fact that the king was indeed infertile – maimed to the extent that any sexual activity might have been painful at best, and impossible at worst. And thus we find that the Grail account and history do walk hand in hand.

Klingsor

In stark opposition to those intent on preserving the Grail, stands Klingsor (or Clinschor), the arch-villain of the Grail account; the embodiment of all evil, intent on acquiring the Grail for his own nefarious purposes.

He is described as a duke magician, someone who practices the Black Art. As he was born into the Grail family, he had asked admittance into the Grail Castle, but had been refused. Like

Perceval, he felt that he was of sufficient stature to be admitted to the Grail Brotherhood. But Perceval realised that he was a fool to believe that only knightly prowess was sufficient for admittance and then went on a quest that would eventually bring him back to the Grail and admittance into the brotherhood. Klingsor had taken his refusal as a clear invitation to oppose the Brotherhood, seeking their demise; he would try to take control of the Grail and therefore set up a rival domain and conspired against the Grail knights. His prowess in the occult arts conjured up attendants for his "Castle of Perdition".

Klingsor thus represents the anti-Grail principles. He appears in Chrétien's account and may just have been used by Wolfram for that specific purpose – he is not necessarily a real person, as it is clear that any story needs contrast. For those fighting for a purpose, the opposing forces are there to destroy that mission. Wut we have so far seen that the main characters are not only incarnations of principles, they are at the same time real people. So is Klingsor merely the symbol of all evil, or could Klingsor be a real person too?

Whereas the Brotherhood holds spiritual aims, Klingsor is only intent on materialistic goals, symbolised by work, the task that has typefied Man's life on Earth. Wolfram adds that Klingsor received his training in magic in Persis, the area where Zoroaster created the *ars magica*: "In a city called Persis magic was first invented. To that place Clinschor travelled, and brought from there the magic art of how to do whatever he will."[119]

Wolfram thus clearly rejects Zoroastrian magic. It is interesting that in the 3rd century, Zosimos was one of those who wrote about the opposition between Zoroaster and Hermes. Zoroaster allowed magic in his teaching, but Hermes was said to find it of no use in man's search of himself: "spiritual man who has recognized himself should not try to obtain something through magic even if he considers the latter a good thing, nor should he do violence to Ananke (compelling fate), but he should devote himself only to the search for himself, and, having recognized God, he should hold fast to the inexpressible Triad."[120]

Wolfram's account differs from Chrétien's, who describes him as a "wise clerk versed in the science of the stars", but Wolfram underlines his wickedness not with astrology, but with necromancy: "Klingsor practiced the art of black magic, and with sorcery he can compel both women and men. Whenever he sees good people, he never lets them go unharmed."[121] But, most interestingly, Wolfram is once again the writer that gives specific details: Klingsor is described as the Lord of Schastel Marvale, with "Terre de Labur", the "Land of Labour" as his domain. Will these details allow us to identify a historical Klingsor?

André de Mandach noted that a historical "Terra Laboris" is known and written about for the first time in 1150. The territory was ruled by King Roger II of Sicily.[122] Before, the land was known as Capoue, which coincides with the name of Klingsor's capital. In 1191, Emperor Henry VI of Hohenstaufen abolished the Duchy of Capoue and replaced it with Terra Laboris, a direct consequence of the resistance of Capoue and Naples against the Germans. The name remained in existence until 1927, when the territory was dissolved by Mussolini.

De Mandach thus identifies Klingsor with Conrad de Querfurt, the legate of Emperor Henry VI in Italy and Sicily. Conrad studied at the "Domschule" of Hildesheim and became chaplain of Frederic I of Barberossa, at whose court he met Philip of Alsace, that other champion of the Grail. It was Frederic who had selected Conrad to be Henry's tutor.

Conrad was later elected bishop of Hildesheim, but would leave Hildesheim for Würzburg, without papal permission, after he had been elected by the canons at Würzburg to their episcopal see. This infuriated Pope Innocent III (1198-1216), who sent a papal decree to the five bishops of Germany, ordering them to excommunicate Conrad if he failed to obey the papal mandates within twenty days.

Klingsor is also said to have been a descendent of Virgil, as well as a practicing magician. Virgil himself was a well-known magician, whose home was Naples, which was of course part of the "Terra Laboris".

But the story of Virgil adds some interesting details about how magic was perceived and practiced. In 19 BC, the Roman Emperor Augustus visited Athens, departing for Rome in the company of Virgil. However, Virgil became ill and died at Brundisium. Virgil had demanded that his bones and ashes would be taken to Naples, to be placed in a tomb, which had already been prepared for him. The tomb is between the first and second mile markers from Naples to Puteoli, on the Via Puteolana. The tomb was in the shape of a small temple, in the centre of which the jar containing his bones was supported by white marble columns.

The location of the bones was subsequently lost, but it was in the 12th century that the tomb and the bones were allegedly rediscovered. During one of the sieges of Naples by the Norman king Roger, it was learned that the city was protected by the hidden bones of Virgil, the city's patron. Many towns possessed the bones of heroes, such as Aristotle, Orpheus, Hector, Plato and others. They were Greek and Roman antecedents of the popular Christian practice of bringing back relics from the Holy Land, which were then incorporated into the churches and cathedrals of Western Europe and would become the focus of worship and pilgrimages, as well as protect the towns from "evil" – either by Satan himself, or from those practicing the black arts.

To break Naples, King Roger employed Ludovicus, an English scholar of the Stoic School, to obtain Virgil's bones through trickery. Ludovicus located the bones, as well as a book, the

Master's *Ars Notaria*. When Naples was without their talisman, the Napoli rose and retrieved the bones from Ludovicus.

They continued to defend the town, when in 1191, Henry VI of Germany marched from Rome to attack Naples. But his army was destroyed by a devastating plague and he was forced to retreat. He returned in 1194, bringing Conrad of Querfurt, chancellor to the emperor, who knew the secret of the bones. It was Conrad who used necromancy to neutralise their protection of the town walls.

The account shows that Conrad was a powerful magician. When Conrad inspected the city's Palladium, where the bones had been kept, he discovered that there was a minute crack in the glass ampoule. With the hermetic seal broken, Conrad's magic had been successful.

He would later go on to state that when the bones were exposed from their dwelling place, the winds would wail and the sea would be whipped into a frenzy, lasting until the bones were restored to their proper resting place.

The main problem with the identification of Conrad as Klingsor is that he is not a contemporary of the events of the Grail. He is, like Rahn's Cathar setting, a century too late.

Nevertheless, it is possible that Conrad served as the inspiration for Klingsor for Wolfram, as the Siege of Naples does predate Wolfram. But if we take Wolfram literally, Klingsor must be located within the larger family of the Aragon kings. He would also have to be present in the proper timeframe, i.e. 1115-1137.

During a meeting with Roger Michel Erasmy, a Luxemburgian former diplomat turned writer specialising in the symbolism of the paintings of the Spanish Surrealist Salvador Dali, I was told that in northern Spain, there was a little-known castle that had attracted the interest of Salvador Dali. Dali often came to the site, specifically to see the sunset over the surrounding hills. The light and scenery, he felt, was magical. Dali tried to purchase the estate, but the sale never materialised. Eventually, Dali bought a castle elsewhere.

The castle of Dali's interest was Quermançó. It is located west of Figueres, near the Spanish Costa Brava and is linked with the stories of the Grail – and specifically with Klingsor. And, most interestingly, local legends state that the castle of Quermançó was the residence of the wizard Klingsor. And nearby is the mountain of Verdera, which in local legend is also linked with the Grail.

The central feature of the castle is the impressive church of St Peter, which dominates the ruin. Though visible from the outside, it was only during a second visit to the site, this time in the company of the owner, Josep Martorell, that we were able to make a thorough inspection. Though the castle was small, it sat on a formidable peak and would have been an excellent defensive position. It is probably best described as a minitiare Montségur.

What was intriguing about the castle of Quermançó was not that it sat in the middle of an area on which the stories of the Grail had been inscribed, but that it had been linked with Klingsor. Furthermore, many sites had been put forward as being the Grail Castle, but few had been identified as the residence of the Grail's nemesis. And equally intriguing about Quermançó was that its history sat within the larger framework of the Aragon family. It could, indeed, be Klingsor's residence. So who was Klingsor?

The castle was in the hands of the descendants of Ponç I of Empúries. This family was known in France as d'Ampurias, and had very noble ancestors. Hugues II d'Ampurias married Sancha d'Urgel, a descendant of Ramiro I of Aragon, which means that they were related to the kings of Aragon – and the counts of Barcelona. Ramiro I, of course, was Titurel, the first Grail king. But despite this relationship, like Klingsor, the "Empurias" often fought their relatives.

In Quermançó, we thus have a family that fits the bill – and local legends underline the castle's Grail connection. The story of the castle begins in 1078, when Hug and Berenguer, sons of Ponç I of Empúries, inherited the castle. Ponç I moved the diplomatic archives of the county to the castle of Quermançó, for security reasons. Over the next few decades, the castle would be mentioned in a number of documents, including one mention under the name "castro Carmanzono" in 1121.

This is the period of the Grail: 1115-1137, and it is within this timeframe that we see the owner of the castle declare war on the counts of Barcelona. In 1128, there was war between Ponç Hug II of Empúries and Ramon Berenguer III, the count of Barcelona – whom we know had strong ties with the Aragon family. Ponç Hug II was attacked, defeated and imprisoned in the castle itself. But like Klingsor, Ponç Hug II did not give up. Ten years later, he started another war, this time against Ramon Berenguer IV, the very man with whom the kings of Aragon had made their alliance, following the death of Anfortas. Again, the counts of Barcelona defeated the counts of Empúries; this time, the peace was sealed with the demolition of the castle. And though this should have signalled the end of their troublesome relatives, in 1154, evidence of castro Carmazone comes to light again, suggesting that though the era of warfare between the two counties had ended, the defensive qualities of the site required the presence of a castle.

The Virgin and the Grail

Wolfram thought that the story of the Grail had its origins in Spain, which is where he cites his sources, whether he invented them or not. Joseph Goering[123] has identified a number of churches in Aragon that have frescoes of the Virgin Mary holding a fiery Grail. Goering points out that the oddity about this depiction is twofold. First, the area in which the Virgin was depicted with a fiery Grail is very small. Second, she was depicted with the Grail fifty years before Chrétien's tale – when the Grail was officially not yet invented as a "literary device".

The earliest example dates from December 1123 and is an apse painting the church of St. Clement in Taüll, in which the Virgin is seen holding a "fiery Grail". The Grail is a dish-like object, from which a red-orange subject rays rise, depicted as if the plate is hot. Goering has not merely traced this object down, he has also linked it with the Virgin, and with a unique position, namely the Virgin hold this in her left hand, the rest of her arm obscured by her blue cloak, while making a hand gesture with the right hand.

Goering concludes that "the image of the Virgin holding a sacred vessel is to be found only here, in these mountain villages, and nowhere else in Christian art before this time" and adds that "the Virgin at the head of the apostolic college is an uncommon artistic theme, and Mary holding a vessel of any sort seems to be attested nowhere else in Christian art before this time."

Yet, these paintings were made at a time when Chrétien had not yet written his book, and it would be almost a century before de Boron would like the Grail with Christian imagery. So where did this painter get his inspiration from? The answer seems as straightforward as it is simple: this type of image was local to the region, so it must have depicted a theme that was only popular in that region. And the only frame – which even Goering had to admit – was de Mandach's conclusion, for, indeed, de Mandach's timeframe for a Grail being in Aragon is precisely in agreement with the facts revealed by these wall frescoes.

The question, of course, is why the Virgin Mary became upgraded amongst the group of apostles and why she became the Grail bearer. Is it possible that these wall paintings were the first attempt, performed within the heartland of the Grail (i.e. Aragon) to see whether a new image could be introduced in religious iconography, namely that of the Virgin holding the Grail. Why the Virgin Mary? Because she was said to be a Virgin… and of course, in the Grail tradition, the Grail Bearer was singled out for being a virgin.

So, in at least eight Pyrenean churches, all located with a small area, stretching from the old boundary between Aragon and Catalonia in the west to the principality of Andorra in the east,, all dating from the same period (ca. 1100-1170), a unique type of religious icon was introduced. In the end, it was never exported, and was abandoned at a date Chrétien still had to commence his Grail book.

Goering goes further, noting that the man these churches were decorated at a time when the bishop was one Raymund, of French origins, but in 1101 invited to the court of King Pedro I of Aragon and elected as bishop of Roda – apparently to everyone's surprise. Pedro's son Alfonso I remained intimately involved with Bishop Raymund, from 1114 until his death from wounds received while accompanying Alfonso on a daring incursion into Andalusia in 1126. Goering notes that Raymund and Rotrou not only fought together, they also appear together frequently in royal charters, "so frequently that one might suppose a real friendship had developed between the two" and adding that "Rotrou may have even been with Raymond on his deathbed".

The identification of a specific family – the Aragon kings – and specific locations in Northern Spain – San Juan de la Peña and Quermançó – show that the territory of the Grail was the kingdom of Aragon, south of the Pyrenees. But it is a French connection, namely the figure of Perceval, the count of "Valle de Perche", which forms the pinnacle of the Grail Code's decipherment. After all, Perceval was the main character of the Grail account and any so-called "Grail Code" fails, or stands, with Perceval – and his identification as a historical character.

Chapter 6: Perceval

Perceval is the central character of the Grail legends. He is the boy who leaves home, to discover himself. In truth, he is on a path towards greater understanding, the events in his life controlled by some "force" of which he himself has been largely unaware. Perceval has thus become the archetypal hero – a larger than life, if not larger than myth hero: a legend.

Legends seem distant from reality. In fact, Joseph Goering points out that "Who is this Perceval? And how did he come to be associated so closely with a lance and a grail? Little scholarly work has been done on these questions. Research has tended to concentrate on the origins of the Grail, with little attention being given to the origins of the first Grail 'hero', Perceval."[124]

So what are we to make of Wolfram's statement that he would talk about the "authentic version, without any addition, of what he had received of his master: he would tell the story of the noble line and children of Parzival, who he had charted just to the height of his fortune."[125]

What if Perceval was indeed a real person? What if someone was able to identify the noble line of Perceval? That was exactly what André de Mandach did, when he put Rotrou II de Perche forward as the likely Perceval. Could the noble family of "Val de Perche" – Perceval – be the "noble line of Parzival"?

History of Rotrou II's family

Rotrou's family is nowadays little known – for many not even a footnote in history. But despite their apparent anonymity, the county of the Perche and its lords became the subject of a detailed study by Kathleen Thompson.[126] Thompson identified that certain families in medieval France quickly rose to prominence, specifically those lords and counties that were on the borders of more important counties. Though history would treat them badly by largely forgetting their importance in later centuries, at the time, the lords of these domains had been important power-brokers. Medieval France was not one vast country, but a collection of individual regions. Some of the regions were large, some were small, some were friendly, some were less so. The "border territories" could be the mortar that glued two large regions together, or the topic of dispute that stopped an alliance from materialising. The county of the Perche was one of these border counties… and one of the most prominent in France.

In November 1135, the English king Henry I lay dying in Lyons-la-Forêt in Normandy. He was surrounded by his nobles. Among these was "Perceval" himself. Rotrou II was the king's former son-in-law, the count of Mortagne, who had participated in the First Crusade and against the Muslims in Spain. Though sometimes referred to as "Mortagne", he was also known as "Percheron", the "Count of Perche", a new political unit that he and his family had created over the preceding decades.

Kathleen Thompson states that the family's history "is essentially that of a lineage which, in the 200 years before the failure of the male line in 1226, rose from apparently obscure origins to considerable prestige and a recognised position among the territorial princes of France."[127] That is not all: "The family was renowned for its participation in almost every significant crusading venture and its members formed, through marriage, religious patronage and landholding, an extensive network of relationships across France, England, Spain and Sicily, extending even into the empire."[128]

The power of the family was centred on the town of Nogent-le-Rotrou, a town that carries the real name of Perceval in its name until today – Rotrou. Rotrou brought the family's wealth and prestige to its highest point and it resulted in a series of lasting donations, as so often for religious causes. The family was thus closely linked with the nearby monastery of Saint Denis and it would be Rotrou II who founded the important religious house of La Grande Trappe.

Throughout their history, the family also remained close to the rulers of Blois and Chartres, a relationship that intensified after 1135, when various members of the family became bishops of Chartres. Chartres Cathedral was – and is – one of world's most important cathedrals.

After the first cathedral of any great substance burnt down in 1020, a glorious new Romanesque basilica, which included a massive crypt, was built under the direction of Bishop Fulbert and later under the direction of Geoffroy de Lèves. However, having survived a fire in 1134, which destroyed much of the rest of the town, disaster struck again in the night from 10 to 11 June 1194, when lightning created a blaze that left only the west towers, the façade between them and the crypt.

Graham Hancock is one of a number of authors who links the Gothic cathedral and its intricate carvings with the Grail.[129] Though the cathedral was built after the death of Rotrou II, Perceval was the person that would bring scholars from Spain to Chartres; his successors would continue on this foundation, resulting in a building that many experts have labelled the most ingenious Gothic cathedral ever built.

But despite their contributions to Chartres, like all other contributors, this family was not meant to be permanently associated with it. Elsewhere, however, the family left stronger links behind.

The de Perche family makes its first appearance in the history books in 1031, when Geoffrey I founded the monastery of Saint Denis in Nogent-le-Rotrou. The town was his power base, though they also controlled the towns of Chateaudun and Chartrain. At Chateaudun, he would found a chapel dedicated to the Holy Sepulchre. In the days before the Crusades, such dedication is rare and scholars believe that it might be an indication that he went on a pilgrimage to Jerusalem.

Though the journey to Jerusalem and back may have been perilous, it was nothing compared to what would happen to him once he may have thought himself safe at home: somewhere between 1035 and 1040, Geoffrey I was assassinated when he left the cathedral of Chartres. Though he was surrounded by several guards, his assassin was able to kill him; the reason for his murder has remained a mystery.

His death left the road open for his son, Rotrou I, who became viscount in ca. 1040. Over the following twenty years, he would forge close relationships with the kings of Normandy. In 1066, Geoffrey II, son of Rotrou I, fought at the Battle of Hastings. The family was also close to de Belleme family, to whom they were related, as well as Roger de Montgommery. Both de Perche and de Montgommery were families that had possessions in France and England – specifically in Wiltshire.

When Rotrou I died in 1079, Geoffrey II and his brother assumed control of his territories. By now, the de Perche family had become a powerful entity in medieval Europe: allied with the kings of Normandy, who had successfully invaded England, Geoffrey II knew that marriage was the primary mechanism to strengthen his foothold. He therefore married Beatrice de Roucy, whose younger sister Felicia was married to King Sancho Ramirez of Aragon. It is with this alliance that the connection between the Perche family and the kings of Aragon was made. It echoes the Grail story, which states that the Fisher King was his maternal uncle. And it was this family relationship that was the reason why Rotrou II, Geoffrey II's son, would later go to Aragon, to the Grail Castle.

It also enables these historic figures to be mapped on the characters of the Grail story, preserving their exact family relationship: Geoffrey II is Perceval's father, and thus Gahmuret; his mother, Beatrice de Roucy, is Herzeloyde; Sancho Ramirez of Aragon is Frimutel, the father of Anfortas, the Fisher King. And

Rotrou II and Alfonso I were thus family, just like Perceval and Anfortas were.

Perceval, the knight

The Grail legends sit around 1115 and speak of how Herzeloyde, Perceval's mother, is distraught when she learns that her son wants to be a knight. Perceval's two brothers had become knights and died in combat; their father Gahmuret had died in grief. It meant that Perceval was the only man in the household, the rightful heir, whose life should be spent taking care of the family holdings. But Perceval can only think of heroic efforts and thus leaves his mother, with her reluctant blessing.

This story fits well within the life of Rotrou II.[130] At a young age, in September 1096, Rotrou II left for Jerusalem, in the company of Robert Curthose, the duke of Normandy. Rotrou's name appears in several French poems, including the *Chanson d'Antioche*. It is known that one of his brothers – and possibly more than one – died in this crusade, just like Perceval's brothers had died in combat.

In 1099, the Christian army conquered Jerusalem, but it was also the year that his father Geoffrey II fell gravely ill – perhaps indeed the result of the grief over the loss of his two sons – and the danger that one of his other sons, Rotrou II, might still die in the Crusade. It would mean disaster not only for his parents, but for the entire family, as there would be no-one left to inherit the estates. Geoffrey II instructed his wife Beatrice to take control of the lands, until the hopeful return of his son. Rotrou II did return home, to find that his father Geoffrey had died in October 1100. He thus immediately assumed the control of the estates and it was expected that from then on, managing the estates and maintaining the family line would be his two key objectives.

In 1104, Rotrou II met King Henry, whereby the king gave his illegitimate daughter Matilda as wife to him. The marriage strengthened the bonds between the de Perche family and the king, but also resulted in the family receiving estates in England. This English connection features prominently in the Grail legends, where they have caused confusion as to whether Perceval was English or French.

The depiction as "Perceval the Welshman" – le Gaullois – came from the work of Chrétien de Troyes. As Chrétien also placed a major emphasis on King Arthur, it suggested that Perceval lived in the 5th or 6th century AD, the timeframe in which King Arthur is normally placed. However, for Wolfram, Perceval was a more recent character; he described him as being an "Anschouwe", an Anjou.[131] And Rotrou II was exactly that: he had married Matilda, the illegitimate daughter of King Henry, who was not only the king of England, but also the Duke of Anjou. He would also politically ally himself with Count Geoffrey of Anjou to the west; in fact, Rotrou died of wounds received while aiding the Angevins at the siege of Rouen.

Having powerful allies often meant you had powerful enemies and it shouldn't therefore come as a surprise that in 1112, Rotrou II was imprisoned. Robert of Belleme visited Rotrou in captivity and King Henry himself intervened and freed him, apparently rescuing him from an early death. It was a test of character, but nothing would prepare Perceval for what would befall him on 25 November 1120. King Henry I was returning to England, with Matilda, his daughter and the wife of Rotrou, joining him on this journey. The ship sank and both the king's son and Matilda drowned. It was a national tragedy, as for the country, the heir to the throne had died. For Rotrou, it was a personal drama, loosing not only his wife, but also loosing her before she had given him a legal male heir.

Her sudden death has also brought an interesting historical enigma to light: at the time of her death, no-one seemed to know where Rotrou was: his whereabouts are unknown. History has recorded that he was "absent", though it has been assumed that he may have been in Jerusalem at the time, as he endowed a church with some relics shortly afterwards. If he was, it would be interesting to know what he was doing there…

But the heroics of Perceval should not be sought in France or England – they refer specifically to Rotrou's Spanish exploits. Rotrou II had visited Aragon in the spring of 1105, at the specific request of the king, his cousin, Alfonso. During this absence, the estates were once again run by his mother Beatrice.

It was the first in a series of visits to Aragon, where it seems his cousin was able to convince him to fight with him against the Moors. It is here that we can see how Perceval and Rotrou's lives overlap once more: rather than focus on his estates, Rotrou was constantly drawn to danger. He had already lost his brothers and most likely all of his comrades of the First Crusade had settled in a lifestyle in which heroic exploits were far from their daily occupations. But in Alfonso and his fight against the Spanish Muslims, Rotrou had found an ally – a cousin – who was still willing to gamble everything – to fight. It left his mother Beatrice no doubt distraught: she was a widow, Rotrou now her only son, who left his wife behind on a life of danger, with the possibility that he might never return. But the Grail legends state that Herzeloyde in the end blessed her son – he was a knight, above anything else.

Rotrou II would return to Spain in 1115, for an 18-month campaign in Andalusia. His troops would aide the king of Aragon in "saving" Spain from the Muslims. Throughout most of this campaign, and definitely in 1123, when he was back in Aragon, he left his sister in charge of the family estates. Like Perceval, he fought, winning victory after victory. His troops conquered Tudelo in 1119, the city that would become the capital of Navarre; Rotrou himself was Lord of Tudelo from 1121 till

1135. For a short period of time, in 1124, Rotrou II was even the lord of the town and castle of Uncastillo, southwest of San Juan de la Peña – the Grail Castle, the capital of his uncle.

As mentioned, in 1135, Rotrou II was present at the death of the English king at Lyons-la-Foret. As the king's former son-in-law, he had the right to be there. He is listed as "comes perticensis", the Percheron count. It is around this time – 1137 – that de Mandach has marked the end of the Grail. And it is, no doubt unsurprisingly, also a turbulent episode in Rotrou's life. He forsook his lordship of Tudelo, though "the reasons for Rotrou's withdrawal from Spain after such a lengthy commitment are nowhere made explicit." Some have argued that it might have had to do with his preparation for a third trip to Jerusalem, in 1140. It would be his final exploit, as he died in battle in 1144. It is believed that he was buried in the monastery of Saint Denis in Nogent-le-Rotrou, though no-one can be sure.

De Mandach lists 1137 as the end of the Grail account and the Grail accounts themselves do not speak of the death of Perceval; Rotrou's death in 1144 as a non-inclusion in the Grail accounts is therefore further confirmation that Rotrou II and Perceval are one and the same.

Beyond Perceval

Upon the death of Rotrou, his son, Rotrou III, assumed the control of his estates. After the death of Matilda, Rotrou had made the statement that he would not remarry. It fits with the statement of Trevrizent, who argued that Perceval had vices, but a lust for women had never been one of them.

Without an heir, the estates would go to Helias, the second son of Fulk of Anjou, the later king of Jerusalem. But Rotrou II did after all remarry, with Hawise, the daughter of Walter of Salisbury. Could the reason for this marriage be found in the Grail mythology itself, where it is said that it is a duty of every knight – and definitely the Grail king himself – to procreate – though in chastity? It was Hawise who, at the time when King Henry died and Rotrou abandoned his interests in Tudelo, gave him a son – Rotrou III.

Ca. 1150, Rotrou III married Matilda of Blois. It would further strengthen the family's alliances with Blois and Chartres, but Rotrou III also allied himself with a new religious order, known as the Chartreux. In 1170, Rotrou founded a Carthusian house – also known as charterhouse – at Val Dieu, this at time when his brother-in-law William was the bishop of Chartres.

Though the Carthusian monks would become a powerful institution in the centuries to come, in 1170, only two houses existed away from the mother house, in Chartreux, near Grenoble, where St Bruno had created his community in 1084: that of Mont Dieu in Rheims and that of Val Saint-Pierre in Laon. The first English house of the order would be founded by King Henry II at Witham (Somerset), in 1181 and Rotrou III may have played a role in the order's extension into England.

In 1188, when king Henry II of England and king Philippe II of France met at Gisors, Rotrou III was pivotal in the negotiations between the two monarchs, as he was related to both of them. The meeting also involved the cutting of a sacred oak tree in a field at Gisors. This enigmatic event has risen to prominence as it was used by a 20th century alchemist, Pierre Plantard, as the event that separated the Knights Templar from the Priory of Sion, the secret society of which he claimed Grand Mastership and which features so heavily in Dan Brown's *The Da Vinci Code*.

With the publication of *Holy Blood, Holy Grail*, by Baigent, Leigh and Lincoln, the fame of Plantard, his Priory of Sion and the event at Gisors have attained the same legendary status as the Grail itself – no doubt aided by the notion that the Grail is mentioned throughout that work. It it is a nice twist of fate that in the fictional accounts of the Priory of Sion and its role as protector of the Grail, we do have the son of Perceval making an appearance… and playing a decisive role.

Rotrou III would die during the Third Crusade, at the battle of Acre, in July 1191. Three decades later, in 1226, the male line of the Perche family would end. A decade earlier, Wolfram had penned down his Grail account, which would be instrumental in maintaining the fame of the legend of Perceval… though the memory of the Perche would soon be largely forgotten.

Mismatches?

Despite the many correspondences, some aspects of the life of Rotrou II de Perche and Perceval do not overlap. In the Grail stories, Perceval is raised as an ignorant fool, shielded by his mother, who hopes her son will not die, like her husband and her other sons, on the battlefield. Even when she realises that she cannot persuade him to stay with her, she advises him to dress in buckskin cloak and mismatching shirt and breeches, so that he will look like a peasant or a fool. She hopes that by making him look like a fool, he may fail in his quest to become a knight and instead return home – disappointed, but nevertheless alive.

At first sight, this might seem to be sufficient reason to label the identification of Perceval with Rotrou II de Perche as a bizarre coincidence: some details are identical, but not all – and hence Rotrou II de Perche is not Perceval.

On second inspection, it becomes clear that what differs, are those aspects that have a very good reason to be different. Wolfram was, despite his willingness to be "accurate" about the events, writing a knightly tale: a tale with a lesson – and the tale of a myst in search of initiation. Indeed, let us not forget that what Wolfram was trying to accomplish was write a story in which the Hermetic principles took centre stage, but equally, to write about the historical Grail Dynasty. Wolfram was not merely writing a biography or family history; he was trying to marry historical facts with eternal knowledge.

Rotrou II by no means can be described as a fool. But Perceval had to be the fool, who might find enlightenment at the court of his uncle. Perceval had to be a fool, like Tat, who will find enlightenment when he speaks to Hermes. Wolfram's story would not have the required impact if Perceval was depicted as a count, already a man of the world, a formidable fighter, yet utterly unfamiliar with the rituals of the Grail that were performed at his uncle's court. The contrast is not big enough… the hero is always an extreme: all good, all evil, all powerfull, or an utter fool. For Wolfram's audience, it would only work if Perceval was an utter fool, whose journey to knighthood teaches him that there is an even higher goal in life – like the audience, he would move from utter ignorance to complete enlightenment.

As a consequence, the tale had to clearly show the lessons his audience had to learn and Wolfram had to use literary devices to get his point across. One of these tools are obvious exaggerations, such as Perceval's mother being able to shield him totally from the world for most of his youth. It would mean Perceval was raised in a cupboard at home, never seeing any friends to play with, nor even seeing the world outside his windows. His isolation is introduced to illustrate that despite every mother's effort, no mother can deny her son his destiny: what will be, will be.

Such details may also have been loaned from other pagan traditions. For example, in section VIII of the Mahabharata, there is the story of a young Brahmin, brought up by his father, Vibhandaka, in a lonely forest hermitage. He is absolutely ignorant of the outside world, and is not even aware of the existence of beings other than his father and himself.[132] Like Perceval, he will go on to perform great things, whereby his specific role was to restore the land to fertility, by performing a sacrifice that would return the rains – a theme that is similar to the story of the Wasteland that Perceval has to restore, because of the infertility of the Fisher King.

But despite such differences, there remains a clear parallel between Perceval and the life of Rotrou II. His mother asked him to be a count rather than a knight, but though he would build an impressive inheritance for his son, Rotrou II was first and foremost a fighter – not an administrator. In spite of his mother's request not to go to Spain and fight with his uncle, he nevertheless did.

Gahmuret's life

The identification of Rotrou II de Perche with Perceval cannot be established solely on the evidence of his family relationships with the kings of Aragon or his heroic exploits. Further evidence comes from the first two chapters of Wolfram's account, which were bespoke to Wolfram and focused on Perceval's ancestry. Indeed, the material has little or nothing of relevance to the actual Grail account and some scholars have pondered why Wolfram worked it into his story. The answer, it seems, is because Wolfram had received that information from the historical accounts of the de Perche family, and no doubt decided to preserve them, by working them into his account.

These opening chapters specifically detail the life of Gahmuret, Perceval's father. He is said to have travelled throughout heathendom, in Morocco, Persia, Syria and Baghdad. During these voyages, he comes to the kingdom of Zazamanc (which some have identified as Seville, others as Ethiopia) and through knightly competition (against the relatives and followers of a former suitor Isenhart), he wins the kingship of Zazamanc and his bride, the black Moorish queen Belacane. A sexual encounter between the queen and Gahmuret leaves her pregnant with Feirefiz, the half-brother of Perceval. But Gahmuret is apparently unaware of this child, having already left the court before he is born. He continues his travels, but eventually finds himself a wife, Herzeloyde, the mother of Perceval.

If Gahmuret is Geoffrey II de Perche, how does this story fit with his life? In short, the answer is that historians do not know what Geoffrey did or where he was between 1066 and 1079, the year he reappears and his name is recording as the witness of an act. It is also in ca. 1079 that Rotrou II is born, and when Geoffrey II assumed half of the estates of his father. These historians find it odd that his father divided the county between two sons – normally the estates would have passed to the eldest child, Geoffrey II, but for some reason, his younger brother received half of the estates.

Here, the Grail account once again becomes an extremely intriguing tool of historical research, or how so-called "fiction" may throw light on "fact". If Geoffrey had left the family estates to travel abroad, his family might have believed that he would never return. Perhaps his father thought he might never return and might therefore have prepared his other son for the succession of the estates.

However, Geoffrey did return from his foreign voyages and his father had to make changes to his plans. But could he leave his younger son without what he had been promised? A division of the county between both sons thus would be seen as logical and acceptable for both parties. Furthermore, the fact that three other brothers got nothing suggests that this was not merely a generous act of their father; it suggests that the eldest son was absent for a long period of time (more than a decade), eventually returning to his estates, forcing his father to make alterations to his will.

Though the absence of evidence for what he did between 1066 and 1079 is not evidence of his travels abroad, it is clear that Geoffrey II's life sits well within Gahmuret's life. History has not preserved what befell Geoffrey II during his absence, but the Wolfram's prologue might. We know that Geoffrey II was unmarried when he left home, and only married upon his return.

We know that Geoffrey II took part in Battle of Hastings in

1066 and like Rotrou II, his son, it seems that adventure and danger were his ally. The Grail account states that Gahmuret reached Mesopotamia, where he offered his services as a warrior to the Baruc, the ruler of Baghdad and travelled around the Baruc's empire, jousting in tournaments.

After winning a great victory in a tournament in the kingdom of Zazamanc, he attracted the attention of Belakane, the queen of Zazamanc; they fell in love and were married. He shared with her the throne of Zazamanc for a time, but peaceful court life in a foreign land was not suited to the young warrior. He grew restless, and decided to leave her; after he had left, Belakane gave birth to Gamuret's first son, Feirefiz, the piebald, later to become the father of "Prester John" – a historical character.

Interestingly, Gahmuret was also in Alexandria, the home of the Hermetica, though, of course, by the 11th century, this was hardly the case.

Gahmuret eventually arrived in Spain, and began to travel around Europe with his cousin Kaylet, king of Spain and Castille. His jousting in a tournament in the kingdom of Waleis (Valais, now in Switzerland) won the heart of Herzeloyde, who convinced him that he should give up the love of the unbaptized Queen in her favour, and they were married. The Grail account therefore specifically argues that Gahmuret married a noble upon his return to Europe, and this is once again a perfect match for Geofrrey II's exploits.

Corridors of the Grail

Kahane & Kahane state that the central question of whether or not the central storyline of the Grail is the Hermetica is this: "how was it possible that Greek text written in the second and third century in Egypt had come to the knowledge of Wolfram in the twelfth century?"[133] They themselves pointed to the presence of the Hermetic tradition within medieval Arab society, but this answer, however correct, has not satisfied many, as it is rather indirect.

But we know that this Spanish-Moorish civilisation was fought against by Alfonso of Aragon and his nephew Rotrou de Perche, showing the real possibility that this is how that tradition entered the Western world, where it would become the corner-stone of a "Hermetic obsession" that would become known as the "Grail mystery" – and which would place Rotrou de Perche at the centre of the Grail tradition; he was Perceval. In short, Perceval and the Fisher King themselves found Hermetic documents during the Conquest of Spain.

Still, other questions remain. One of these is how Perceval could be linked with Arthur, even though it is a link that is stressed by Chrétien de Troyes, and less so by Wolfram. The answer is that Rotrou II twice married English women. His brother-in-law was none other than Robert of Gloucester, another illegitimate son of Henry. And he was the person who commanded the *Historia Regum Brittaniae* of Geoffrey of Monmouth. It is this book that has been identified as the first written Arthurian tradition – on which all others would be based.

There is therefore a strong link between Arthur and Rotrou II; he must have been one of the first people in France to know about the book and perhaps he himself was instrumental in promoting the Arthurian stories, after Geoffrey had written them down in 1138.

Geoffrey of Monmouth's book was adapted into French in 1155 by the Anglo-Norman poet Wace, in his *Roman de Brut*.[134] The emphasis was on Arthur's military victories, but it was specifically *Erec and Enide* by Chrétien de Troyes himself, written in ca. 1170, that was the first romance that focused on Arthur's knights as individuals.[135] All of Chrétien's literature was heavily influenced by the Arthurian story, which he consequently also wove into his Grail story.

Might it be the numerous references to Arthur that so angered Wolfram in Chrétien's work? And there is a major problem about the relationship between Perceval and Arthur in Chrétien's story, which few have identified: though Arthur is present in Chrétien's story, why is Perceval missing from Geoffrey of Monmouth's account? It is clear evidence that Perceval is not part of the original Arthurian tradition and that the two were only linked by Chrétien de Troyes, who is a known devotee of the English hero, time and again introducing him in his stories.

The historical Rotrou II – the legendary Perceval – could thus be an important link between the English Arthurian stories and their promotion in France. And it is not a stand-alone event… Rotrou II is also the missing link between the Arab schools that existed in Spain at the time of the Reconquisita and the School of Chartres. The town of Tudelo, ruled by Rotrou II from 1121 onwards, had an important intellectual and literary tradition, with the Jewish and Arab quarters of the town housing scholars such as Yehuda ha-Levi, nicknamed "el-Tutila" ("from Tudelo") and Abraham ibn Ezra. It was one of the greatest centres where translations of Arab and Hebrew texts into Latin were carried out, before the famous school of Toledo, which developed from 1135 onwards – and which would provide Wolfram with his "UrParzival".

When Alfonso and Rotrou II conquered Tudelo in 1119, the texts that were used in the schools of that town fell into the hands of Rotrou. Rather than burn them or oppress them, it is known that Rotrou decided to export the knowledge of the school – and some of its teachers – to France, to Chartres. It was this knowledge that in the end would contribute to the construction of its cathedral.

The birth of a legend

Rudolf Steiner spoke of how Chartres was the meeting point of the Arthurian impulse from the West and the Grail impulse from the South. Bernard D. Haage identified that the ideology expressed by Wolfram of Eschenbach showed evidence of the "old learning" and the "new learning", whose focus was the School of Chartres.[136]

The "official" rediscovery of the Hermetica in the 14th century is seen as the birth of the Renaissance. But AJ Fegustière states that France knew a "12th century Renaissance", which showed a great interest in the Hermetica.[137] Indeed, direct knowledge of the Hermetica existed in the 12th century and was derived from the Latin form of the *Asclepius,* which was studied at the School of Chartres.

The awareness of this School's knowledge of the Hermetic treatises coincides with the exploits of Rotrou II de Perche. Thus, even if Rotrou would not be Perceval, Rotrou II is nevertheless the instrument that leveraged this body of learning from the Arab world into France. In short, he was largely the man responsible for the creation of the "12th century French Renaissance".

Would it be a stretch of the imagination to assume that the man responsible for this effort would consequently be made into a character in the story itself? There are hundreds of examples of real people that have been worked into novels or paintings. It seems logical to assume that a French or German author, who wanted to write a Hermetic treatise and who realised its true origin, would work the character of Rotrou II into the volume.

And identifying Rotrou II with the myst on search of his initiation is exactly what seems to have happened. The story of Perceval in Wolfram's *Parzival* is foremost the story of a myst, but the details of his character match the known life of Rotrou II. What are the statistical chances that Rotrou II's relationship to Alfonso matches perfectly with Perceval's relationship with Anfortas – and that Anfortas is the Grail king who resides in the Grail Castle, whereas Alfonso is the king of Aragon who resided in San Juan de la Peña, which is a known Grail site?

Furthermore, we need to ask the question about what the chapters about the exploits of Gahmuret and his travels abroad have to do with the story of the Grail. Irrelevant of what the Grail may be, these opening chapters of Wolfram's story bear no relationship at all with the main storyline: Perceval and the Grail. So why *did* Wolfram include it? The only logical answer is that Wolfram incorporated it because it was part of his source material. The "UrParzival" would thus be the family history and exploits of the counts of the Perche, into which the Hermetic story of the myst was woven.

There is further evidence that proves that Wolfram was intimately aware of the importance of the School of Chartres – and that he knew much more about it than most of his contemporaries.

First, students from the School of Chartres that discussed the Hermetica include Hugh of St Victor (1097-1141), Theodoric of Chartres (who died between 1148 and 1153) and John of Salisbury (1115/20-1180). The latter's ideologies were unknown in Germany at the start of the 13th century, but his philosophy is nevertheless written down by Wolfram – showing that Wolfram was aware of his teachings.

Wolfram was therefore familiar with John of Salisbury's writing, and we need to ask how. But that is not all. Rotrou's second wife was Harvise de Salisbury; the link with John of Salisbury is therefore straightforward. And it shows that as Wolfram knew the Hermetic teachings of John of Salisbury; he must have known – by default – of Harvise de Salisbury and her marriage to Rotrou II de Perche. As such, John of Salisbury had known Perceval – who would become the main character of Wolfram's Grail account. Thus, when Wolfram states that he has relied on better source material than Chrétien de Troyes did when he wrote about Perceval, we should, once again, trust Wolfram, as the historical records confirm his reliability.

More than a legend

Wolfram's Grail account has achieved mythical status. Over the centuries, layer upon layer of symbolism and adaptations have transformed it into *the* legend of the last millennium. But the account itself is fundamentally a family history, retelling the famous exploits, first of Gahmuret and later of his son Perceval. It is a tale of its time, about a knight and his travels.

Rotrou II was a powerful lord – and a notorious knight. He had fought in the First Crusade. It was his reputation as a knight that had persuaded his cousin Alfonso I to use him for the Reconquista. If no knightly tales were told about Rotrou II, it would be very strange indeed.

After Wolfram von Eschenbach had completed *Parzival,* he worked on the epic poem *Willehalm,* which he finished ca. 1220. This poem is Wolfram's adaptation of the French poem *Aliscans,* which had been composed about 1185 and which was based on an earlier "Song of William". Once again, Wolfram made specific mention that this poem was based on a true story, about a knight who became a saint. Unlike with *Parzival,* no-one has doubted this specific claim, perhaps because William is easily identifiable: it was Guillaume – i.e. Willehalm – who was made Count of Toulouse by his cousin Charlemagne in 789. Four years later, Guillaume was defeated by invading Muslims in the battle of Alischanz. Guillaume then assisted Charlemagne to take back Barcelona, which they succeeded in doing in 801. Guillaume then spent the last six years of his life dedicated to God as a Benedictine monk near Montpellier, before he died in 812.

But if Perceval is the story of a wandering knight and his fight against the Moors along the Spanish border, then there are clear parallels between *Parzival* and *Willehalm*: both stories are the accounts of a French noble, fighting against the Moors, in attempts to liberate Spain from the Moors. In the early 13th century, when Wolfram wrote, the struggle between the western world and the "Islamic threat" was a topical debate – as it is at the start of the 21st century.

The central question that remains is whether someone did indeed write a story about the exploits of Rotrou II; if someone did, this would thus be the "UrParzival" – the document that was used by Wolfram to write his account. Such an account could have been written either in his home county of the Perche, or the town of Tudelo – or both. The exploits of the ruler of the county and the town would literally have been the exploits of "the Perche", or "Perceval".

Rotrou II was one of the most famous and illustrious knights of his time. It is remarkable that there are no accounts of his exploits, even though other members of his family were the subject of knightly tales – and yet their exploits were less spectacular than his.

Eustorge, the bishop of Limoges from 1106 till 1131, ordered the *Chanson d'Antioche* from Guichard Bechada. We already noted that Rotrou II's name appears in this knightly tale, though he is not its main character; that honour goes to Gouffier, the lord of Lastours, a hero of the First Crusade and the Fall of Mara. Gouffier's second wife (after 1125), was Marguerite de Perche, Rotrou II's sister.

Guichard composed the *Chanson d'Antioche* for the sister of Perceval. Is it therefore possible that another poem may have been written to honour Rotrou II? However, this would not focus on Rotrou II's exploits in the First Crusade, however remarkable they were, but more on his role in the Reconquista. It is the story about a French knight who comes to Spain, to the court of the King of Aragon, where he witnesses bizarre events, involving an enigmatic "stone", known as the Grail. In short, it is the story of a knight abroad and the events that befall him there.

The family background of Rotrou II, his Hermetic knowledge and his apparent initiation into a Hermetic brotherhood at the court of his cousin, King Alfonso of Aragon, would thus become the storyline of *Parzival,* itself based on an "UrParzival". That this source is now lost, should not come as a major surprise. In 1226, roughly the period of Wolfram's storytelling, the male line of the counts of the Perche ended. Any family histories would have been scattered – even if they survived in some libraries, they hardly mattered: there were no descendents who desired to hear the exploits of their forefathers.

If the accounts of the Perche family had been written in Tudelo, then the tale of the wandering knights of the Perche Valley would have been written in ca. 1135-7 – when Rotrou II forsook his control over the town, and when de Mandach claims the story of the Grail ends. Coincidence? Note that Wolfram wrote that "Kyot found the adventures of Parzival in Arab texts."[138]

It is clear that in Rotrou II de Perche, we are indeed in the presence of the real Perceval, who witnessed the strange events surrounding a precious relic while he visited his cousin's castle in San Juan de la Peña. There, his family was involved in the worship of a container, which would be known ever since as "The Grail".

Chapter 7: A prehistory of the Grail

The story of the Grail is therefore not an invention of the 12th century, but goes back further in time, confirming what Wolfram wrote: "Thus Flegetanis wrote of it. Kyot, the wise scholar, began to seek for that tale in Latin books, of where there might have been a people fitting to tend the Grail and embrace such chastity. He read the chronicles of the lands, those of Britain and elsewhere, of France and Ireland. In Anjou he found the tidings."[139]

This is a vital, and often overlooked, piece of information present within Wolfram's *Parzival.* It identifies Flegetanis as the first source, who on his turn inspired Kyot. Kyot tried to find out who these servants of the Grail could be; he searched across Europe, but in the end noted that it spoke of the lords of Anjou – and hence why Perceval becomes "the Angevin".

But even though he identifies the people featuring in the Grail account as being of Anjou, it is not in Anjou that he found that information. Kyot, instead "found in Toledo, lying neglected, in heathen script, this adventure's fundament. The abc of those characters he must have learned beforehand, without the art of necromancy." It is an interesting contradiction that even though Kyot knew they were the lords of Anjou, he seems to have known this before he was able to read the Arab document – he had to learn Arabic to discover what this family had done with the Grail, and finding this out, was obviously incentive enough for him to learn Arabic. Finally, Wolfram states that it was this document that was the source of his book, his "adventure".

We are therefore confronted with two sources. One, Flegetanis' account was one or more Hermetic treatises, as well as his identification of the Grail in the constellations, and the fact that there was *a* brotherhood, in France, who had preserved the doctrine. Two, the document Kyot found in Toledo was the story of the de

Perche family, which he identified as the actual family who had preserved – and were members of – this brotherhood, which he combined with Flegetanis' account, to result into *Parzival*.

Richard Barber too concludes that "what [Kyot] found enabled [Wolfram] to tell the history of the Grail dynasty, Parzival's kin, and of their guardianship of the Grail."[140] But, to this, he adds: "Wolfram is writing in the light of an interest in or knowledge of the kind of scientific learning that had come from Arabic Spain in the twelfth century. This reintroduced the thinking of the Greek philosophers to the West [...]."[141]

That Kyot's contribution is that of the Grail – de Perche – dynasty is clear. But it is impossible to know whether or not and how close Wolfram stuck to his source material. It seems that he stuck closer to Flegetanis' than Kyot's account, as there are discrepancies – though only in unimportant details – between the de Perche family history and Wolfram's account.

Several factors can be held responsible for this. For one, we still know relatively little about the de Perche family and certain historical details are either unknown or might be erroneous themselves. Secondly, Wolfram may have introduced, or perpetuated, errors. We note that Kyot had to learn Arabic in order to comprehend their family history. This implies that he may not have been the best versed in the language and certain details may have been misinterpreted by Kyot himself, before passing it on to Wolfram.

Furthermore, everyone who has ever had to translate or write a document knows that reason plays an important part in interpretation. If Kyot did not understand a section clearly, he will have used logical deductions to interpret those passages. On occasions, errors must have occurred, which were then transmitted to Wolfram, who on occasion must have made errors in certain details also.

Finally, Wolfram joined this family history with Flegetanis'

Hermetic material, whereby there must have been a number of issues in one account, which meant that incorporation of certain material became problematic. Wolfram will have had to choose and "smooth" his account so that the reader would "get" the message, and no doubt, the Hermetic material, because of its universal and moral meaning, took precedence over historical accuracy.

Today, the scientist will argue that historical veracity needs to rise above any mythical context, but the storyteller, whether J.K.Rowling, Dan Brown or George Lucas, will argue that archetypical imagery will always need to take precedence over fact for the story to have appeal. And hence, indeed, Wolfram seems to have chosen to stick with the Hermetic messages and downgrade the family account when there was a conflict of interest for the purpose of good storytelling.

In the end, we have a work – *Parzival* – that is a mixture of three sources: Flegetanis, Kyot and Wolfram himself. Which sections of this masterpiece originates from what, can become the subject of future analyses, but at present, it is more important to identify what the Grail was. And for that, we need to look, firstly, to Flegetanis' Hermetic material. As Richard Barber wrote: "Wolfram is writing in the light of an interest in or knowledge of the kind of scientific learning that had come from Arabic Spain in the twelfth century. This reintroduced the thinking of the Greek philosophers to the West […]."[142] And it is the history of the *Corpus Hermeticum*, its origins and reintroduction in Western Europe, that are a vital piece of our quest for the origins – and nature – of the Grail.

The Florentine Renaissance

The Florentine Renaissance was one of the most fascinating periods of time in human history. During the Florentine Renaissance, there was a huge development in the arts, architecture, literature, science, government, and many other fields of knowledge. It was also the time when the *Corpus Hermeticum* made its appearance in Western Europe, even though more and more evidence is now uncovered that the Hermetic literature was known in Europe before.

Even though it may have been known before, the fact remains that there was one person who was instrumental in exposing Western society to its content: Cosimo de Medici, the man behind the emerging economic power of the Italian city of Florence.

1401 was the year in which Florence's wool merchants' guild announced that it would sponsor an artist to make a new bronze door for the city's baptistery. The rise of Florence was the result of wool, imported from the 11th century onwards from Northern Europe. Rare dyes from the Mediterranean and the East resulted in specialised weaving and dying techniques that would make the wool trade the city's main source of income. By the 14th century, Florence was Europe's richest city, the florin becoming the first common European currency, widely accepted and circulated because of the purity of its gold content.

The rise of Florence was not appreciated by everyone. Dante, born in the city in 1265, labelled the city as a "glut of self-made men and quick-got gain". But though there were those who sought fame and fortune, only to loose both equally quickly, some families carved out a lasting powerbase.

Cosimo was the head of de Medici family, the richest family in Italy, one of those who had benefited from the invention of credit banking. The family ruled Florence almost continuously from 1434 until 1737.

The family's wealth had begun to grow in the 13th century, increasing towards the end of the century when one of the members of the family served as gonfalero, the bearer of a high ceremonial office. It was Savestro de Medici who led the people of Florence in revolt against the ciompi, the small artistanate, and became so popular that he was made defacto dictator of Florence. Though an elected dictator, he suffered the fate of so many other dictators, when he was banished in 1383.

It was left to Giovanni Bicci de Medici to regain the family power by making the family the richest family in Florence, then Italy, and possibly Europe. His bank was even entrusted the collection of papal revenues. Economic power was transformed in political power when he became gonfalero in 1421. It would be his son, Cosimo de Medici, often nicknamed "the Elder", who would be the real founder of the family's fortune... and the man who would give the Hermetica to the world.

In 1434, Cosimo controlled the government in Florence. He would rule the city for sixty years, even though he had no official title. He did hold office in Florence's highest magistry, at the same time managing interests in banking, trade and industry. Florence thrived under his rule and the fact that the city became the centre of Renaissance, which would give the world painters such as Leonardo da Vinci, Michelangelo and Botticelli, is in essence only thanks to him. Throughout his rule, Cosimo spent lots of his money on the city and the support of artists and sculptors. Churches were built and many large libraries were constructed for the books he collected.

Amongst the many books he sought, Cosimo was mostly intrigued by Greek texts, specifically Plato. He used his extensive network of contacts to trace and buy copies of documents that many had thought to be lost. But amongst the many books he recovered, there was one very special: the *Corpus Hermeticum.*

It is unknown how Cosimo exactly learned about the document. As a consequence, some theories have been advanced. In 1439, a Byzantine scholar named Georgius Gemistos was present in Florence for a special papal gathering. Born in Constantinople about 1355 and thus in his eighties, he had changed his name to Plethon out of veneration for Plato. He combined the teaching of Plato with Oriental mysticism and magic (Zoroastrism), apparently under the influence of Muslim teachers. He openly abandoned Christianity and sought to substitute paganism for it as the model according to which one should live his life. At the Council of Florence, he was one of the six champions of the Orthodox Church.

The problem of the Council was an urgent one. Since 1422, Sultan Murad II had laid siege to Constantinople. Every day, the Turks tightened their control over all approaches to the city. Only a new crusade could relieve the Byzantine Empire from its looming fate.

But before such a crusade could be organised, the many religious differences between the Catholic and Orthodox Church needed to be addressed before the Catholic world would lend any help to their Orthodox brethren.

Many of these differences were about doctrine. The Catholic World was largely self-contained, intent to continuously repeat that what it already knew. The Orthodox Church was regularly rejuvenated by the incorporation of Greek mythology and other Middle Eastern religious doctrines. It was clear someone had to bow and in the face of the power of the oncoming Ottoman force, the Greeks declared themselves Catholics, signalling a formal reunion of the two churches. Despite the successful reunion, the Orthodox congregation was unwilling to adopt the unification – even the people of Constantinople seemed more willing to face Turkish rule than be labelled "Catholic". And even though a crusade was mounted, the army was totally defeated at Varna in 1444.

Though the Council therefore had no real positive outcome, it would plant a seed of rejuvenation at the heart of Europe. In Florence, Plethon spent most of his time lecturing on Platonism and Zoroastrianism to the Florentines. Some of these lectures were attended by Lorenzo de Medici, Cosimo's grandson. Cosimo himself was often a guest at the house of Agyropoulos, where the lectures were often the topic of further discussion. Plethon spoke to Cosimo and inspired him to create a Platonic Academy, dedicated to the study of ancient texts.

Though Plethon returned to the Peloponnesus in 1441, he left behind a number of very talented young men in Florence, including a monk, named John, named after the Egyptian hermit Bessarion. It was John Bessarion who was commissioned to read the Greek redaction of the Act of Union on 6 July 1439, in the cathedral of Florence. Bessarion briefly returned to Greece, but during the same year is found once more at Florence with Pope Eugenius IV, who, in the consistory of 18 December 1439 (according to others 8 January 1440), created him cardinal of the title of the Twelve Holy Apostles.

Cosimo, Plethon and John Bessarion were those that planted the seed of the Renaissance; now it had to grow.

Marsilio Ficino was only six years old when the papal delegations united in his home town. He was the son of the physician of Cosimo de Medici and would serve three generations of that family. He studied philosophy and medicine, before being elected as the president of the Platonic Academy. He thus walked in the footsteps of Plethon and became a propagator of Platonism, going so far as to argue that Plato should be read in the churches, and claiming that Socrates and Plato were fore-runners of Christ. It is said that he kept a light burning before a bust of Plato in his room.

In 1460, the Italian monk Leonardo da Pistoia brought a Greek manuscript to Florence from Macedonia.[143] Some place the arrival of this manuscript, known as the *Corpus Hermeticum* in 1460, though others suggest a slightly later date of 1462. Whatever date, everyone agrees that Cosimo de Medici ordered Ficino to stop all other translations, so that he could focus exclusively on the *Corpus Hermeticum*. He accomplished the translation of the work in a matter of months, which meant that the Platonic Academy was now able to read the "Body of Hermes".

Erik Hornung, professor emeritus of Egyptology at the University of Basel, Switzerland, has underlined the importance of Ficino's injection of Egyptian material into the Western world, a topic which he has labelled "Egyptosophy", i.e. the conceptualisation of various artistic, literary and esoteric devotion to Egypt. He rightfully points out that the introduction of the Hermetic doctrine in the Western world has resulted in a centuries-long interest – sometimes bordering on an obsession – with all things Egypt.

Even though the *Corpus Hermeticum* sits closely with the Greek philosopher Plato, Ficino believed that the document was first written in Egyptian and was later translated into Greek to reveal to the Greeks the Egyptian mysteries.[144] Though unaccepted by many, in recent years, more and more scholars are beginning to share this point of view, namely that the texts were written for a Greek audience, but were renderings of the Egyptian initiation rites.

Hornung himself anchors the Hermetic perspective in Egypt's 12th Dynasty (ca. 1800 BC), at the Temple of Thoth in Hermopolis. He sees the origin of the *Corpus Hermeticum* as the *Book of Two Ways*, a religious document on the afterlife. Thoth, the central figure of Egyptosophy, was a judge, a winged messenger god (hence his identified with Hermes), the scribe of the gods, whose priests were authors of the famous sacred writings, the "Books of Thoth". By the Ptolemaic period, when Manetho was tasked with reformatting these Books in such manner that the Greeks could comprehend the Egyptian religion, Thoth had become the primary Egyptian god of magic, incantations, and spells whose name was not to be spoken.

Dubious origins

Though the *Corpus Hermeticum* contains Egyptian material, most scholars still believe that it was not composed in Egyptian times. It is possible that the actual collection of treatises that make up the Hermeticum only dates from the 11th century, when Michael Psellus is known to have edited individual Hermetic texts. Like Plethon, Psellus was a child of Constantinople. A lawyer and judge, he became imperial secretary under Emperor Michael V (1041-2), though under his successor, he also began to teach philosophy at the new Academy of Constantinople. Soon, Psellus aroused opposition amongst ecclesiastical professors, as he preferred Plato to Aristotle – a preference that Plethon himself would display three centuries later.

It is indeed likely that it was Plethon who collated a small selection of specifically worthwhile documents into one document, thus creating the *Corpus Hermeticum*. It is in this collection that we find the "Grail chapter", dealing with the Cup of the Monad. Hence, from the 11th century onwards, this new compendium of Hermetic lore would have been able to inspire stories of a magical Cup. It is known that Psellus was familiar with the "Grail chapter", as he repeatedly spoke about this fourth chapter.[145] That before others, including Wolfram, had been exposed to this chapter, is now evident.

Though the above, conservative timeline allows for the appearance of Hermetic material in Wolfram's *Parzival*, more recently, there is a growing tendency to place the collation of the *Corpus Hermeticum* further back in time, in Graeco-Roman times. For example, an early work called *The Hermetic Definitions* was known to the Neoplatonist Porphyry, who wrote about this ca. 300 AD. Other collections from the 5th century are also known, and in Vienna there are fragments of papyruses of ca. 300 AD with Hermetic texts being listed as "tract 9" and "tract 10", suggesting they are part of a larger collection.

Though scholars continue to find new evidence, constantly redefining the date for the creation of the *Corpus*, it is clear that Hermetic documents were in circulation in the 11th century, and possibly much earlier. But that is not the central question; the question is whether it is possible that the kings of Aragon possessed a copy of this document in the 12th century, which at that time was apparently only circulating outside the realm of the Catholic world.

The Dutch collector of Hermetic documents Joost Ritman has recently been able to prove that other copies of the Corpus existed in Europe pre-1460. He was able to buy a Greek manuscript, which had originally been bought in June 1458 by Cardinal John Bessarion.[146] It shows that even in Florence, there were older copies in circulation than that translated by Ficino.

Still, with this new evidence, we remain within the small circle of Florence's Platonic Academic. It is therefore important to show that other people in Europe had access to Hermetic material prior to the 15th century – and that is the case.

Albertus Magnus, the great Dominican scholar, the bishop of Cologne and teacher of Thomas Aquinas, lived in the middle of the 13th century. In his writings, he frequently cites Hermes Trismegistus, "Hermes Thrice Great" – the "author" of the *Corpus Hermeticum*. Albertus Magnus had discovered a copy of one of the Hermetic texts, the *Asclepius*, around 1250. Some have argued that he had only heard about this document, but this ploy to keep the dogma that the Hermetica only resurfaced in Europe in the 15th century alive, is inadequate to explain Magnus' familiarity with the *Asclepius*, which was far greater than that of any of his contemporaries, except Thomas of York, who died ca. 1260. Not only does Albertus quote from this text more often than any other Hermetic work, he does so more often than most other authors' citations of the Hermetic corpus as a whole. He therefore must have had first-hand knowledge of the Hermetic writings, although he did also draw on other sources, such as Augustine, for some of his information on Hermes.

John the Baptist, the herald of the Grail?

The *Corpus Hermeticum* could therefore have fallen into the hands of Flegetanis, and the kings of Aragon, by the 12th century. It would have made the kings of Aragon the precursors of the Florentine Renaissance, and there are indeed some apparent parallels between the kings of Aragon in San Juan de la Peña and Cosimo de Medici in Florence.

Both were phenomenal rulers, instrumental in restructuring the monastery and the town of Florence to their own liking. In the case of the kings of Aragon, they created a Grail Brotherhood; Cosimo created the Platonic Academy. Both had been exposed to foreign cultures – from where they had taken their pagan knowledge. The only difference between his Spanish predecessors and the Italian Cosimo was that the latter was a businessman who had made his way into politics; the right to rule had not been his birthright, or the result of a formidable military power. He would, however, soon correct such a genetic problem and transform his family into a ruling dynasty. Both courts were equally "enlightened"; they possessed a certain quality to it, which is also typical and has become known as a "Grail court": a place of higher learning, where certain moral values ruled that were above the norm of their time. For Florence, that was symbolised by the Renaissance – the rebirth of Hermes.

We can only wonder whether it is a coincidence that San Juan de la Peña and Florence also share the same patron saint: both are placed under the protection of John the Baptist. This seems to be a coincidence, but it becomes an intriguing coincidence when we note that one vital component of the Grail tradition is the role of baptism, echoing Hermes' dictum: "Know that the secret, and the life, of everything is water."[147]

Throughout two millennia of Christianity, John the Baptist has been little more than a footnote. He was the one to whom God had sent a messenger, saying he would one day baptise the Messiah.

Years later, John the Baptist would indeed baptise Jesus in the waters of the river Jordan, thus fulfilling his destiny and opening the Christian Era. And that seems to be all.

But it seems that for some, John the Baptist might have been much more. The role of John the Baptist in a Western European "underground stream" came to the forefront in 1997, with the publication of Lynn Picknett and Clive Prince's *The Templar Revelation*, the book that served as a major source of inspiration for Dan Brown's *The Da Vinci Code*.

The authors argued that throughout Western civilisation, a small group of people had known about the true origins of Christianity: that Christ was not the Son of God; that neither he nor his teachings were unique; that the teachings of Christianity had been borrowed from other religions... and that Jesus' doctrine had been copied from John the Baptist's teachings, who was nothing more – or less – than a missionary, trying to convert the Jews to the Egyptian religion.

There is indeed evidence to suggest that John the Baptist was not an isolated preacher, but that he and the leaders of his community received instructions and directions from Alexandria, the capital of Egypt, where the Egyptian high priests were not only responsible for the spiritual welfare of the Egyptians, but may have decided to export their religion to neighbouring areas; the region where John the Baptist and Jesus preached was well within the reach of Alexandrian missionaries.

That the Baptist had a far more important role than the Bible provides for, is clear, but how precisely he and Christianity slot into each other, is at present a non-requirement to slot his role into the Grail tradition. All that is needed, is what he was credited for in mainstream Christianity as well: the role of herald.

John the Baptist's role of the herald of Christianity became reinterpreted within the pagan doctrine, where the Phoenix bird was the herald of a New Age. In the Hermetic doctrine, the

Monad was sent down, with an angel as its herald. For those who followed the Hermetic path within the Christian Western world, John the Baptist became the herald of their quest – a Christian veneer on top of a pagan tradition.

In the Hermetic doctrine, the role of the herald is to preach the message, but it is left to our free will whether to follow or ignore it: "To follow will lead to eternal life, to ignore, will lead to death. Ignorance will result in a state whereby Mankind remains unaware by whom and for what purpose we have been made."[148] We are thus confronted with two paths, one that will lead to good, the other to evil. And it is not God who is responsible for evil, but Mankind, as evil is the outgrowth of ignorance.

Like John the Baptist proclaimed the New Age of Christ in Christianity, the heralds of the Grail proclaimed the possibility to ascend to God, by proclaiming the presence of the Grail and the existence of a brotherhood that serves it. In the Hermetica, the herald states: "Dip yourself in this Krater, you who are able; you who believe that you will ascend to Him who sent this Krater down."[149] The herald is therefore the person who calls to be baptised, which in Christianity is of course the role of John the Baptist. That the Baptist would therefore become an important figure for the Hermeticists is clear; his association with the Monastery of San Juan de la Peña should therefore not be seen as a coincidence, but as a sign – a herald – of careful planning.

Egyptian origins

The Hermetic doctrine is based on the belief that Egypt was the original home of all knowledge. The great Greek philosophers had all visited the land that stretches along the river Nile and had conversed if not studied with Egyptian priests; hence, the Greeks were the heirs of Egyptian knowledge. Still, most scholars assume that the link between the *Corpus Hermeticum* and the Egyptian Mysteries is very much like the link between the superstar and his fans: they know of each other, but what they know of each other is often erroneous or exaggerated.

Despite this standoff, in recent years, scholars have argued that the origins of the Hermetica should not be located in the first centuries of the Christian era, but instead half a millennium earlier, after Alexander the Great's Conquest of Egypt. This makes the case for the validity of the inheritance much stronger, as it allows for a direct transmission; it is where we find Manetho as the key enabler of this transmission.

When Alexandria had become the capital of Egypt, the city immediately became a centre of learning, where Greek philosophy merged with Egyptian mysticism. Its status as a centre of learning was symbolised by the great Library of Alexandria.

One of the Greek philosophers who owed a debt to Egypt was the great Plato himself. Though often identified as the archetypal Greek philosopher, Clement of Alexandria stated that Plato did not "deny importing anything from abroad the best parts into his philosophy and admits a visit to Egypt", showing that what many considered to be typically Greek, was in fact on loan – or inherited – from Egypt.

According to some sources, Plato actually stayed in Egypt for thirteen years. Clement claimed that Plato became the disciple of an Egyptian priest Sechnuphis of Heliopolis. When the Greek historian Strabo toured Egypt in the first century BC, he was shown the places where Plato and the Greek mathematician Eudoxos had supposedly lived and studied.

And it was Egyptian knowledge, particularly the "knowledge of Thoth", which Plato incorporated as the cornerstone of his Platonic Academy, which he founded in Athens in 387 BC.[150] The origins of the School of Chartres and the Florentine Academy can thus be found more than a millennium before. But these academies themselves were the children of the Egyptian centres of learnings, spread along the shores of the river Nile, affixed to the various temples dedicated to the pantheon of Egyptian deities.

With the arrival of the Greeks as the rulers of Egypt, the government asked if not demanded that the Egyptian doctrine and knowledge should be written down and distributed amongst all the people. The Greek concept of democracy versus the Egyptian merocratic regime had come to a head. Still, the Egyptians obliged as in essence initiation had always been open to anyone, provided they had to willingness and perseverance to learn.

It is perhaps not coincidental then, that the world's largest library came about in Alexandria. The building of the library seems to have been an attempt to safeguard the teachings of the ancient Egyptians. Their empire was in decline and over the previous centuries it had become clear that their knowledge could soon be completely lost. Instrumental in building the library was an Athenian exile, Demetrius of Phaleron. Demetrius had been a ruler of Athens for ten years and was one of the students of Aristotle, along with Alexander the Great. After Alexander's death and the resulting power struggle, Demetrius had fled Athens, to settle in Alexandria, where he was converted to the Serapis cult, a new cult that had become formed upon the Greek conquest of Egypt.

It was Demetrius who persuaded the king to translate the Septuagint, the Hebrew bible, into Greek. 72 Rabbis were brought in to oversee the translation, which came about as the Jews of Alexandria, like the local Egyptians, had gradually lost the knowledge of their ancient language and many had adopted the Hellenistic culture. It was Demetrius who told the king to build the temple of the Muses, which would hold the library.

According to Strabo, at the heart of this structure was a Great Hall and a circular domed dining hall with an observatory in its upper terrace; classrooms surrounded it. This layout resembles that of the Serapeum. An estimated thirty to fifty scholars were probably housed there permanently, sponsored by the royal family and later, according to an early Roman papyrus, by public money. It is clear that Florence in the 15th century was merely copying what had occurred in Alexandria so many centuries before.

Alexandria also had a second, smaller library, connected to the Serapeum, the temple of the cult of Serapis. Both seem to have been closely related, as the major library was next to the Museum, with the Head of the Museum also being the High Priest of Serapis; both jobs went together. It therefore suggests that, not surprisingly, the maintenance of this knowledge was considered to be a sacred task, given to the high priest.

The High Priest of Serapis was thus the heir of the sacred literature that had been placed under the Egyptian god Thoth, the Greek Hermes and it is from this that we get the so-called "Hermetic texts".

The Cult of Serapis

Who was Serapis, who suddenly had become the most important deity of the Land of the Nile? History books say that the cult of Serapis was an invention, a creation of Ptolemy I Soter, the Graeco-Egyptian ruler of Egypt from 305-283 BC. His requirement was for a new religion that was acceptable and accessible both for his Egyptian and Greek subjects.

One of the most learned and respected scholars on Serapis is the Dutch Hermetic specialist Bruno Stricker. For Stricker, the Ptolemies created a single god by incorporating the two chief deities of the respective pantheons: the Greek Zeus and the Egyptian Osiris. This new "one god" was then named Serapis. The Greek writer Plutarch confirmed Stricker's conclusion: "Serapis being none other than that common name by which all those are called who have thus changed their nature, as is well known by those who are initiated into the mysteries of Osiris."[151]

In light of the transformative power of the Grail, the reference to "those who are called who have thus changed their nature" is intriguing. After all, it was said that the Grail had called for certain people to serve it, and that they had become changed men.

The change of nature to which Plutarch refers applies to the initiatory death that the initiates of the Mysteries of Osiris had to overcome. The God Osiris himself had died, only to be resurrected and become the Everlasting Ruler of the Underworld. The initiate symbolically "died" to the normal world, to become "born" into another world – distinguished only from the old world by his chosen allegiance to the highest principles decreed by his doctrine.

The Serapis cult was therefore a mixture of the Greek Zeus and the Egyptian Osiris, the god of the Afterlife, the god of resurrection. Plutarch continued: "It is better to equate Osiris with Dionysos, and Serapis with Osiris, since the latter acquired this name when he changed his nature. For this reason Serapis is common to all, and this is true also of Osiris, as the initiates know."[152]

Of course, the king could not merely state that he had invented a new deity. A "magical occurrence" had to be created that lay at the origin of the new worship. We know that Serapis was linked with temple sleep. The story therefore goes that whilst Ptolemy was meditating, he had a dream in which he saw a colossal statue of some god. The god told him to relocate the statue to Alexandria.

According to Plutarch,[153] he had never seen such a statue and he knew neither the place where it stood, nor to whom it belonged. One day he mentioned the dream to Sosibius, describing the statue, upon which Sosibius declared to have seen a statue like it at Sinope. Tradition identifies this town with the Sinope on the Pontus and states that the inhabitants of the city were unwilling to part with it. But the statue, after three years of waiting, left by itself, walked into a ship and arrived in Alexandria after a voyage of merely three days. The idea that statues can walk seems absurd, but in the Hermetic literature, there are frequent references to walking and talking statues and it was seen as evidence that a god was resident inside the statue. And it was a good mechanism to explain how Serapis arrived in Alexandria.

It is interesting that Plutarch and Tacitus write that Ptolemy consulted the Egyptian priests for an explanation of this dream, but they are unable to offer one. Instead, it were Timotheus and Manetho who told him that they recognised the deity in the dream as Serapis, and that the dream meant that Serapis wanted Ptolemy to establish his cult in Alexandria. This would seem to have revealed an agenda on the part of Timotheus and Manetho.

They were charged by the king to respectively preserve and codify the Eleusian mysteries and the Egyptian religion in an acceptable and accessible manner to all the people of Egypt. Manetho was handpicked for this task as he was the High Priest of Heliopolis. The priests of Heliopolis were in charge of the worship of the sun god Ra and are seen as the main influence as to why the Third and Fourth Dynasty rulers of Egypt – two millennia before Manetho – began to construct pyramids.

The importance of baptism is also stressed in the cult of Serapis, where it served as the symbol of initiation. P.M. Fraser wrote that "early in the Ptolemaic period the cult of the Nile, itself closely associated with Osiris, seems to have been joined to that of Serapis and Isis in Canopus."[154] The town of Canopus was a suburb of Alexandria. Situated at the mouth of the river Nile, it was a key religious site: "In two dedications of the third century from Canopus, Serapis and Isis are associated with Nilus, who from an early date was personified, and received a semi-divine status in which he was associated with Osiris. [...] It is significant that these dedications are from Canopus, where, [...] apart from the notable shrine of Serapis, there was also a Greek cult of Osiris himself, and a separate cult of Nilus." The conclusion is therefore that in Greek times, the Egyptian god Osiris was linked with Nilus, the God of the Nile [in Egyptian times known as Hapi], to create Asar-Hapi, or Serapis.

Though there is agreement that Serapis codified both the cult of Osiris and Hapi, there is some dissent on whether this amalgamation was done by the Greeks, or whether it already existed in Alexandria before the Greek conquest of the country. John Stambaugh states: "It is surely best to avoid the common assertion that Serapis was 'created' by the Ptolemies. The ancient sources never say that Ptolemy created Serapis, and in fact Athenodorus, Tacitus and Pseudo-Callisthenes state clearly that his cult had been conducted on the hill of Rhacotis *from high antiquity*." (emphasis added)[155] He continues: "Not even the name 'Serapis' was completely new, for pre-Ptolemaic documents of the fourth century address Osiris-Apis of Memphis as 'Osorapis'. The expanded use of the name in connection with the god of Rhacotis did not imply the discovery or invention of a new god; rather it represented a new understanding both of the Greek Pluto and of the Egyptian Osiris."[156]

Whatever its specific origins, the region of Alexandria was definitely its homeland. From there, the Serapis cult exploded in popularity. It would spread across the Greek world, with a Serapeum being built in Delos in 205 BC, dedicated to "Serapis in Canopus", opening the path of official recognition by the Greek rulers, which occurred at the beginning of the 2nd century BC. Originally, the cult was of course centred on Serapis, but as popularity grew, particularly abroad, the Egyptian goddess Isis was added to the religious corpus. In the end, Isis would become the more popular of the two gods – at least outside of Egypt's former borders.

Serapis and John the Baptist

The Egyptian town of Alexandria, the first cosmopolitan and the second largest city after Rome, is only mentioned once in the New Testament. Why? Why is it so absent, even though John the Baptist sent his prominent disciple Simon Magus to Alexandria for an advanced education? Furthermore, why was Alexandria for the apostles not the main focus for converting souls to the new religion? Why instead opt for the barren lands in which Jesus and his disciples proposed to preach?

Also, why did a peculiar – almost unchristian – form of Christianity grow in Alexandria – and nowhere else? Why, in fact, was it specifically this branch of Christianity, a mixture of Neoplatonism and Gnosticism, which would become the main focus of suppression of the early Christian Church of Rome? How was it possible that before St Paul started the first preachings of Christianity, various "Gnostic Christians" were already practicing their religion in Egypt? From whom had they learned the message of "Jesus Christ", if no-one had proclaimed it yet to them, according to the accepted origins of Christianity?

These are questions that few Christian scholars have asked... as they are very difficult to answer when leaving the originality of Christianity intact. The situation becomes even more intriguing when we know that these Gnostic Christians actually denied that Jesus had died by crucifixion. They did not believe Jesus' resurrection was a physical event, but rather a symbolical one.

But to return to John the Baptist: we know that Alexandria played an important role in the life of the Baptist. An important question with which Christianity has always struggled, is the question in whose name John the Baptist baptised. After all, Christianity did not yet exist. As we mentioned, Picknett & Prince have argued that John the Baptist's teachings were based on a cult that had its centre in Alexandria. If so, then it is more than likely that John the Baptist was a priest of Serapis, sent "into the desert" to convert the neighbouring people of Egypt to the nation's religion.

For Alexandrian Christians, Jesus was never more than a footnote in their religion. In recent years, it has become obvious that throughout the Middle East, there were many "Christian" groups that have survived throughout the ages, even though they have been repressed by both Muslim and Christian communities alike. But through Christian in name, these people did not worship Jesus, but instead held John the Baptist in high regard. They did not consider Jesus Christ to be the Son of God; they considered John the Baptist as the man who had brought the teaching of their religion to them.

Victorian explorers called them "St John's Christians".[157] Known to the modern world as Mandaeans, they claim that their doctrine originated in ancient Egypt; their holy books do contain Egyptian words. They stated that John the Baptist was the greatest in a long line of priestly prophets, though they do not believe he was divine.[158] In an intriguing parallel with the title of "Fisher King" that is present in the Grail tradition, John the Baptist is called "The Fisher of Souls" by his followers.[159]

Could it be that Jesus was a follower of Serapis – seeing he was baptised by John the Baptist – and that Christianity was a corruption of the Serapis cult? In 175 AD, the Platonic philosopher Celsus stated that Jesus was a Galilean who had learned the techniques of magic in Egypt. The Jewish Talmud also states that Jesus was a magician, who had received his education in Egypt. Jesus' Jewish opponents also proclaimed him to be a magician. Many scholars have shown that Jesus' miracles are identical to those found in Graeco-Egyptian magical texts. Furthermore, the philosopher Porphyry stated that Serapis was "the ruler of demons, who gives spells for their expulsion".

It is beyond any doubt that Jesus' teachings were "un-Jewish".

Many literary analyses have revealed that the Jewish elements of the gospels, rather than the pagan elements, were added later. The early Christians were prosecuted by the Jews because they had introduced foreign elements into the Jewish religion. But outside of the Jewish communities that seem to have been the focus of a group of Egyptian priests that tried to convert these people to a new religion, observers have noted that it was almost impossible to distinguish between Serapis worshippers and Christians...

When archaeologist Shimon Gibson did his investigations of the "Cave of John the Baptist", where most likely John the Baptist began his preaching, he also discovered depictions of what is most likely John the Baptist himself. The saint is depicted with a staff and serpents, which Gibson identifies as John the Baptist holding a caduceus.[160]

The name caduceus literally means the "herald's wand", and at first, such a depiction appears to confirm the Baptist's role of the herald, of Christianity. But what is intriguing is that in these ancient depictions, dating back to the first part of the first millennium, John the Baptist is not depicted with a shepherd's crook, as is currently the norm, but with a herald's wand, which not all depict him as the herald of Christianity, but identifies him with Hermes – the god identified with a caduceus. Gibson adds that the image seems to indicate that John was "thus portrayed as the 'messenger' of God".[161]

There is more evidence to show that John had Hermetic alliances. On numerous depictions, the river god is depicted on scenes of Jesus being baptised by John.[162] This is remarkable for at least two reasons. Within a Christian context, there is no room for a belief in spirits of the river, and hence no such figure should be depicted. But within an Egyptian context, the river god would be identified with Hapi, the god of the Nile – and thus with Serapis.

Finally, one tradition states that after the Baptist's body was buried in Sebaste, a local uprising largely burnt the remains of the saint. Some bones were however rescued and sent to Alexandria, where a patriarch is said to have placed part of these recovered bones in the temple of Serapis. Why the bones of the herald of Christ would be deposited in a temple to Serapis is an intriguing question; it could have a simple answer.

Our central question is how an underground stream, aware of the fact that Christianity is not unique, but instead was the descendent of an Egyptian mystery tradition, coded this knowledge. What could be their call-sign, their "key"? In the Bible, it is John the Baptist who is linked most closely with Alexandria, the home of this cult. It is also clear that John the Baptist was the teacher, who initiated Jesus in this cult. Some time afterwards, Jesus himself began to preach the teachings he himself had learned from John the Baptist – and possibly other priests of Serapis. In this scenario, John the Baptist was a teacher of the Hermetic doctrine… and for any underground stream in Europe, the two would forever go hand in hand. It explains why John the Baptist became such a key personality in Florence, why Leonardo da Vinci incorporated him in so many paintings, and why he is of equal importance in that other bastion of Hermetic faith, the monastery of San Juan de la Peña, under the patronage of the kings of Aragon.

Serapis and the Renaissance

The link between Serapis and the Hermetic tradition is not just the fruit of 20th century scholarship; it was known to the Florentine scholars: Marsilio Ficino, the translator of the *Corpus Hermeticum* and leader of the Platonic Academy at Florence, stated that the Christian cross was a symbol of Serapis.[163] More than a century later, in front of the inquisition, Giordano Bruno equally proclaimed that the cross was not a Christian symbol, but was in fact "known in the time when the religion of the Egyptians flourished, about the time of Moses, and that this sign was affixed to the breast of Serapis."[164]

Centuries before, the Roman Emperor Hadrian made the remarkable statement that "those who worship Serapis are likewise Christians; even those who style themselves the Bishops of Christ are devoted to Serapis."[165] Though deemed by some to be enigmatic and interesting, the quote is, in essence, simple. Serapis was the resurrected god, based on the resurrected god Osiris. The Greeks had reinvented the god Osiris and had labelled him Serapis. Jesus Christ was also a god of resurrection and the resurrection from the dead formed the basis of the Osiris, Serapis and Christian religions. However, Hadrian's wording does suggest that the comparison did not stop there, apparently stating that Christ's religion was somehow linked to or based upon the Serapis cult. Was he suggesting that Christianity was not a new religion, but instead descended from the Serapis cult? If the answer is yes, then Hadrian possessed the same knowledge as those of the "underground stream".

Whereas Hadrian stated that the worship of the Christians was identical to that of Serapis, by the time of the Renaissance, Christian priests like Ficino were more interested in Serapis than in Jesus Christ. Their emphasis on the Antiquity of the *Corpus Hermeticum*, which they claimed pre-dated Christianity and was of higher value than the teachings of Christ, did not sit well with the ruling elite. As a consequence, the Hermetic texts were subjected to detailed analyses, in particular by one of the most respected scholars of the 17th century, Isaac Casaubon. Casaubon disagreed with the Hermetic scholars, stating that the texts were written by the Greeks and thus postdated Christianity. But specifically, Casaubon argued that "such knowledge" could not have been known or revealed by God before the arrival of His son, Jesus – "those people" were simply not enlightened enough. It was, of course, not a scientific argument, even though it got accepted as one.

Casaubon's dating of the Corpus to the 2nd or 3rd century AD remained scientific dogma until the middle of the 20th century. It was Bruno Stricker who pointed out how historians felt that the Greeks were deemed to have a superior philosophy, and hence no-one was ever interested in the Corpus, unwilling to accept that it might be Egyptian.

Stricker explained that the reason for this bizarre situation had to do with the surviving records of Egyptian texts. Half of those records are copies of the *Book of the Dead,* a text that never changed over the millennia of Egyptian civilisation. The other half of surviving Egyptian records amounts to very little and is hence of little interest. With only the *Book of the Dead* to show for millennia of civilisations, historians stated that the Greeks were superior, producing more advanced philosophical debate, in much less time.

The absence of surviving written evidence was, therefore, taken as evidence of absence – once again showing how the "scientific approach" practised by the less intelligent of scientists is bound to destroy and give a warped view of factual history.

Stricker was one of the first to fight against this scientific windmill. His remarkable conclusion was that the *Corpus Hermeticum* had originally been the "sacred literature" of the Serapis cult, also underlining that most of ancient Egypt's knowledge was passed on orally, and hence that there would be little evidence of this knowledge in a written format – furthermore, the total destruction of the Alexandrian Library, containing information that had eventually been written down by the gyptians, didn't help either.

This, of course, makes the connection between Serapis and the Hermetica at its most intimate. Furthermore, Stricker was not the only modern scholar to hold such views. M.W. Bloomfield, in

1952, stated that he felt that the Hermetic writings "were perhaps the bible of an Egyptian mystery religion, which possibly in kernel went back to the second century BC."[166] In Antiquity, Clemens of Alexandria and Origen, both natives of Alexandria, spoke with respect about the Corpus and considered it to be an authentic codification of the Egyptian religion. The North African Lactantius agreed with their conclusion.[167] Iamblichus in *De Mysteria,* stated that "the books said to be of Hermes, contain Hermetic doctrines, even though they use the language of the philosophers [i.e. Greek]." He considered the Corpus to be Greek in form, but Egyptian in content. Iamblichus actually referred to the Committee that wrote the Corpus, stating they were "men not unexperienced in philosophy."[168]

Iamblichus' opinion would later be echoed by Marsilio Ficino. In his opinion, the Corpus was first written in Egyptian and was later translated into Greek to reveal to the Greeks the Egyptian mysteries.[169] This is, of course, exactly the task that Manetho was given to do. And is it not interesting that Manetho is the only person in history believed to be named as such? His name literally means "Gift of Thoth", and he was indeed the person who created the *Corpus Hermeticum,* the bible of the Cult of Serapis, which was a re-codification of the ancient Egyptian religion, of which he was one of the primary pylons, being the High Priest of Heliopolis.

Manetho is therefore the "patron" of Wolfram's *Parzival*: Manetho was his predecessor, who had codified the Egyptian mysteries as part of the cult of Serapis, hoping they would thus survive. Wolfram followed in the footsteps of Manetho: at a time when the *Corpus Hermeticum* was unknown in European literature, he used one of the Hermetic texts and incorporated it into his *Parzival.* This would eventually mean that his figure of Perceval would become the archetypal initiate, in search of knowledge. For the following two centuries, the Grail mythology would become one of the best-known tales that made their way around medieval Europe. It was the most defining aspect of Western literature until the advent of the Renaissance, which largely should be seen "merely" as the continuation, the next stage, of the exposure of the Western world to the ancient "truths" of the Corpus Hermeticum.

In the 15th century, the political power of Christianity was waning in Europe, though over the following centuries, the balance between religion and politics would often change. In the late 16th century, men such as Giordani Bruno prophesized the advent of a New Age, one which would see the Renaissance of the Egyptian cult of Heliopolis.

Interestingly, the rise of the Hermetica went hand in hand with the decline of the Grail legends. Though the Grail would remain a popular theme, its message of knightly heroism was no longer a message of the new times – an era largely void of knights and their heroic efforts. The new heroes were no longer knights, but the explorers, men who set off in convoys in search of new horizons.

It seems that once the Hermetica was reintroduced in Christianity under its own name, there was no longer a need to use the Grail as the focus of a mystery tradition. In a strange twist of fate, that which had made men dream, now became ever more forcefully cemented into the traditions of the Christian church: the Grail, in its incarnation as the Cup of the Last Supper, became a powerful tool for the Church to try and convince an ever more unchristian Western world of the validity of the Church's teachings, and the central role of Jesus Christ. San Juan de la Peña thus became a centre for pilgrims, not in search of enlightenment by the Grail, but in search of validation of their Christian beliefs.

Chapter 8: The Egyptian Grail

Erik Hornung has coined the term "Egyptosophy", which is the idea that Egypt was the fount of all wisdom.[170] It does not mean that Egypt *is*, merely that people *believe* it is, and thus treat it as special.

Many people, for many centuries, have run to the borders of the river Nile to seek answers to all questions. Even Napoleon, whose expedition at first seems to have been merely one of conquest, was nevertheless said to be equipped with an armada of architects and engineers, who mapped the ancient Egyptian pyramids and temples in extraordinary detail. He himself apparently asked to be left alone inside the Great Pyramid and allegedly had a major revelation while inside the King's Chamber.

We too have to make the jump from medieval Western Europe and the Grail to the Gift of the Nile, but it is not a leap of faith or part of Egyptosophy. We have shown that the story of the Grail was taken from the Hermetic tradition, which was a codification of the ancient Egyptian religion in the last centuries of that country's existence. They were made to impart the knowledge of the Egyptians to Jews and Greeks at the time of the Ptolemaic rule.

Almost two millennia after they had been written down, the documents were to be incorporated in the medieval Grail legends, though its real moment of "international fame" came in the Renaissance, when the Western Europe's fascination with Egypt truly began. Despite the fact that it is millennia old wisdom, ancient Egypt continues to inspire people, as its spiritual message seems to be "more" than that of many institutionalised religions; it seems to be an eternal wisdom.

The question that remains to be answered is whether what made its way to the Aragonese king was "merely" a Hermetic text – the story of the Grail – or whether the actual Grail – an actual object – was also present in San Juan de la Peña. In both scenarios, we need to know what the ancient Egyptians thought the Grail – the Monad – described in the fourth Hermetic treatise was, and whether they considered this crater to be an actual object or merely a symbol of some "eternal truth".

Origins of the Hermetica

It was the High Priest of Heliopolis Manetho who had been in charge of the codification of the Egyptian religion into the *Corpus Hermeticum*, which in general was a codification of the Egyptian religion, but specifically of the creation myth of Heliopolis, focused on the gods Atum and Ra.

The priesthood of Heliopolis has been the main driver behind some of Mankind's greatest accomplishment, and their presence in the codification of the Corpus, the original Grail account, should not come as a surprise. It was another High Priest, Imhotep, who was responsible for the creation of the first pyramid (that of Zoser). Imhotep lived in ca. 2980 BC and is seen as the father of medicine. This title is further confirmation of the connection between the priesthood and the role of healers and medicine, which is also at the forefront of the Corpus, and Wolfram's Grail account.

Imhotep was a known scribe, chief lector, priest, architect, astronomer and magician and for the next 3000 years, he was worshipped as a god in Greece and Rome. Even early Christians worshipped him as the "Prince of Peace".

Though today, Hippocrates is largely known as the Father of Evidence, given today's knowledge, one is a hypocrite (pun intended) not to give this title back to its rightful owner, Imhotep. This honour was confirmed by Sir William Osler, who said he was the "first figure of a physician to stand out clearly from the mists of antiquity."

According to some scholars, the biblical Moses, who led his people out of Egypt, to create the state of Israel, was also a high priest of Heliopolis. The story of Moses was also preserved by Josephus and attributed by him to Manetho; it tells of the struggles between a rebellious Egyptian priest named Osarseph, i.e. Moses, and Pharaoh Amenhotep and his son "Ramesses also called Sethos". Osarseph, according to the story, seized control of Egypt for thirteen years, instituted a reign of terror, and destroyed Egypt's religious institutions. The Pharaoh fled from Egypt and hid his son away for safety. Later, the son returned and expelled Osarseph from Egypt. This Osarseph, says Manetho, was Moses, the biblical hero.

Most Egyptologists and biblical scholars reject the identification of Moses with Osarseph. Some scholars, like Gary Greenberg, nevertheless argue that the Exodus occurred during the co-regency of Ramesses I and Sethos, and that the confrontation between Moses/Osarseph and "Ramesses also known as Sethos" arose out of a struggle for possession of the throne at the death of Pharaoh Horemheb.[171] The story underlines the importance of the Heliopolitan priesthood, showing how they were able to influence, if not control, if not overpower, the Egyptian rulers.

On his travels, the Greek Plutarch, himself a priest of the Delphic oracle, observed that the "priests of the Sun at Heliopolis never carry wine into their temples, for they regard it as indecent for those who are devoted to the service of any god to indulge in the drinking of wine whilst they are under the immediate inspection of their Lord and King. The priests of the other deities are not so scrupulous in this respect, for they use it, though sparingly."[172]

When Herodotus had visited and met the Heliopolitan priests, he equally praised them for their wisdom. But Strabo, in a visit in 25 BC, wrote: "At Heliopolis we saw large buildings in which the priests lived. For it is said that anciently this was the principal residence of the priests, who studied philosophy and astronomy. But there are no longer either such a body or such pursuits."[173] Indeed, by 25 BC, it appears that the priesthood of Heliopolis had not so much died out, but instead, that Manetho had accomplished a transformation of their cult into the cult of Serapis, and had relocated to the new capital Alexandria – no doubt in an effort to remain close to the new Greek rulers. Whereas many Egyptologists have used these examples as evidence of the shrewdness with which the Heliopolitan priests were able to toy with the kings, one could of course also ask the question whether there was something that these priests possessed that the kings wanted or needed.

The benben stone of Heliopolis

The centre of the cult of Heliopolis was the benben stone, on which the bennu bird – the Phoenix, a mythical creature symbolising rebirth to the ancient Egyptians – was said to return. Wolfram too identifies the Grail with the process of rebirth, regeneration, adding "Such powers does the Stone confer on mortal men that their flesh and bones are soon made young again. This stone is also called the Grail."

The connection of the Phoenix with a stone also conforms precisely with Wolfram's account, when he wrote: "I will tell you how they are fed: they live from a stone whose Essence is pure [...] It is called lapis exilis. By virtue of this stone the Phoenix is burned to ashes, in which she is reborn. Thus does the Phoenix molt her feathers, after which she shines dazzling and bright, and as lovely as before."

Wolfram's Grail stone should therefore be identified with the benben stone; the phoenix is the Egyptian bennu bird.

That no-one has made this straightforward identification before, should not necessarily come as a surprise. Though the story of the benben stone is central in the Egyptian creation myth, the Western world only truly came to know these texts after the decipherment of the Egyptian hieroglyphs and the translation of the *Pyramid Texts*.

The *Pyramid Texts* were funerary inscriptions that were written on the walls of the early Ancient Egyptian pyramids at Sakkara. These date back to the 5th and 6th dynasties, approximately 2350-2175 BC. However, because of extensive internal evidence, it is believed that they were composed much earlier, circa 3000 BC, making them therefore essentially the oldest sacred texts known.

But despite their age and status as being the oldest sacred texts known to us, it was only in 1952 that Samuel Mercer was the first to produce a complete English translation of these texts. Furthermore, it was also the first complete translation in any language.

The Mercer translation was followed by the R.O. Faulkner translation in 1969, which is considered the standard today. It has thus been only very recently that the Western world has had direct knowledge of these creation myths, even though via secondary sources, of which the *Corpus Hermeticum* is one, the story has been known for centuries. But that no-one has identified the identical nature of Wolfram's Grail with Egypt's benben stone, should not come as a major surprise.

It is not the only problem that knowledge of the Egyptian Grail had to contend with. Until recently, Heliopolis was portrayed as the centre of the solar cult, dedicated to the sun god Ra. Heliopolis, now lost under the modern streets of Cairo (and not to be confused with the modern district of Cairo named Heliopolis), does mean "city of the sun", but this Greek name is different from its Egyptian name: Iunu, Pillar City. This name refers to the pillar, on which the benben stone sat, underlining the central importance of the stone, rather than the sun.

Egyptologists have long been distracted by the Greek name, as if the Greeks knew better what the Heliopolitan tradition was about than the Egyptians themselves. But the recent re-centralisation of the creation myth as the core of the ancient Egyptian beliefs has readdressed the balance, moving it away from the role of Ra and towards the role of the creator deity Atum.

Atum was the head of the Heliopolitan pantheon, their creator god. In this Heliopolitan creation myth, the world was submerged in water. All things originated from a primeval ocean (nun), out of which rose a primeval mound or island, on which the creator god Atum rose, and from where he created the world.[174] In Utterance 600 of the *Pyramid Texts*, we read: "O Atum-Kheprer, you became the high hill; you rose as the benben stone in the mansion of the benu-bird in Heliopolis."

Hence, the benben stone was seen as the primary manifestation of creation, the stone – the seed – of Atum from which the world had been created. By extension, this is the true nature of the Grail stone: the primary manifestation of creation, the residence of God – which is precisely what Wolfram had said the Grail is: the Stone of God.

With such a straightforward identification, hopes may be high that archaeologists have since located this stone – and by extension that of the Grail. But alas: just like nothing remains of Heliopolis, nothing has survived of the central shrine of the benben. Nevertheless, the archaeological record is not totally blank.

It is believed that the temple, known as the Mansion of the Phoenix, was within the precinct of the Great Temple of Heliopolis. It contained an open courtyard, in the centre of which was the stone pillar, holding the benben stone. R.T. Rundle Clark added that "the temple which enclosed the benben stone was the centre of calendrical rites as well as the scene of the rising of the High God. It was the place where the mysteries of creation were ceremonially repeated."[175]

These Mysteries of Creation that were held in Heliopolis are comparable if not identical to the Grail procession that occurs in Wolfram's *Parzival*. Details of the ceremony of the benben are scant, but if possible (its weight is unknown), it is most likely that the benben stone would have been ceremoniously carried around the city. Failing that, a procession will have occurred, which would have originated and/or finished underneath the benben stone, as this object would have been central in the ritual.

Another important characteristic common to the Grail accounts and the Egyptian creation myths is the role of sacred kingship.

In many societies, particularly those of ancient China, the Middle East, and South America, the ruler was identified with a particular god or as a god himself. Thus, we find that a legend in the Westcar Papyrus relates that the first three kings of Egypt's Fifth Dynasty (Weserkaf, Sahure and Neferirkare) were offspring of the god Ra and a lady named Radjeded, wife of a priest at Heliopolis.

The kings of ancient Egypt have been regarded as incarnations of the sun god, though this is not exactly correct. The Pharaoh was seen as the incarnation of Atum-Ra; the sun, Ra, was seen as the visible aspect of the hidden creator Atum, who was felt to be out of reach without the mediation of Ra.

Though priests assumed important functions at the festivals centred on the fertility of the soil irrigated by the Nile and the life-giving warmth of the sun, the Pharaoh, i.e. the sacred king, embodied the continuity between the realm of the sacred (i.e., the transcendent sphere) and the realm of the profane (i.e., the sphere of time, space, and cause and effect). His presence at and involvement in many of the festivals was therefore required.

As the benben ceremony was the most important festival of the Egyptian calendar, it is likely that the Pharaoh participated in the ceremony. Most likely, the Pharaoh had to play the role of the creator deity, Atum, whose emissary he was on Earth. In *The*

Twilight of Ancient Egypt: First Millennium B.C.E., Karol Myśliwiec reports on a 5th or 4th century BC papyrus, containing "instructions of a liturgical sort concerning the celebrations conducted annually to mark the anniversary of a king's assumption of power. The prayers and the instructions for the priests that it contains enable us to reconstruct the entire ceremony and even the layout of the buildings between which the procession moved. The frequent references to the god Atum allow us to conclude that the ceremony took place in Heliopolis, the principal center of his cult. This is not surprising, for Pharaoh was identified with no other god as completely as with the Lord of the Two Lands at Heliopolis."[176]

The ceremonies began at dawn; when the Pharaoh awoke, he was ritually purified, dressed, and "the ceremony of the royal house of the morning" was read to him by the master of ceremonies. A procession was formed, making its way to the temple, where the priest stood in for the Pharaoh. When this part of the ceremony was completed, the act of "the approach of the earth to the benben-palace" was carried out. This entailed bringing a container of sand from the primeval mound located in the temple of Heliopolis. The sand in the container was sprinkled around the royal stand-in, so that the latter would be placed under the protection of the "intimates of Atum". A protective zone of purity and holiness was thus created around the priest, and his place was now taken by the king himself. Returning to the procession, the king then marched past flags decorated with representations of various deities, while the party approached the "pavilion of the House of Life that is in the Great Seat". The opening ceremony ended with entering the temple, with both the priest and the Pharaoh making a food offering to the resident deities.

After this relatively public aspect of the annual ritual, the king spent several days inside the temple, where he was subjected to a series of ceremonies, many of which were magical in nature, and which were meant to confirm and strengthen the safety of the ruler for the entire year to come

The closing ceremony saw the entire party return to the House of Life, where nine live birds were presented, in a ceremony that began with a prayer to the sun god Ra. After a series of ritual anointments, the birds were set free, so that they were both emissaries and protectors of the king, whereby the entire festival ended with a prayer to these birds of Ra, who granted life and health to the king for the coming year. The king, and his kingdom, was reinvigorated for yet another year; he was "fit" to rule.

The aspect of such sacred kingship is prominent in both Chrétien and Wolfram's story, even though the ceremony does not go as smoothly as it should. Whereas it is clear that all the ingredients for success, including the presence of the Grail/benben stone itself, are present in the Grail Court, the Fisher King is unable to be granted life and health for the coming year – as a vital role, to be played by Perceval, is never performed correctly during the ceremony.

It is here that the role of King Arthur also becomes important, for Arthur was the symbol of the sacred king par excellence. Many writers have made a straightforward link between the Grail and Arthur, but it is my contention that the Grail authors used Arthur as a symbol: he symbolised an era when sacred rule still existed over the land. As the Christian era was largely void of such "sacred kingship" – if only because the concept is not part of the Christian doctrine – the story of Arthur was re-engineered: to become an example of a sacred king, within the Christian era. In this context, Arthur was the Christian equivalent of the ancient Egyptian Pharaoh, whose symbolism incorporated his status as a divine ruler, repeated over the millennia of Egypt's existence: the king was "fit" to rule.

This was indeed the "hope" of the Grail and the Grail king: that he would be able to transform "the Waste Land" and make it into a kingdom that was ruled in accordance with the ancient principles of sacred kingship, in which the ruler was both king and high priest – the emissary of the creator god.

Many scholars have identified the presence of the sacred kingship tradition more easily in Chrétien's work than in Wolfram's. Though Wolfram did remain closer to the source, by quoting from largely unavailable Hermetic texts, it also meant that his audience did not understand, whereas everyone understood Chrétien's references to King Arthur; his audience was aware of the wave of Arthurian tales flooding in from England; it also touched the inherent Celtic nature of the French as well… Egyptian Hermetic thinking on the other hand was not in vogue in medieval Europe; that craze would ride on the wave of the Renaissance in the centuries to come.

Further correspondences

So far, it is clear that the Fisher King's mission was to restore sacred kingship, and that Wolfram identified the Grail with a stone, and made specific references to the Phoenix's role, who was reborn from his own ashes upon this "firestone". This allows the identification of the Grail stone with the Egyptian benben stone, which formed the centre of the Egyptian Creation myth, focused on Atum.

But there are many more parallels between the Egyptian primeval mound and the Grail. For one, it is the place where there was an assembly of the gods, mimicking the assembly of the Brotherhood in the Grail Castle. Some of these assemblies had the specific purpose of restoring the divine kingship of Egypt – similar to the Grail and Perceval's role in restoring the Fisher King back to health, and his divine task to assume the role of Grail king himself.

The benben stone was also the site from where the Egyptian gods ascended, the "Rising of the High God", identified by

Wolfram with the Grail as the location where angels ascended and descended. In this respect, the angels were nothing more than the old gods of the ancient Egyptians, known as the Ennead, or Nine Principles. In essence, it is the assembly of the nine most important gods – the Council of Gods, and is echoed in the Grail by the assembly of the Grail Brotherhood; the infamous Round Table of King Arthur, in which the number was changed from nine to twelve, no doubt to correspond better not so much with the twelve apostles, but with the twelve signs of the zodiac.

Though the Grail is the medieval name for the benben stone, the Stone of Creation, the Seed of Atum, it is clear that in the Grail accounts, the seed of the Fisher King is exactly what is causing the problem his country faces: it is "not working". Hence, the Grail Procession is organised to restore the balance, but as it is left to the foolish Perceval, who fails to play his proper role and ask the proper question, the king has to endure one more cycle of pain before someone might relieve him – restore his seed, relieve his pain. In the end, that cycle is concluded when Perceval returns to the Grail Castle and is now knowledgeable enough to ask the proper question. As such, the wrong of Perceval's previous cycle was righted, and all was well, that ended well.

This part of the Grail story repeats the Egyptian belief that through rites and ceremony, the power of the Pharaoh and by extension the gods would be restored. In ancient Egypt, this belief was specifically focused on the myth of Isis and Osiris.

In this myth account, Osiris is the divine king of Egypt, until at a meal, his evil twin brother Seth killed him and then had Osiris' body dismembered into 14 parts. Osiris's sister and wife Isis searched the lengths of the river Nile, collecting all parts, except Osiris' penis. Knowing she had to create an heir to rule in Osiris's place, Isis was therefore forced to craft a wooden penis, and was able, by using magic, to conceive a child from that union, Horus, the divine offspring that would restore the balance and continue the sacred kingship over Egypt.

The parallels with the Grail account are obvious: Anfortas had received his wound from the evil Klingsor; Osiris had been murdered by his evil brother Seth. Anfortas' nephew had to heal him, whereas it was the task of Isis to restore Osiris, just like Isis had to restore Lucius from an ass to human form – a story that we know lies at the root of Chrétien's *Le Conte du Graal*. Just like Horus would eventually avenge his father Osiris, we see that Perceval will eventually avenge his uncle by defeating Klingsor.

The Egyptian story also reveals the important role of magic: though Osiris is seedless – and by all accounts dead – through magic, Isis is still able to conceive. In the Grail story, magic plays an equally important role: by uttering the correct words – a question – the seedless king will be healed again.

It may come as a surprise to some, but magic is primarily defined as the repetitive uttering of the same words, which is in evidence in the *Pyramid Texts*. One part of the *Pyramid Texts* is the so-called "Declaration of Innocence Before the Gods of the Tribunal", in which the Pharaoh states: "I am Pure. I am pure. I am pure. I am pure. My purity is the purity of this great Phoenix that is in Heracleopolis, because I am indeed the nose of the Lord of Wind who made all men live on that day of completing the Sacred Eye in Heliopolis in the 2nd month of winter last day, in the presence of the lord of this land. I am he who saw the completion of the Sacred Eye in Heliopolis, and nothing evil shall come into being against me in this land in this Hall of Justice, because I know the names of these gods who are in it." Apart from the repetitive nature of the "I am Pure" reference, which is the tell-tale sign of magical utterings, this specific text of course also contains references to the Phoenix, and Heliopolis.

Richard Barber has stated that "There are many stories in folklore and literature which revolve round the finding of an answer to a question, but stories where the crux is the *asking* of the question in the first place are rare in the extreme. I have not as yet been able to find any satisfactory parallel for this daring leap of invention, for such it must be."[177] Equally, he believes it is "not about mysteries or objects, but is a straightforward declaration of human sympathy."[178]

The love for fellow Mankind is exactly what the servant needs to display – and it is what Perceval omitted in his first encounter: by showing sympathy with the king, the king is healed. But, contrary to Barber's conclusion, it is very much like the Mysteries, as what Isis performs on the body of Osiris is not an act of love, but a sacred task. The presence of a wooden penis and a dead body makes it clear that Isis is not performing some form of necrophilia; her task is to produce a child, and this she accomplishes through magic. There is no pleasure in her union with her dead husband.

This, of course, also underlines the role of "sacred sex": the task to procreate, which in the Grail tradition was identified as an important task to be performed in one's lifetime, and said that the sexual act itself could nevertheless not be enjoyed – very much like Isis will not have enjoyed the wooden phallus.

There are still further parallels between ancient Egyptian myths and the Grail account. In the story of Isis and Ra, the sun god Ra is laid low by the bite of a serpent which was placed on his path by Isis, who this time plays the role of the evil nemesis. Ra's heart and limbs are stricken by pain and like Anfortas, he calls out for the gods, to come to his aid. Only Isis can remove the poison, and she argues that she will agree, but on condition that Ra reveals to her his secret name. By surrendering his secret name, he in essence would surrender all his power. When he agrees, she removes the poison from his body and permits him to live. In the Grail procession, we see that though Perceval is without malice (unlike Klingsor), once he has healed the Fisher King, he has nevertheless become Anfortas' successor and like Isis, it is Perceval who is now the focus of the Grail court.

The parallels do not end there. One ancient Egyptian spell states that "Sekhmet's arrow is inside you, the magic of Thoth is inside you. Isis condemns you, Nephthys punishes you, the spear of Horus is in your head."[179] Thus, the imagery of the spear, which has wounded Anfortas, is itself present in the ancient Egyptian texts. It underlines that the Grail tradition, based on the *Corpus Hermeticum*, is indeed a medieval incarnation of ancient religious doctrine.

The Pyramids

Though Atum's cult was centred on Heliopolis, many Egyptologists have too narrowly focused on the town – excluding the Gizeh plateau and its pyramids as part of the bailiwick of the Heliopolitan priests. Even though Strabo mentioned that Heliopolis was situated on top of a noteworthy mound, it seems likely that the pillar on which the benben sat was not the true primordial hill, but that this was located at Gizeh, on the hill where the greatest of Egyptian pyramids rose. That same conclusion was picked up by the popular author Robert Bauval, quoting Robin J. Cook: "The Gizeh group probably represents a symbolic expression of the Heliopolitan myth."[180] One of the deans of Egytology, I.E.S. Edwards, described how the Sphinx was said to guard the "Splendid Place of the Beginning of All Time", which is none other than the primeval hill – the Mound of Creation.

The Gizeh plateau is a natural rocky outcrop rising quite high above the Nile and as such is an ideal candidate for "first land rising from the Abyss" and the waters of nun, who must have found their parallels in the waters of the Nile, specifically at the time of the annual flooding. This is no idle speculation, for Diodorus Siculus, in ca. 60 BC, wrote that the Great Pyramid took twenty years to build and how "a cut was made from the Nile, so that the water turned the site into an island". The need to make the plateau into an island was therefore a specific human intervention – one with a specific purpose, as the "cut" was no small engineering feature. At the time of the Flooding of the Nile, every year, the primeval hill of Gizeh would rise out from the Waters of Chaos, the waters that had flooded Egypt. It were these waters that restored the land of Egypt – which had become the Waste Land – to its fertility.

As the primeval hill was a place of descent for the Creator God, was the myth of Atum descending to Earth related to the Gizeh plateau? There is the account of how Khufu, the builder of the Great Pyramid, mentions that an old sycamore tree[181] that grew near the Sphinx was damaged "when the Lord of Heaven descended upon the Place of Hor-em-Akhet", the latter translated as "the place of the Falcon God of the Horizon", most often identified with the Sphinx – even though this monument is not known for its bird-like appearance. This tree was linked to Atum and in Heliopolis there was a chapel to "Atum of the Sycamore Tree".

Abdel-Aziz Saleh mentioned that there were several sacred trees at Heliopolis: the ishd(et) tree in the House of the Phoenix, the shendet (acacia) tree in the sanctuary of the goddess Iusas, on the primitive high mound of sand, north of the temple of Ra, as well as the sycamore tree mentioned above.[182] This suggests that Gizeh and Heliopolis were two parts of one whole, namely the cult of the Creator God Atum. A sacred road furthermore connected the Gizeh plateau to Heliopolis, enforcing the notion that the pyramids were related to the cult of Atum. Further confirmation comes from the work of Dr. Gerhard Haeny of the Swiss Institute of Archaeology in Cairo, who stated that the pyramids of Gizeh align to the obelisk of Heliopolis, which in later times had replaced the Temple of the Phoenix, where the benben stone had previously been kept.[183]

The primeval mound was therefore the location where the Lord of the Universe resided – or ascended and descended, as his presence on Earth was not constant. Rundle-Clarke wrote that "his throne is placed upon the creation mound, which the deceased now reaches in what he calls 'this city'". The Egyptian word for "mound of creation" is "niwt", which means the numinous centre of the universe, the seat of God.[184] It is from where God ruled the universe. In the Grail tradition, it is the Grail Castle, from which the representative of the creator deity on Earth, the Grail King, rules.

So what is the Grail? The benben stone was the crystalisation of the seed of the Creator God. Egyptologist Henri Frankfort wrote that "the pyramidion on top of the obelisk is called bnbnt, and the bnbn stone had originated as a drop of seed of Atum or of a bull [...]; hence it is likely that the obelisk did not serve merely as an impressive support for the stylized benben stone which formed its tip but that it was originally a phallic symbol at Heliopolis, the 'pillar city'."[185] Similarly, the pyramidion on top of the pyramid was called "bnbnt". The pyramid itself was thus a representation of the benben stone, resting on the Mound of Creation, the Gizeh plateau.

The Egyptian Perceval

Not only did the ancient Egyptians have traditions about magical stones, the Egyptian literature also had stories that are on par with Perceval's Grail Quest.

The Hermetica was the "Body of Hermes", in ancient Egypt known as the *Book of Thoth*. [186] A *Book of Thoth* has recently been found, written in demotic and dated to the later stage of Egypt's existence. It contains a conversation between Thoth, Osiris and a student. Thoth imparts information on the netherworld, ethics, the sacred geography of Egypt, secret language and mysteries.

The text has been labelled largely "Greek" in nature – even though it is written in the Egyptian language. In one instance, the name of Thoth is qualified by the triple adjective "wer", meaning "great" and thus equating him with Hermes Trismegistus – thrice great.[187]

The *Book of Thoth* was said to contain all the knowledge of the universe. As a consequence, it was a very prized possession. In ancient Egypt, there were many stories of people going in search of it, trying to unlock its power and its knowledge. Most often, the protagonists of these tales were princes – a setting very similar to Perceval, a cousin to the king.

It is at this point that we need to trade in Dan Brown's *The Da Vinci Code* as our favourite example of comparison, and, rather than Indiana Jones, look towards tombraider Lara Croft, and the 2003 movie, *Lara Croft Tomb Raider: The Cradle of Life*.

The plot revolves around Croft's quest to find Pandora's Box, an object from ancient legends which supposedly contains one of the deadliest plagues on Earth, before evil Nobel Prize-winning scientist Jonathan Reiss can get his hands on it. The key to finding the Box, which is hidden in the mysterious Cradle of Life, is a magical luminous orb that is supposed to be some type of a map. While exploring the submerged Luna Temple off Greece, she recovers the orb, which sets her on a series of mini-adventures, before she is able to learn that the Cradle of Life is in Africa, near the Kilimanjaro. There, an African tribe protects the access to a mysterious cavern, at the bottom of which is a small box.

As fictional as Croft's adventures are, they are taken – sometimes word by word – from historical legends; and Croft's quest for Pandora's Box, is but a modern rendition of an ancient Egyptian story... that forms the origin of the Grail Quest.

One Egyptian legend states that an old priest had told prince Naneferkaptah that there was an iron box on the bottom of the river Nile. Inside was another coffer, of copper, containing a series of further boxes, until finally a golden one, containing the *Book of Thoth*. The boxes were guarded by serpents and scorpions and thus presented a veritable challenge for anyone going in search of it.

The rest of the story can best be described as an Egyptian – and thus the original – version of Perceval's Grail quest: the prince left in search of the book, battling his way towards his goal. Using magical spells and rituals, he kept on defeating the serpent, to finally find the book.

Fortunately, this Egyptian rendition clarifies some of the unspoken attraction of the medieval Grail. In *Parzival,* the Grail is considered to be the panacea of all things, but Wolfram is scarce on details as to what the possession of the Grail allowed. In ancient Egyptian sources, what the *Book of Thoth* accomplished was however carefully written down.

After reading the first saying, prince Naneferkaptah was able to speak the language of the animals, the birds and the fish. After the second saying, the gods of the sun, moon and stars appeared to him in their true form.

Naneferkaptah was clearly on his way to becoming all-knowing. But the prince had a prize to pay for this knowledge. After a series of tests, the prince drowned himself in the Nile and was buried, together with his precious book. Thus, it showed that knowledge of "everything" was not only a difficult quest; once found, it was for many impossible to continue living with the power and knowledge, opting for suicide – but at the same time informing the reader that if he or she so wanted to, he could himself go in search of the tomb of prince Naneferkaptah, where he would find the *Book of Thoth,* and could partake of its knowledge.

The Egyptian series of "Grail quest stories" does not end here.

Like Wolfram would inspire others to continue writing about the Grail quest, such as *The Younger Titurel,* so would this Egyptian story inspire other accounts. One of these was the story of Setne Khamwas, son of Ramses II, who also wanted to find the *Book of Thoth.* He discovered the tomb of the prince, but was stopped by the spirit of the prince when he tried to remove the book. They decided to settle the standoff with a game of chess. Setne lost three matches and was almost totally buried in sand, but due to magical spells and amulets given to him by his father, he was able to release himself and eventually leave with the Book.

Setne kept the book in his possession and organised readings from it, even though his father Ramses II did not approve. Then, one day, Setne was blinded by the sight of an astonishingly beautiful woman. It is a clear parallel to the Grail stories, in which human shortcomings – temptations of the flesh, which are present with Anfortas and Perceval – prevent the proper handling of this divine knowledge.

Hence, Setne murdered his children and gave away his possession to be able to spend just one single night with her. But when that night came, he saw her disappear as if she was a phantom. Setne was dazed and confused and when Ramses found him in this state, he convinced his son to return the book. It was clear that Setne was not ready to partake in the knowledge – and the events that could befall him. When Setne agreed, he immediately realised that the entire event had been a dream, but still decided to return the book to the tomb of Naneferkaptah, resealing the tomb – where once again it would remain in wait for those who felt drawn to this knowledge.

Both stories are warnings, in which both princes are like Perceval: fools. They feel that they are both of sufficient nobility and capability to find, read and keep the *Book of Thoth.* In the case of Perceval, there are repeated references that he feels himself more than worthy to be a member of the Grail Brotherhood, as there are few better knights than he. But on his first test, Perceval fails. The same fate befalls Setne, though in Setne's and Perceval's case, it is not fatal, as is the case for Naneferkaptah. In all stories, it are human shortcomings that will end the seeker's quest – though Perceval will have another opportunity, when he has realised his earlier mistakes; he is given a second chance, and succeeds.

Both Wolfram's account and the Egyptian stories also show that though many feel called to the Grail, in truth – says Wolfram – the Grail itself calls by name those whom it feels will serve it properly. This is underlined in the Egyptian accounts, which are clearly Grail quests performed by princes who were not ready, and thus failed…

The Egyptian Fisher King

So as there were Egyptian Percevals, is there an Egyptian Fisher King? The answer is yes, and we have already come across him.

The story of the Fisher King is that of the ruler of the land, who is maimed by an evil opponent. This results in his inability to reproduce, whereby Perceval is looked upon not only as the initiate that will heal the king, but who will also become his successor.

Why this king is nicknamed "Fisher King" has been the centre of great speculation. To some, it is merely a reference to Jesus, a fisherman, whereby the fish was a symbol of the early Christian Church. To others, it is nothing more than the fact that Perceval first meets the king when he is fishing and only later does he realise that the fisherman is actually the king.

Again, this is a piecemeal approach, rather than taking the story as a whole. When we do the latter, it is clear that this story resembles the myth of the death and resurrection of Osiris, the most famous of all maimed divine rulers. In that Egyptian account – which is an integral part of the Mysteries of Isis, as well as the Hermetica – we have the ruler of Egypt, the god Osiris, invited to a banquet – a ceremonial meal, not unlike the meal that is held inside the Grail Castle. During the meal, Osiris is murdered by his evil brother Seth – from which derives the name Satan. As already noted, Osiris' body is scattered across Egypt, but through love (of his wife Isis) and magic, he is reassembled again. However, the fish of the Nile have eaten his penis, and hence Isis will have to create a wooden phallus to make sure Osiris is able to procreate offspring.

The story has many parallels with the Grail legend: a king impossible to reproduce, one who is called "Fisher King", the other where fishes have been responsible for the problem itself. Then there is the search for a successor, Perceval and Horus, who will guarantee the succession of divine – enlightened – rule over the country.

With so many parallels, it becomes clear that the image of the Fisher King also has its origins in ancient Egypt and that the name "Fisher King" in Egypt referred to the maiming of the king by fish. This resulted in his infertility, which not only had serious consequences for his dynasty, but for the land itself, as it was believed that the "royal seed" somehow contained the divine seed of Atum, the seed of creation.

Jessie Weston, without referencing Osiris specifically, stated: "I hold that we have solid grounds for the belief that the story postulates a close connection between the vitality of a certain king, and the prosperity of his kingdom; the forces of the ruler being weakened or destroyed, by wound, sickness, old age, or death, the land becomes Waste, and the task of the hero is that of restoration."[188]

It is clear that when we are talking about Anfortas and Perceval, we are merely creating new characters in a story that was known and that formed the backbone of the Egyptian religion. In short, the origins of the Grail can be traced back to Egypt… The Grail is Egyptian; it is the Stone of Creation.

Chapter 9: The Protectors of the Grail

To the romance writers, the Grail was something secret, something mysterious, the exact knowledge of which was reserved to a select few, and which was only to be spoken of with bated breath, and a careful regard to strict accuracy. This makes the Grail Brotherhood appear to be a secret society, like the Freemasons from the 18th century onwards, or perhaps even the Knights Templar, if some of the stories about this brotherhood of warrior-monks is to be believed. But both postdate the Grail romances. If we need to find precedents, then we need to look to the mystery schools of Antiquity, which were often linked to religious institutions, e.g. the temples of ancient Egypt.

Is it a coincidence that the School of Toledo also studied the Hermetica, or that it was Rotrou II de Perche – Perceval – who exported the concept of a "mystery school" to Chartres, where it would soon underpin the construction of the most phenomenal cathedrals ever built in Western Europe?

It is a fact that the School of Chartres was very Hermetica-orientated, which is in evidence in the figure of Thierry of Chartres. He himself was still somewhat reluctant to speak repeatedly about Hermes, but pupils of his school would later speak about Hermes as if he was part and parcel of the Christian religion: a clear precedent of what would happen in Florence in the 15th century. But as the Corpus was officially unknown in Europe in Thierry's time, someone had obviously introduced the learnings of Hermes into the School of Chartres, and it is now clear that this man was none other than Perceval himself – Rotrou II de Perche.

There are further interesting parallels. The School of Chartres lay at the foundation of the building of the Gothic cathedral of Chartres, just like the Heliopolitan priesthood lay at the foundation of the Pyramid Age. Both were amazing building projects and many have made a direct comparison between both eras of religious building activity, as each use a body of knowledge, which was not purely religious in nature, but which incorporated, as the *Books of Thoth* made clear, knowledge on architecture, especially "sacred principles" that have contributed to an eternal appeal of these monuments, as they used what is perhaps best described as principles of ethernal aesthetics.

John Julius Norwich commented that "in 1194, the master-builder of Chartres outlined new principles which would inspire all the great architects of the 13th century."[189] Indeed, Chartres' cathedral was built between 1194 to 1260, had sprouted from de Perche's seed, and was constructed at a time when Wolfram was writing his *Parzival*. Like the Grail would inspire many authors, so would the Gothic cathedrals, whose principles seemed to belong to a different era – which is indeed from where they came.

In his novel, *Notre Dame de Paris,* set in perhaps the best-known and definitely most visited Gothic cathedral, Victor Hugo spent a whole chapter[190] on the idea that architecture is the great book of humanity, and that the invention of printing and the proliferation of mundane books spelled the end of the sacred book of architecture. Indeed, among the many books, that of the *Book of Thoth* has become lost…

The Grail Brotherhood

Mystery schools existed in Moorish Spain, and the court of the Aragon kings was obviously such a place of study. As in Florence, interest in and exposure to the Hermetic teachings was normally reserved to the highest levels of society. Details of San Juan de la Peña's mystery school are also apparent in the preparation of Perceval for his initiation into the brotherhood. Perceval learns everything in the "hermit cave" of Trevezent, "three-all wise", and stays with him for 14 days in a one-on-one relationship of teacher and pupil. He is healed of his ignorance and learns about the Grail. The initiation in the Hermetic texts is always one-on-

one, and in San Juan de la Peña, it was no different. Indeed, there seems little difference between Trevrezent and Marsilio Ficino, the "High Priest" of the Florentine Academy…

Still, if there was a Hermetic mystery school of San Juan de la Peña, it was different than most. It would be a bad mistake to argue that the Grail Brotherhood is nothing more than a mystery school. The Grail was served and protected by a "noble Brotherhood… who, by force of arms, have warded off men from every land, with the result that the Grail has been revealed only to those who have been summoned to Munsalvæsche to join the Grail Company."

Julius Evola saw the Grail Brotherhood as a heroic society where an elite group pursued spiritual transcendence while at the same time defending the material world from the powers of chaos and darkness.[191] The Grail Brotherhood was there to make sure that those called for duty would gain entrance to this exclusive community… and that those trying to enter without such invitation, were turned away… apparently forcefully, if necessary.

In truth, the Grail Brotherhood was even more than this. For the Aragonese nobles, the Grail Brotherhood was about the protection of an object (the Grail) which featured in a plan to install sacred kingship, based on the Hermetic doctrine. Hence, the teachings of the Hermetica in San Juan de la Peña were but the first stepping stone in a much larger, and more ambitious plan; seeking spiritual transcendence was a requirement for entry, not the end goal of those who had entered.

The brotherhood was limited in number as it was not up to Man, but to the Grail itself, to dictate who would serve. Normally, this is a charismatic act, as Nous – wisdom – will only be given to those with the right moral disposition. Yearning and effort are insufficient for acceptance into the Grail community, "unless he is known in heaven and he be called by name to the Grail."[192]

Though only knights are chosen to guard it,[193] knightly prowess alone will not suffice. Perceval himself argues that on his mastery of the sword alone, he should be admitted: "I fought wherever I found a battle, and in such a way that my armed hand had highest honour within its reach. If God is a good judge of fighting, He should summon me by name to the Grail so that they may come to know me."[194] But his teacher Trevrizent makes it clear that this is not how the Brotherhood works: it is not a society of fine swordsmen, but a brotherhood fighting for a higher cause, blessed by the Grail. Repeatedly, his teacher tells him that his thinking is his greatest vice, one he should shake off if ever he hopes to gain admission: "Pride has always sunk and fallen."[195] To enter the Brotherhood, the initiate needs to have humility.

The Brotherhood has high ideals, but that in itself is not good enough to become a member. Whereas the Hermetica suggests that salvation and unification with God is open to all men, Wolfram states that "those who are called to the service of the Grail are always noble men."[196] Their name appears on the Grail stone: "on the stone, around the edge, appear letters inscribed, giving the name and lineage of each one, maid or boy, who is to take the blessed journey."[197] This makes the Brotherhood an interesting contradiction: it is egalitarian between the two sexes, but is socially exclusive, only open to noble families. It is conform to the medieval social matrix, in a somewhat non-conformist manner.

The social exclusivity of the Brotherhood seems a dramatic departure from the Hermetic principle. Initiation into the Hermetic Brotherhood had always been exclusive, but the defining factor was Intellect, not birthright. Wolfram thus limits membership even further, defining it by birth and Intellect. As a consequence, we should wonder whether he contradicted the central message of the Hermetica: that anyone, provided he acquired Gnosis – Wisdom – could ascend.

There is no doubt that Wolfram does fall short of this Hermetic dogma. But the question is why; if it was his own invention, it lacked logic or social conformance. For example, the Brotherhood does admit female members. Apart from Repanse de Schoye, there is Conduiramurs, Herzeloyde, Sigune, Cundrie and others. This inclusion of women is possibly the best evidence of the group's Hermetic nature, as in medieval times, women were unlikely to be admitted into a brotherhood – as the name itself suggests.

Wolfram elsewhere refers to both "maid or boy" whose name may appear on the stone.[198] Despite this equality, there is a difference between the sexes, as he adds that "the maids are sent out openly from the Grail and the men in secret, that they may have children who will in turn one day enter the service of the Grail, and, serving, enhance its company."[199]

This is a most important statement. On a basic level, it means that women do not need to make a secret of their membership of the Grail Brotherhood. Male adherence is however secret. When knights leave the Grail Castle, they do not want to answer any questions about their allegiance with the Grail Brotherhood: "Upon the Grail it was now found written that any Templar whom God's hand appointed master over foreign people should forbid the asking of his name or race, and that he should help them to their right. If the question is asked of him they shall have his help no longer. All keepers of the Grail want no questions asked about them."[200]

It is here that we find the basis as to why the Grail Brotherhood might have been accessible to nobility only. In Aragon, the Grail had returned to the dual nature it had in pre-Ptolemaic times: it was not merely a symbol for the ascent of the soul, as written in the Hermetica, it was also a physical object, i.e. similar or identical to the benben stone. And though the preservation of a physical object is not what made the Grail Brotherhood restricted to noble men and women, the role of the benben stone in the sacred kingship of Egypt, transposed on the Grail stone in the aim to attain sacred kingship in Aragon, is.

That there was an ambition to export "the Grail bloodline" is obvious already in Wolfram's statement about how female members of the Grail are allowed to reveal their membership, yet men are not. But there is much more to it than this, and when taken together, the evidence clearly suggests that the Grail Brotherhood's ambition was the installation of a pan-European Grail Kingdom, ruled by the Grail king, and managed by the Grail Brotherhood working both openly and behind the scenes. In short, the ambition of the Brotherhood was the transformation of Europe into a theocracy… back to the good old days of ancient Egypt, with the Grail king being the new Pharaoh.

Thus, as first step, we find that Wolfram argues that the race – the bloodline – needs to be continued. This is actually in line with the Hermetica, which states: "The begetting of children is held by those who think aright to be the most weighty concern in human life, and the most pious of deeds. That a man should depart from life and leave no child is a great misfortune, and a great sin; such a case is punished by the demons after death."[201]

Commentators have thus concluded that children are apparently to be conceived in chastity, as "any man who has pledged himself to serve the Grail must renounce the love of women."[202] In *Parzival*, we thus read that "Children begotten in true chastity, I believe, are man's greatest blessing."[203] If this command is not met, it will lead to misery, of which Anfortas is the best example: his wounds are the result of his pursuits of the love of a woman, whereby he was wounded in a jousting match. Wolfram also writes that "Amor [love] was his battle cry. But that cry is not quite appropriate for a spirit of humility."[204] So: "if any Lord of the Grail craves a love other than the writing on the Grail allows him, he will suffer distress and grievous misery."[205]

The Grail therefore also functions as a marriage broker – it states whom the nobles serving the Grail will have to marry. Such type of forged marriage is typical of the European medieval courts. But it is clear that within that large body of European nobility, a small subsection seem to be an even closer clan, whereby alliances are built by the Grail itself.

It is also made clear that the Grail is in the hands of one family, with the Grail king in charge of that dynasty. Trevrizent informs Perceval that "When Frimutel, my father, lost his life, they chose his eldest son to succeed him as King and Lord of the Grail and the Grail's company. That was my brother Anfortas, who was worthy of crown and power."[206] Later, it will be Perceval himself who will inherit that title from Anfortas – as will Feirifez, his half brother. The account states that the sons of Perceval and Feirefiz will also be Grail knights, including Lohengrin, the son of Perceval and Conduiramurs: "My son is destined for the Grail and there he must submissively devote his heart, if God permits him to achieve the proper spirit."[207]

As Anfortas did not have a son, the Grail Dynasty was in peril. The inheritance of the Grail was apparently more important than the future of Aragon. We have already seen how Alfonso I – or the Grail – had made preparations for Rotrou II to continue the Grail dynasty, whereas he had made no such provisions for his kingdom; indeed, we will soon see how his ambitions for Aragon were part of the "Grail plot" he hoped to achieve.

That it is the Grail who is in charge of the selection of the Grail king's successor, is made apparent when Perceval himself says that even though he himself may have a son, that child will also have to "achieve the proper spirit" for him to become his successor as the Grail king.

At the time of Perceval's own first visit to the Grail Castle, the only certainty is that Anfortas will die without offspring. Any antics by Trevrizent and the possibility of a child, which may or may not achieve the proper spirit, is simply too risky; the Grail does not gamble. And this is specifically why Perceval is identified as the successor to Anfortas as Grail king. Thus, we find that worked in the Grail dynasty is not merely the normal system of inheritance of one line to the next, but also the all-important question whether the genetic heir is equally of the proper spirit, has been called by the Grail. If not, he will be passed over as the next Grail king, replaced by someone who must have a bloodline link to the Grail dynasty, but who also specifically has the proper "nous" to rule as a sacred king.

Apart from marriage broker, the Grail apparently functions as an outsourcing company for nobility, providing countries where a dynasty has ended with a nobleman from the Grail Brotherhood: "Of anywhere a land loses its lord, if the people there acknowledge the hand of God and seek a new lord, they are granted one from the company of the Grail."[208] This, of course, should be interpreted as the masterplan, engineered either by the Grail or the Brotherhood to provide Mankind with enlightened leaders and transform Europe into the Grail kingdom, ruled by members of the Grail Brotherhood. For wherever in Europe vacancies are filled with members of the Grail Brotherhood, the final outcome would be that over time, all countries will be ruled by members of the Grail Brotherhood, and the Grail itself will successively rule the world. The masterplan is divine rule, with the Grail – which is assumed to be the earthly representative to God – at its top.

Templeise

It seems that in the roll-out of this masterplan, they were helped by an organisation of people that had equally turned away from the pleasures of women, even though they were not necessarily nobles or noble enough to be part of the Grail Dynasty itself. Whereas the Brotherhood served the Grail and provided its noble lineage, the other group – the protectors – were a worldly power that had to support the efforts of the Grail and its Brotherhood in accomplishing its masterplan. Who were they? Apparently, they were the infamous Knights Templar.

In *Parzival,* Wolfram labels these protectors "templeise". Most scholars have straightforwardly identified the group as the Knights Templar, if only because the clothing of the real Templars and Wolfram's "templeise" is identical. In French, the organisation was known as "templiers", whereas in Aragonese Catalan, they were known as "templés". It once again reveals the Aragon connection between the Grail story and its historical foundation.

The word "templeise" is mentioned by Wolfram six times.[209] Some scholars do not agree with the identification of the "templeise" as the Knights Templar. Perhaps it is too straightforward, which is indeed a problem if your main argument is that Wolfram's account was purely fictional.

Some argue that the "templeis" is a generic reference and that the Knights Templar's profile was not high enough to be referred to as such by Wolfram. It is true that the Templars in Germany had a low profile in Wolfram's days, but Wolfram is not writing about Germany, but about the Grail – a story which is not German in nature, but comes from abroad. And this may indeed be the very reason why Wolfram is writing about the Templars: he is writing about a country – the kingdom of Aragon in northern Spain – where the Templars *were* an important and well-known order. That he identifies them by name may exactly be because a German audience would in general not be too familiar with them.

Others have debated the issue because they try to date the accounts of the Grail as occurring in the 6th century – the time of King Arthur, whereas the Knights Templar were an organisation that existed between 1118 and 1307. But in the framework of André de Mandach's historical research, the Grail story captured a period of 17 years, from 1120 to 1137, and this period sits perfectly within the framework of the Knights Templar.

The Knights Templar were warrior monks, an unusual composition of a man who had entered a religious community to serve God, but was equally willing to kill in his name. Still, the concept of a warrior-monk was not totally unknown at the time: in Roman times, there is the example of the Salii, who formed a college of priests, twelve in number, dedicated to the service of Mars, the god of war. It seems possible that the Knights Templar were even modelled on them.

And if the number twelve in the Salii priesthood might have had stellar connotations, what are we to make of the possible coincidence that the founders of the Knights Templar numbered nine – conform to the Nine Principles of Heliopolis.

The Poor Fellow-Soldiers of Christ and of the Temple of Solomon, to give them their official name, were among the most famous of the Western Christian military orders. The organisation existed for approximately two centuries and was founded in the aftermath of the First Crusade of 1096, to ensure the safety of the many Europeans who made the pilgrimage to Jerusalem after its conquest.

At the dawn of the 14th century, the Knights Templar had become Europe's dominant religious order. They were more than 7,000 members strong and held almost 900 castles; equally, they controlled unimaginable wealth in land and gold. Even though they were originally there to maintain power and tranquillity for pilgrims to the Middle East, after the loss of Jerusalem, they had continued to grow in Europe, thus becoming a genuine threat to the likes of the French king, who had massive debts to the order.

Today, they are best remembered for their controversial demise, which was engineered by the French king Philip IV, in league with Pope Clement V, the only authority to whom the knights had to answer. The French king ordered their arrest, which was executed on Friday, October 13, 1307.

Their end signalled the beginning of endless speculation about the true motives of the king and the real belief of the Knights Templar – who had been labelled heretics at the time of their arrest. But amidst this speculation, one strand of research has never been followed: whether the Knights Templar were following a masterplan. If not, is it a coincidence that their wealth accumulated to the extent that they were largely the bankrollers of European society? Indeed, if the pope and the French king had not engineered their demise, what would have happened sooner rather than later, was that the Knights Templar would have been in control of Western Europe, and that they could have engineered the collapse of several nations, with the new rulers puppets following their Templar masters. If this were part of someone's masterplan, then this master would have succeeded in uniting Europe, very much in line with modern Europe, which equally originated out of a sharing of economical and monetary assets. The next question to ask, therefore, is whether there was a hidden master behind the Knights Templar, and/or whether there was a masterplan.

The early origins of the Poor Knights of Christ and the Temple of Solomon are unsure. Guillaume de Tyre states that it was in the year 1118 that a minor French noble Hugues de Payen presented himself, with a number of companions before Baudoin II, the King of Jerusalem. It would be ten years before the rule of the order was endorsed at the Council of Troyes, in 1128, marking the official foundation of the order.

The period between 1118 and 1128 has been labelled a "mysterious period", about which is little known. What were the embryonic Knights Templar doing in Jerusalem? Were they really intent on keeping the roads clear for pilgrims and if so, why were there only ten-odd of them – an insignificant number when trying to protect thousands of miles of road. Is it possible that they had some other raison d'être, such as digging below their lodgings on the Temple Mound, which had been the location of the Temple of

Solomon... and the location where centuries before the Ark of the Covenant had rested?

In the absence of evidence, speculation has run wild. Perhaps between 1118 and 1128, those who had created the order had felt that it had been a good idea at the time, but how to continue from there? Every idea has a period of inception, and perhaps that is what those ten years were: thinking time. Still, it is known that at some point before 1128, Hugues de Payen wrote to Bernard of Clairvaux, the leader of the Cistercian Order, a new religious power.

The first Cistercian abbey was founded by Robert of Molesme in 1098, at Cîteaux Abbey – from which they took their name. Two others, Saint Alberic of Cîteaux and Saint Stephen Harding, are considered co-founders of the order, and Bernard of Clairvaux is associated with the fast spread of the order during the 12th century.

The keynote of Cistercian life was a return to a literal observance of the Rule of St Benedict, rejecting the developments the Benedictines had undergone, and tried to reproduce the life exactly as it had been in Saint Benedict's time, indeed in various points they went beyond it in austerity. The most striking feature in the reform was the return to manual labour, and especially to field-work, which became a special characteristic of Cistercian life.

Hughes is supposed to have asked St Bernard if he would sponsor the embryonic order, including the creation of their rule. But documents found in Seborga in Northern Italy largely prove that St Bernard had a direct hand in the formation of the Templars as early as 1118, suggesting that St Bernard and Hugues de Payen knew each other much earlier than most are willing to concede. Some have even suggested they were kinsmen.

St Bernard had been responsible for creating a monastery in

Seborga in 1113. The documents suggest that Bernard went to this monastery in 1117, in order to release two monks from their vows: Hugues de Payen and Bernard's uncle, André de Montbard, two of the founders of the Knights Templar. Of course, such a stunning conclusion has been met with scepticism, some arguing that as Bernard himself only entered monastic life in 1113, it would have been extremely unlikely that he would already have created a monastery in Northern Italy in the first year of his new lifestyle. This controversy therefore furhter underlines the level of speculation and mystery that surrounds the organisation, before and after their official lifetime.

What is definitely incontestable is that in 1128, Bernard of Clairvaux was championing their cause. He wrote a long document, "In Praise of the New Knighthood", arguing that a group of monks whose purpose was to fight and kill others was required. Bernard managed to convince not only his fellow monks of this need, he also managed to persuade the pope to back his idea.

The purpose of the Council of Troyes was to settle disputes regarding the Bishops of Paris and other relevant Church matters. But Bernard hijacked the Council to push through the rule of the Templars. He had previously adapted the rule of St Benedict to suite his Cistercian monks; he had now reworked the latter into a format that would fit the Templar Order.

By the time Pope Honorius II sat down to convene the Council of Troyes, he was faced with a fait accompli: he could not risk offending the local rulers of Champagne, who were also blood tied to the kings of Jerusalem. Most likely, the idea of the Templar Order actually impressed the Pope, since this armed group of knights would be responsible only to him and his successors. The Knights Templar had become his private army, though it is clear that he or any of his successors were seldom able to exercise any control over the organisation. Which begs the question was supposedly was in control of this organisation.

The Templars and the Grail kingdom

The area of our interest, of course, is not Europe in general, but specifically Aragon and surrounding countries. From 1132 onwards – four years after their official foundation – the power of the Knights Templar was firmly embedded in the Languedoc-Roussillon, with the preceptory of Mas Deu, just outside of Perpignan, being the nerve centre for the Aragon region.

The Preceptor of Mas Deu was said to be acknowledged both by the King of Aragon and the sovereign Count of Roussillon as equals. Under King Jaime I of Aragon, the Templars held territory from Montpellier to Barcelona, including the Balearic island of Mallorca. Researchers have even argued that by 1143, the order had conceived of a plan for an independent Templar state, with Mas Deu – or perhaps more likely Perpignan – as its capital.

Still, by 1307, this idea had not materialised, though some have speculated that it was a contributing factor to Philip's aggression towards the order, when he realised that he not only had tremendous debt with this organisation, but that the organisation could soon become a nation, whereby economically, France would be reliant on this new economic power to the South. One possible scenario was that this new country could actually take over France in the not all too distant future.

This state of affairs overlaps impressively with the ambitions of the Grail Dynasty, as described by Wolfram. The masterplan called for the infiltration of countries, by outsourcing Grail Dynastic nobles, while at the same time using the Grail protectors – the Knights Templar – to physically extend the Grail Kingdom.

The actions of the Grail King, Alfonso I, also fit perfectly within this plan. "Anfortas" was an admirer of the military orders of Jerusalem, specifically of the Knights Templar. In his testament, made in Bayonne in 1131, and confirmed on the eve of his death,

4 September 1134 at Huesca, he states that a third of his kingdom was left to the Knights Templar, as well as his horse and arms. The other military orders each received a third as well. (It is an intriguing aside that these documents refer to him as "Anfortius".)[210]

Hence, Anfortius had made sure that the Grail Dynasty would continue via Perceval, whereas his own country would become the first step in the masterplan of transforming Europe away from a conglomerate of kings, and run by the Protectors of the Grail, the Knights Templar.

But Anfortas must have known that this situation was precarious at best. Indeed, when the will was challenged, the loyal nobles persuaded Alfonso's brother to take the crown, so that not everything would be lost. After the birth of his daughter Petronella and her marriage to Ramon Berenguer IV of Barcelona, the Kingdom of Aragon thus remained intact. The new king of Aragon also compensated the Order by giving them the town of Monzon, where they turned a former Moorish fort into one of the most extensive military works in Spain.

Centuries later, the castle and the order itself would inspire a young Spanish man, Escriva, to create Opus Dei, the controversial organisation whom many have seen as the 20th century religious revival of the medieval Knights Templar – and leading antagonists in Dan Brown's *The Da Vinci Code*.[211]

Though it might seem strange that the king of Aragon would leave his estates to the new orders, such decisions were not unique; large donations of land across the entire Western world were done in favour of military orders that truly were new powers on the map of Europe.

But apart from the ambition of establishing Europe as the Grail kingdom, Alfonso I actually had better reasons than most rulers to donate freely to the Knights Templar. And that reason also suggests that Alfonso I was the unknown master of the order –

which thus confirms that Wolfram was indeed right to identify the Knights Templar as the protectors of the Grail.

From its inception in 1128 till 1136, Hugues de Payen had been the Grand Master of the Knights Templar. Hugues de Payen was a member of the lesser nobility of Champagne, the homeland of Chrétien de Troyes. Bernard of Clairvaux was also close kin to the ruling house of Champagne, a powerful elite which the Pope did not wish to provoke at the time of the Council of Troyes. André de Montbard, one of the original nine knights and a future Grand Master, was an uncle of Bernard of Clairvaux, clearly showing the close family connections between the Knights Templar and their champion. Like the Grail Brotherhood, the genesis of the Knights Templar was a family affair.

But what is less known, is that if one were to combine the Grail Brotherhood and the Knights Templar, one would get a family affair too. Through Ramiro Sanchez I's marriage to Felicia de Roucy, the king of Aragon had not only become related to the de Perche family; both families were also related to Hugues de Payen. The conclusion is that there is a family connection between the Grail king Anfortas and Perceval and the founder of the "templeise", the protectors of the Grail. This connection is never made explicit by Wolfram, but *is* the relationship of its historical characters.

These family connections allow for new intriguing questions, specifically as to the true purpose of the Knights Templar. The official version, that the Knights Templar were there to protect the pilgrims and travellers to the Holy Land, has always been labelled as ridiculous. As we mentioned, during the first ten years of their existence, nine knights and their helpers could not guard the thousands of miles of road that connected Western Europe with the Holy Land. The Order's acquisition of territories across Europe, the foundation of commanderies across Western Europe, from northern Scotland to southern Spain, did not aide in this purpose either. If anything, it meant that the Templars were scattered all over Europe, rather than be able to concentrate on the stretches of road the pilgrims had to negotiate outside of Europe. Long before Jerusalem fell to the Muslims, the Knights Templar had become a new power in Western Europe, answerable to none, except the pope – in theory.

The creation of the Knights Templar has been seen as the concerted effort of a group of Champagne noblemen, but their family links to the Aragon kings has largely gone unnoticed. If it had been known that the Aragon kings were the historical Grail knights, perhaps this alliance would have been highlighted.

Within this new framework, we see the masterful hand of the king of Aragon, using his French family connections to create an organisation that would serve his purpose – just like he had relied upon his French family connections to find a successor as Grail king. Furthermore, it was within the Champagne region itself that we see both the origins of the Knights Templar and the first writings of the Grail. It was in Troyes, the capital city of the Champagne region, that the Knights Templar were officially recognised... and the name Chrétien de Troyes says it all.

With this information in hand, it is clear that the purpose of the Knights Templar fits precisely within the project that Anfortas and the Grail Brotherhood had in mind, in the period of 1104-1137. That upon his death, the project did not continue as he had hoped for, does not invalidate the original scope of the project. Furthermore, it is clear that the role of the Knights Templar within this project continued and was extremely successful for almost two centuries. What may have contributed to the collapse of that part of the project may have been the fact that whereas the protectors of the Grail were going from strength to strength, the Dynastic Grail Brotherhood itself had been largely unable to attain its goals. Hence, by 1307, the Protectors of the Grail were more powerful than ever, but what they were protecting, the Grail and the Grail king, might have been weak – so much so that pushing through the secret agenda was no longer on the cards. It meant that the French king, with the acceptance of the Pope, was able to destroy the entire project, by arresting the Protectors, the Knights Templar.

The Templar heresy

Though the Knights Templar fit neatly within the masterplan, one important question remains: where did the allegiance of the Knights Templar lie? Were they indeed "merely" warrior monks, or did they instead adhere to a Hermetic worldview, which would make them the heretics that they were long held to be?

Though the Knights Templar were arrested on heresy charges, the exact nature of the heresy was never made clear. In both war and legal affairs, the first victim is often truth. Thus, whether the suspicion of heresy was the true reason for the arrest or a carefully constructed legal argument – the only argument that would work for King Philip to convince the Pope of the wrongs of his organisation – is difficult to identify. The Knights Templar were said to trod on the cross, deny Jesus Christ as the true Saviour and many other transgressions against the Bible. Even if they spat on the cross or denied Christ, why did they do so? What was it that had made them that way?

Though not all knights were arrested and not all arrested Templars were tortured, some were. During these, many made confessions, including the disclosure that they had worshipped an idol known as "Baphomet", an idol apparently in the form of a human head, sometimes bearded, sometimes with wings and cloven feet, and sometimes even attached to the upper body of a woman. Whatever it was, it is obvious that the idol was not even loosely based on an image of Jesus Christ.

One of the brothers who spoke of the idol was Jean Taillefer of Genay. He was received into the order at Mormant, one of the three preceptories under the jurisdiction of the Grand Priory of Champagne at Voulaine. He said that at his initiation, "an idol representing a human face" was placed on the altar before him. Hughes de Bure, a Burgundian from a daughter house of Voulaine, described how the "head" was taken out of a cupboard in the chapel and that it seemed to him to be of gold or silver. Brother Pierre d'Arbley suspected that the "idol" had two faces, and his kinsman Guillaume d'Arbley made the point that the "idol" itself, as distinct from copies, was exhibited at general chapters, implying that it was only shown to senior members of the order, maybe even only on special occasions. The treasurer of the Paris temple, Jean de Turn, spoke of a painted head in the form of a picture, which he had adored at one of these chapters.

People will admit to anything under torture. But it is clear that the detail of the admission is quite specific and largely identical across the various testimonies. What is even more important is that the allegation of "idol worship" did not originate solely from the interrogations following their arrest in 1307. After the Templars' stronghold in Jerusalem had been overrun by the Muslims in 1244, sultan Baibars inspected the castle. Allegedly, inside the tower, he found an idol, in whose protection the castle had been placed – obviously without much success. Even though the Baibars' story is not the strongest of evidence, the evidence for a Baphomet idol itself is largely coherent, and does require further analysis.

The opinions on what Baphomet represents vary from scholar to scholar. The name "Baphomet" itself has caused great controversy. Some believe it is a corruption of "Mahomet", i.e. Mohammed. The Templars fought both with and against Muslims, but this possibility collapses when we know that Islam forbids all forms of idolatry. It is why the heads of many ancient

Egyptian deities has been scraped off or why ancient monuments in Afghanistan and surrounding countries have either been shot off, or blown off. Thus, if the Templars were secretly Muslim, they would not have expressed their faith through the worship of an idol.

One possible explanation suggests that Baphomet is derived from two Greek words, Baph and Metis, meaning "Baptism of Wisdom". This is, of course, the concept expressed in the Grail: the drinking of the Grail involves the initiate to be baptised into knowledge. As protectors of the Grail, this is exactly what the Knights Templar would do. Idries Shah furthermore argues that Baphomet could be a corruption of the Arabic "abufihamat" (pronounced in Moorish Spanish as "bufihimat"). The word means "father of understanding".[212] It could also mean "source" or "seat" "of understanding"... or "Wisdom".

This explanation is underlined by a different, but in essence similar, analysis of Hugh Schonfield. Schonfield showed that by applying the Hebrew Atbash code to the name Baphomet, the name Sophia, the goddess of Wisdom, is revealed. The Greek writer Plutarch identified Sophia with the Egyptian Isis, whose magic was allied to the wisdom of Thoth, the God of Knowledge. Again, we are in the realm where Knowledge and Wisdom are the key concept of the Grail quest: the search for Wisdom, but it is also the bailiwick of Thoth – the Egyptian Hermes.

It thus seems entire possible – if not likely – that the Knights Templar coded their belief in "Wisdom" by using a Hebrew codification system, giving them the name of a new deity: Baphomet. Baphomet thus becomes the latest incarnation in the line of Thoth, Hermes and Serapis.

Religious idols often have multiple layers of symbolism – that is their purpose. One thing can mean many things to many different people. This is *exactly* why the Grail is such a popular symbol today, as it is for many purely an undefined symbol, whereby the individual can define it for himself. For a Greek audience, Baphomet could be a baptism into Wisdom; for an Arab audience, it would be the source of Knowledge; for cryptographers, it was Wisdom.

In the final analysis, it is clear that there is clear convergence towards the likelihood that Baphomet was indeed "Wisdom". It also means that they were worshippers of the Grail, and that they were indeed an order that was created to protect the Holy Grail... as Wolfram von Eschenbach had stated in the early 13th century. But though it identifies Baphomet with Wisdom, what are we to make of the apparent identification of Baphomet with a head – something that seems to ill-fit the Hermetica.

Some authors have speculated that "Baphomet the head" was none other than the severed head of John the Baptist, based on allegations that the saint was revered by the Order. This is the general train of thought of Lynn Picknett and Clive Prince's *The Templar Revelation*.

During their many conquests in the Middle East, the Knights Templar are said to have found the right index finger of John the Baptist, the finger that had identified Jesus as the Messiah. The sacking of Constantinople during the Fourth Crusade in 1203-4 also resulted in the retrieval of numerous relics from the chapel of the Boucoleon Palace, which supposedly contained the head of John the Baptist. Jacobus de Voragine in *The Golden Legend* gives some details on both body parts of this saint, claiming that the index finger was the only part of the corpse that escaped destruction by Emperor Julian. He said that it was brought to France by St Thecla. The Baptist's head had apparently been buried under Herod's Temple in Jerusalem, the site of the Knights Templar's headquarters.[213]

Though it is a possibility, there is no conclusive evidence that the head of the Baptist was or was not the Baphomet. Like the "Head of Wisdom", it could be. However, in the framework of the Grail, the problem is not one of mutual exclusivity. If the Baptist was indeed the "code" the Knights Templars used for the h"erald who called upon Mankind to be baptised in Wisdom" – as he would have done if he was indeed a priest of Serapis – then the Knights Templar could equally be worshippers of John the Baptist and Wisdom; in the tradition of the Grail, they are compatible, not mutually exclusive.

A major stumbling block in a straightforward identification of Baphomet with John the Baptist's head is the secret nature of the rituals involving the Baphomet head. There was nothing that would have stopped the Knights Templar from taking out their head or even replica heads of John the Baptist and worship them in public. He was their patron saint and parading him or his head about would have met with near universal acclaim from the Christian community – not condemnation. Even if their interpretation of their patron saint was vastly different from mainstream Christianity, they still could – and most likely would – have taken the head out of its cupboard during public displays. As they did not, it strongly suggests the head was not that of a Christian saint.

The 19th century Orientalist Joseph von Hammer-Purgstall believed that Baphomet was indeed a head. But rather than work within a Christian framework, he found 24 examples, in the form of Greek two-handled "kraters" which were associated with these heads. This makes the connection between the Baphomet head and the Grail very strong, as of course the Grail was a krater too.

Furthermore, when discussing these kraters, he states that "after this there can be no doubt that this is that most famous cup of the middle ages known under the name of Holy Graal, which signifies the symbol of the Templar community of Gnostic wisdom."[214] In this one statement, several pieces come together: the image of the krater and the head of Baphomet, linked via Greece, to the image of the Grail. I would argue that the case is closed…

Heirs of the Johannite Church?

Still, the link between John the Baptist and the Knights Templars is not finished here. The Knights Templar travelled in the Middle East, where it is known that groups of "Johannite Christians" roamed the territory. "Johannite Christians" had preserved a specific type of Christianity, in which the role of Jesus was subordinate to the role of John the Baptist, who was considered to be the true messenger of Christianity. However, Johannite Christianity does not substitute Jesus with John the Baptist; it considers the Baptist to be the truer messenger – herald – of the message of illumination – Wisdom.

Though often described as small bands of people, the movement seems to have had some structure. It is claimed that the Grand Pontiff of the "Johannite Church" was one Theocletes. Specifically, it is claimed that he became acquainted with Hugues de Payen. The latter learned of their religion and was initiated into the mysteries of his church. The legend goes that he eventually was designated as Theocletes' successor. This would make the first Grand Master of the Knights Templar also the High Priest of the Church of John the Baptist.

If true, then it also explains the importance of why Wolfram makes it explicit that the Grail can only be seen by baptised men. Though this may at first look like a typically Christian reference, opening the way for a Christian interpretation of the Grail legend, in this framework, it is not. Here, we are confronted with a belief that John the Baptist was a preacher of the cult of Serapis, the cult of Wisdom – the Hermetic Way. The Grail Brotherhood argued that baptism was important, for baptism was an important ritual for the Hermetic myst; though it appeared to be Christian, it had a different meaning…

In 1804, a doctor, Bernard Raymond Fabré-Palaprat founded the

Ancient and Military Order of the Temple of Jersualem, who claimed that his Order was ordained by the Charter of Transmission of Larmenius. The Larmenius Charter was allegedly written in 1324 by Johannes Marcus Larmenius, who claimed to have been appointed Grand Master of the Order by Jacques de Molay, officially the last Grand Master of the Knights Templar, himself.

The document has it critics, though some authors have concluded that the document is possibly genuine – which does not mean it is genuine, merely that the evidence of the critics has been laid to rest.[215] What is intriguing, is that Fabré-Palaprat also possessed another document, the *Levitikon*, "a version of John's Gospel with blatantly Gnostic implications".[216] Fabré-Palaprat used the document as the Bible for his Neo-Templar Johannite Church, which he founded in Paris in 1828.

This convergence of the Knights Templar and the Johannite tradition is intriguing, but even more so when we note that the *Levitikon* argues that Jesus was an initiate of the mysteries of Osiris – the original Serapis.[217] Such claims in the early 19th century are intriguing, as they predate the conclusions drawn by Stricker and others by more than a century, as well as the discovery of various Gnostic documents, such as those at Nag Hammadi

Karl Luckert, in *Egyptian Light and Hebrew Fire*, states that two Greek philosophers, Plotinus and Origen, developed "Neoplatonism" from Egyptian teachings told to them by Ammonius Saccas, yet another priest of the Heliopolitan tradition. Ammonius himself fled Alexandria in 391 AD, when Alexandria's Egyptian religion was attacked by Christian mobs, at a time when the Gnostic – Hermetic – aspect that was present in Christianity was forcefully removed from the record. It forced many Gnostic writings to be hidden, as was the case in the famous Nag Hammadi documents.

The Nag Hammadi library is a collection of early Christian Gnostic texts discovered near the town of Nag Hammadi in 1945. That year, twelve leather-bound papyrus codices buried in a sealed jar were found by a local peasant named Mohammed Ali Samman. The writings in these codices comprised 52 mostly Gnostic treatises, but they also include three works belonging to the *Corpus Hermeticum* and a partial translation of Plato's *Republic*.

Subject expert James Robinson suggests that these codices may have belonged to a nearby Pachomian monastery, and were buried after Bishop Athanasius condemned the uncritical use of non-canonical books in his Festal Letter of 367 AD. About the dating of the manuscripts themselves there is little debate. Examination of the datable papyrus used to thicken the leather bindings, and of the Coptic script, place them ca. 350-400 AD.

The Festal Letter, "enforced" by the burning of several libraries and the hunting down of its preachers, is not only reminiscent of the Cathar crusade that would occur a millennium later; it also meant that the Hermetic doctrine was removed from public circulation and could now only survive underground – secretly. That it was easier to survive in a Muslim country or within Orthodox Christianity than in those countries subject to the Catholic Church is a matter of historical record. It is from there that the *Corpus Hermeticum* would make its re-entry in Europe, first at the courts of the king of Aragon, later in the Florentine residence of Cosimo de Medici.

If the Larmenius Charter is correct, then it seems like there was not only a Johannite handover from Theocletes to de Payen in the 12th century; after the demise of the Knights Templar and their Grandmaster Jacques de Molay, it was handed down into the hands of "Larmenius" – a nickname – who most likely passed it onwards throughout an underground stream in Western Europe, to find its way to the surface again in 1804.

In this scenario, a lot of investigation could go on as to what happened after 1307, whether de Molay did indeed pass on his rule to an heir, who Larmenius was, whether he indeed received it, and what happened in the following centuries. But in this scenario, there is a history that precedes the foundation of the Knights Templar, which is far more interesting, and which makes the Knights Templar not just a group of warrior-monks that protected the roads, but an organisation that was built upon, heirs and protectors of, a sacred knowledge, which they had received during their travels in the Middle East.

The scenario also suggests that others, before Hugues de Payen, might have gone to the East, and may have established initial contacts with the same group of Johannites… which might be what happened to Gahmuret, Perceval's father, who was said to have travelled extensively in the Middle East, before returning home to father Perceval.

The remaining question is whether this meeting between Theocletes and Hugues de Payen did indeed happen. Even if the meeting happened, would it be likely that Theocletes gave Hugues de Payen the title of high priest of his order?

If Theocletes and Hugues de Payen met for the first time, at best, Hugues de Payen might have been initiated – though at first, de Payen would most likely have listened incredulously to the stories Theocletes would tell him: that Jesus was not the Son of God – not literally. That John the Baptist was a popular baptiser, offering people initiation into a wisdom tradition that had gone underground for almost one millennium.

It would take many years before Hugues de Payen would ever be accepted as heir to the pontiff – the Johannite Pope. If Theocletes would ever crown Hugues, it would not have been ca. 1118, when Hugues was in essence a total nobody, not at all destined to become a somebody. It would be ca. 1128 before his possibility of greatness was realised. Though it is known that Hugues de Payen may have travelled to the Middle East before

1118, it is clear that this transmission of power will have taken many years. And thay may be the real reason why it took the Templars a decade to get their house in order, from their initial idea, to their official foundation; it may also be the real answer as to what the real mystery of the Knights Templar is all about: the Knights Templar were nothing more – or less – than a group of Hermetic Brothers… which is in essence what Wolfram said they were.

Again, the story of the Grail itself may shed further light here. After all, we know that the Grail had come from the East, and had been entrusted to Titurel, Alfonso's grandfather. We previously argued that the creation of the Knights Templar fits within the Grail masterplan, directed by the kings of Aragon. So…

If Theocletes did crown Hugues de Payen as his successor, it is clear that something had happened before, which would have allowed this succession to occur. Though de Payen may have been a perfect student, Theocletes must have had students closer to him that were on par with Hugues. Furthermore, his "local students" would surely be better equipped to guide his flock, as de Payen would surely go back to his homeland.

But what if Hugues de Payen was specifically sent to the Middle East to make contact with Johannite Christianity? What if this was merely one phase of the Grail masterplan? What if he was told to appear in front of the King of Jerusalem, asking him to recognise his order of Knights Templar? If so, it is ironic that the power of Christianity that had forced the Johannites to go underground, would now be the instrument used to reconquer Europe so that the lost tradition could flourish once again.

There is an even more intriguing conclusion. We know that the Grail came from the East. Its arrival occurred in the second half of the 11th century. It therefore predates the First Crusade. Should we see the Crusades as part of this masterplan, perhaps engineered by the Grail itself? Was the Grail perhaps at one point in the hands of these Johannite Christians, but given to the Aragon dynasty so that the Grail could help them in the design and execution of the Grail masterplan?

Cover-up

From 1128 till 1307, the Knights Templar and the Cistercian monks would remain close allies. When the order was abolished in 1307, many knights simply entered Cistercian monasteries, as they were after all monks, and often members of the Cistercian order already.

Interestingly, scholars, including John Matthews,[218] have identified that the story of the Grail as a Christian Cup was carved into the public's mind through a literary campaign that was specifically sponsored by the Cistercian order.

It was the Cistercian chronicler Helinandus of Froidmont, who, in 1204, in his universal history under the date of 717 AD, mentions a vision in which a hermit was shown the Cup used by Jesus at the Last Supper, and about which the hermit then wrote a Latin book called *Gradale*.[219]

The entry reads: "At this time in Britain, there was shown a hermit, through the help of an angel, a miraculous vision of Joseph [of Arimathea], the decurion who took the Lord's body from the cross, and concerning the vessel in which the Lord ate from with his disciples, [and from this vision] the hermit proceeded to write a history called 'Of the Grail'. The Grail, called 'gradalis' or 'gradale' in French, is a wide and deep saucer, in which precious mater [food] is ceremoniously presented, one piece at a time, richly provided in the various courses. This is called in the vernacular 'greal'. as it gratifies and is welcomed at such a meal, is made of silver or some similar precious metal, and so because of its content, an overwhelming succession of expensive delicacies. This history I have not found in Latin, but so far only written in French in the possession of certain chieftains, and not even then in a complete form."

Rather than just speak about the Grail apparition, Helinandus feels he has to educate his people that this vision is actually the true origin of the Grail. Furthermore, he suggests that he did not find this text in Latin, but in French, in the possession of unnamed chieftains, but not even in a complete form. In short, Helinandus is stating that no-one will ever be able to consult his source – they will just have to take his word for it. It is amazing that so many scholars have done just that, whereas what he is asking us to do is trust him far beyond the level of trust Wolfram von Eschenbach desires of his readers. Trust, it seems, is a knife that often cuts irregularly.

So, with one obscure entry of an unnamed hermit from a distant past, the Grail had become the Cup of Christ. The question needs to be asked whether this entry is indeed true, or entirely fabricated, and if the latter, whether it was to suit a specific goal – the Christianisation of the Grail.

When people note that no-one will ever be able to find their original source, it normally means that they are protecting themselves, from being labelled a liar or an inventor – and that is what Helinandus most likely was doing: inventing a Christian precedent for the Grail.

Frederick Locke has observed that *La Queste del Saint Graal*, compiled by – indeed –Cistercian monks in the 13th century, "is first and foremost a Christian book, and nothing in it suggests a conscious use of any pagan mythology, ritual, or folklore in their primitive forms...." Any pagan imagery – whether Gnostic, Hermetic or Celtic – was absent from its pages.

Some have argued that the *Queste* could not be written by the Cistercians, as they were not allowed to "make rhymes", but there is evidence that the Cistercians did stray from the strict ideals of Bernard and went as far as "making rhymes".[220]

In the *Queste*, the Grail is the dish from which Christ ate the

Passover lamb with his disciples. It was brought to Britain by Joseph of Arimathea and was guarded by his descendants at their castle of Corbenic. Its hero is Galahad, the son of Lancelot, whose quest for the Grail becomes a search for mystical union with God. Only Galahad can look directly into the Grail and behold its divine mysteries.

This Grail account would become the best-known version of the Grail story in the English-speaking world. It was the basis for Sir Thomas Malory's famous late 15th century *Le Morte d'Arthur,* which would become the source for much of the film *Excalibur* and the musical *Camelot*. By cleverly introducing more people and more castles in different locations, identifying the truth that sat at the core of the story became more and more muddled… Coincidence, or design?

Joseph Campbell in *Creative Mythology* stated that "it is certain that the Cistercian monk who was the author of the *Queste* had been greatly inspired by the confirmation at the Fourth Lateran Council, in the year 1215, of the Catholic dogma of the Real Presence of Christ's body in the sacrament of the altar (the Host in the ciborium)." An alternative explanation is that our Cistercian monk was not such much "convinced", but "ordered" to adopt the tale and set it within a proper Christian framework.

Over the course of the next century and a half, until 1399, the "Grail" that had once been in San Juan de la Peña had thus become firmly identified as the "Cup of Christ" – and nothing else; like the Grail was supposed to transform the land, the true pagan Grail had, by human manipulation, transformed itself into the ultimate Christian relic.

The hand of the Cistercians in this transformation – or cover-up – is visible everywhere. *Perlesvaux* was written at the request of Lord of Cambrin, near the French city of Lille, for Jean de Nesle, the castellan of Bruges. He had founded a Cistercian monastery at Noyou in Picardy.[221] In *Perlesvaux,* the Grail is the vessel in which the blood of the Saviour was gathered on the day of his crucifixion. Intriguingly, there are no longer any mysteries involving the Grail, which are at the core of Wolfram's account.[222]

Why did the Cistercian Order contribute so much to the "Christianisation" of the Grail? A century earlier, it had been their founder, Bernard of Clairvaux, who had created the Knights Templar, who Wolfram had identified as the protectors of the Grail. It was that same order that would later be labelled "heretical". But if the Knights Templar were labelled "heretics", should the Cistercians, who apparently shared their beliefs, not be labelled similarly? The only real difference lay in whether the Cistercian monks lived a contemplative, or warrior lifestyle. The question that needs to be asked is whether, with the rising popularity of the Grail, the Cistercian Order commissioned itself to deflect attention away from the heretical nature of the Grail, in an effort to protect both themselves and the Knights Templar. By doing so, the Grail would merely become another Christian relic, which would bring its protectors, the Knights Templar, back into a clean, safe Christian fold.

Thus, at a time when Wolfram von Eschenbach is stating that he is setting the record straight and is going to write the ultimate account of the Grail, we find that the Cistercian monks were hard at work as well. They were defining the Grail as a purely Christian relic.

Just like Wolfram's *Parzival,* the *Queste* makes numerous allusions to the Knights Templar too. Even though Galahad isn't called a Templar; he is a secular knight. However, at a monastery of white brothers – the Cistercians – he does receive a white shield with a red cross on it that once belonged to Joseph of Arimathea. It were of course the Knights Templar that had white mantles marked with a red cross.

Though the *Queste* makes it clear that the Grail is "good

Christian stuff", it may actually have revealed one part of the masterplan. In the *Queste*, the Grail knights go to Jerusalem with the Grail, as their quest has already ended. When Galahad, Perceval and Bors reach the Grail castle in Jerusalem, they encounter nine more knights who have equally achieved the Grail. Are we here face to face with the original nine knights, who went to Jerusalem, where in 1118 they asked the King of Jerusalem to create the Knights Templar? Rather than consider 1118 the beginning of a story, it was perhaps part of a phase of a masterplan, a plan that had begun much earlier. Coincidentally, that is also what the author the *Queste* says…

Chapter 10: The realms of the Grail

Wolfram's Grail account differs from Chrétien's treatise in that the former lists a series of events that had gone before Perceval's Grail quest. Scholars have often overlooked the information presented in this "prequel", as it is not deemed to be of core value for the story itself.

The prequel tackles events that led to the existence of a Grail Brotherhood and the exploits of Perceval's father on his foreign travels, before returning home, marrying, and Perceval's birth. As Wolfram's account is deemed fictional, these scholars have not seen any value in analysing the information of the prequel, instead opting to label it a "unique trait" of Wolfram's account. Full stop.

However, if the Grail is historical, rather than fictional, then the information contained in the prequel should be analysed and could reveal important further clues, specifically about the origins of the Grail Brotherhood.

There are two main areas of potential research: the story of Titurel and his discovery of the Grail in the East, and the adventures of Perceval's father in the East, which resulted in the birth of a half-brother, Feirefiz. It is the latter's exploits that is also unique to Wolfram, written down as a "postscript" once Perceval has been crowned Grail king.

Both the prequel and the postscript can be seen as being derived from Kyot's source material: the family history he was able to rescover. Still, it would be imprudent to argue that both prequel and postscript derive from this source. Whereas the prequel clearly reveals the knightly prowess of Perceval's father and could therefore be part of a family account, the postscript is of a different nature, detailing a much later period. Here, Wolfram may not have relied on Kyot, but instead on his own research, or even a third source. However, before delving into the end of the story, let us look at the beginning first.

Titurel

Observers have noted that each of the line of Grail kings is specifically "crafted" to display a key talent: Perceval is the fool seeking enlightenment; Trevrizent is wisdom; Anfortas represents extreme sickness and suffering; Titurel, the first Grail king, represents extreme old age.

That is the moral, Hermetic message; when we read the story on a historical level, Wolfram states that the Grail had been brought from the East by Titurel, Anfortas' grandfather. In *Parzival,* Trevrizent states that "he was the first to be entrusted with the banner of the Grail and the charge of defending it."[223]

Though Titurel was the founder of the Grail Dynasty, most authors have paid little attention to him. André de Mandach has identified him with Ramiro I, the first king of Aragon. That Titurel and Ramiro I are at the origin of a dynasty, that of the Grail and that of Aragon, is another intriguing "coincidence", which is actually further confirmation that both dynasties are one and the same.

Ramiro I was the illegitimate son of King Sancho III of Navarre. During his father's lifetime he governed the small valley of the river Aragon and was made king of that land by his father's will in 1035. In 1045, he annexed the territories belonging to his brother Gonzalo upon the latter's death, which were the kingdoms of the Sobrarbe (the central north strip of the modern province of Huesca) and the Ribagorza (the northeast corner of that province).

Ramiro I had married to Gilberga Hermesinda de Conserans on 22 August 1036 in Jaca. She was a daughter of Bernard Roger de Conserans, Lord of Foix, Count Bigorre and Conserans, himself the son of Roger I of Carcassonne. She died in 1054.

Titurel himself died at the siege of Graus on 8 May 1063, a

battle of the early Spanish Reconquista. He was slain by a frontier-dwelling Moor named Sa'dada who could speak Aragonese and had so penetrated their lines to drive a lance into Ramiro's face. As a consequence, the Muslim king of Zaragoza, Al-Muktadir, defeated the king of Aragon, dashing the immediate hopes that Christianity would defeat the Muslim rulers of Spain.

Titurel is depicted as alive at the time of Perceval's visit to the Grail castle. This represents a historical problem for de Mandach's theory, as Ramiro I reigned over Aragon from 1035 until 1063. This means that Ramiro I was long dead by the time Perceval arrived at the Grail castle at the beginning of the 12th century. What are we to make of this inconsistency – one which was well-known to de Mandach but nevertheless did not stop him from making this identification.

In Wolfram's *Parzival,* Titurel is an enigmatic character; he is said to have partaken of the Grail so many times, that he should have been dead, but is not; the Grail continues to keep him alive. Nevertheless, though alive, he never leaves his couch, from where he issues his wisdom.

What does this mean? The most logical explanation would be that André de Mandach is incorrect in his identification of the Grail family – or at least of Titurel with Ramiro I. The second possibility is that Wolfram was erroneous – or his sources were: Titurel was in fact dead, not alive. The third possibility, the most fantastical of all, is that Ramiro I was indeed alive, contrary to the historical record, and living inside the monastery of San Juan de la Peña, being kept alive solely by the power of the Grail – he was beyond death.

There is a fourth explanation, which is the most likely: that Wolfram may have decided to show the power of the Grail, and used Titurel as an example of the otherworldly powers that the Grail could achieve. It would mean that Wolfram departed from a historical account to make his point. In short: for someone to display the Hermetic characteristic of extreme old age, you need to make some live for a very long time. When no-one like that is available in history (neither in the Grail Aragon dynasty, nor anywhere else), what to do?

Titurel was at the origin of the Grail Dynasty, but it would be his descendants who would have the solemn task of keeping the dynasty alive, and abide by its stringent rules. Titurel thus had handed his kingdom to his son, Frimutel, but this son was not wise. His death was reported as "till in the service of love he met his death in a joust." Earthly desires thus failed him. "He left four noble children, of whom three are in misery; the fourth lives a life of poverty as a penance in the name of God: he is called Trevrizent. His brother Anfortas is crippled: he can neither ride nor walk, nor lie down nor stand up. He is the host of Munslvaesche: and misfortune is his lot."[224]

Titurel is alive, but rather than enjoy extreme old age, he is in mental distress: his son and heir is dead, his grandson is incapable of creating offspring. He himself is wise, but too old. In short, Titurel is portrayed as the intelligence that is removed from the physical world, whose wise words can only help his family in trying to continue the Brotherhood that he created so many years ago – but which already seems to have gone awry when the first heir became Grail king – and almost immediately failed in the challenges posed by that office.

Against this background, we see how Wolfram's story is actually the story of the righting of this wrong, whereby Perceval will restore the Wasteland that Titurel's children have created.

It seems that Wolfram modelled Titurel on the god Kronos/Saturn, an identification that was made many decades ago by F.R. Schröder.[225] In the *Corpus Hermeticum*, Kronos is identified as the prototype of the Hermetic ecstatic.[226] Hermes states that Kronos was his ancestor – like Titurel is Anfortas'.

Furthermore, Kronos is considered to be the "old god", who rules from behind the scenes, only able to offer advice, but unable to carry out his own desires. Like Titurel, Kronos was depicted as full of wisdom, yet sleeping, dreaming; Titurel is bedridden, lame. It was "a lameness for which there is no help. Yet he has never lost his fresh colour, for he sees the Grail so often that he cannot die."[227]

Titurel's lameness is the result of podagra (gout) and according to the astrological tradition, people born under Saturn/Kronos often suffer from podagra, with Saturn himself described as suffering from it.[228] It is in such details – which to the untrained eye may seem incidental – that the true mastery of Wolfram's writing comes to fruition and that it becomes obvious that Titurel is indeed modelled on Saturn, and that he shares all characteristics with this deity, including those he was given in the Hermetic literature. Though it may argue against the historical accuracy of the account, the most likely explanation is that Wolfram kept Titurel alive, so that he could adorn him with the attributes of Saturn, as well as show the immortality-giving aspect of the Grail.

But physical immortality is "merely" the acquisition of great age – not necessarily wisdom. In mythology, there were cycles of time, each ruled by one deity. And in mythology, the gods of the previous cycle remained alive – gods cannot die. Saturn was the ruling deity of a previous cycle, and he too, though no longer the active ruler of the current era, remained available to guide the current ruling deities in their task – with wisdom, his experience of his own rule.

Within the framework of the cyclical nature of time, we have also returned to the role of the Phoenix, whose chief role it was to mark the completion and start of one era by returning to the benben stone, and rising from his own ashes.

The Phoenix symbolised the reborn man, but he also symbolised the initiate, not in his change from mere mortal to initiate, but from initiate to Grail King. The old name for Kronos is Phaeinos – "shining" and is directly linked with the Phoenix. It explains why Saturn was seen as the "Old God", the god of a former era. And that is specifically the role of Titurel in the Grail accounts: the ancient ruler, still present, able to disperse wisdom, but unable to rule himself. He can only guide the Grail court, but in the end, it is up to Perceval to become the person who would restore order to the Dynasty.

In the Egyptian tradition, the Phoenix bird was not only the bird of the sun, but the Pharaoh himself was identified with the Phoenix bird: each new king was "reborn", rising from the ashes of his predecessor. The ancient Egyptians adhered so strongly to the cyclical nature of renewal that every New Year festival was an expression of the original act of creation, as was shown above. Should kings have the fortune to reign for several decades, a specific ceremony of "rejuvenation" occurred, known as the Heb Sed festival. Originally, this occurred once a king had reigned for a period of thirty years and thereafter, every three years, though in theory, the king was allowed to hold this festival whenever he felt it necessary to demonstrate his fitness to rule.

Both in the New Year ceremonies and the Heb Sed festivals, the rituals were meant to bring back the harmony between the king and the universe. Like the New Year rituals, the Heb Sed ceremonies started with an impressive procession. Afterwards, the celebratory rituals were carried out in an open courtyard, often specifically constructed for this purpose. The open court of the Step Pyramid at Saqqara is believed to have been used for the function of Djoser's Heb-Sed Festival. Here, the king would run around the field (or within the Sed courtyard), carrying several ritual articles in his hands, and shooting arrows towards the four cardinal directions. These physical displays proved the king's vitality and ability to rule. It is in sharp contrast with the Grail court, where Anfortas cannot show his vitality: he is unable to run; his wound causes him so much distress that even moving about on his couch is painful.

Though Titurel displays the characteristics of Kronos, some attributes of Saturn were given to Anfortas. The wound of Anfortas is said to have been caused by a spear, and is most painful when Saturn is prominent in the sky. A lot of speculation exists as to what this spear might be, as some Grail accounts put great emphasis on it. Some identified it as the Holy Lance that pierced Jesus' side when the Roman soldiers tried to confirm his death on the cross. However, in Wolfram, the spear is not linked with any Christian imagery.

Wolfram instead opts for mythology and astrology. In medieval times, Saturn was often depicted with a spear and an arrow in his left hand.[229] Wolfram is therefore using the spear as further confirmation that the wound is related with Saturn, underlining that, if anything, Wolfram, or his sources, were well-versed in astrological lore.

Saturn is also the astrological ruler of Capricorn and the ancient ruler of Aquarius. Evidence that Wolfram's story is firmly set within the context of astrology is obvious when astrology states that Saturn rules responsibilities, restrictions and limitations that a person is apt to encounter and the lessons that must be learned in life. This is Anfortas' challenge. It often describes the rules that a person has established for himself, and/or the external limits and restrictions that are necessarily imposed for the growth of individual consciousness, which is of course the goal of the Grail initiate.

It is Anfortas' wound that ties him to this world – that to him is a reminder of the pain of this realm. For his part, Titurel's reminder of the pain of this realm is experienced through his gout, which keeps him, like his grandson, bedridden. In astrology, Saturn's issues are about being a physical human being in a physical body coping with physical needs and dealing with the consequences of previous physical actions. Thus, Anfortas, with the help of Perceval, wants to relieve himself from this pain, so that he can dedicate himself completely to the Grail.

It should thus not come as a surprise that Saturn is often identified as the planet with which the Hermetic scholar has to battle. Marsilio Ficino himself used the planet in such manner, as he had this planet on his ascendant in his astrological chart. In the understanding that he had to overcome the limits and restrictions imposed by this planet, so that he could seek enlightenment, Ficino devised methods to break up the rigidity of Saturn.

Ficino found that this preoccupation was also present with other Hermeticists, and wrote: "The Pythagorean maguses seem to have been extremely cautious in this matter, when they would become frightened that their constant philosophizing was the tyranny of Saturn, so they would dress up in white garments, and each day sing songs and make music with Jovial and Apollonian things, and in this way they lived a long time under Saturn." Ficino stated that for those who suffered from this influence, they should turn to Jupiter, "Jove", to balance these energies by using "joviality", to act as the remedy.

In astrology, Jupiter is linked with a sense of well being; it gives a feeling of being ageless, living forever, being immortal, the very attributes that Anfortas tries to attain, in his struggle with Saturn. Jupiter also makes an appearance when Feirifez is united to Repanse de Schoye; he is receiving "knowledge of joy" – Repense in Old French has the meaning of "thought, reflection".[230] The marriage that was the ambition of the Grail Dynasty, was therefore the marriage of Saturn and Jupiter – a most important theme in astrology.

By extension, Jupiter symbolises social drives for expansion and improvement, the very goal of those who have heeded the call of the Grail. When the Grail announces that a knight might come forward who, if he asks the proper question, will heal him, the court is filled with hope. Hope is the intermediate, which beckons the possibility that pain will be turned into joy. Perceval will thus not so much alleviate his purely physical pain – but the enquiry about Anfortas' physical ailment will also resolve his spiritual wound: the continuation of the Grail Dynasty.

With the connection between Saturn, Titurel and Anfortas, the Hermetic contents of *Parzival* are once again clearly illustrated. A link between stars, Saturn and wounds is definitely not customary for 12th century European writers, who had yet to experience the wave of Arab astrology that would soon take hold of the European continent. The Hermetic stellar correlations between events on Earth and the stars – often summed up in the statement "as above, so below" – would result more and more in the fame of practical astrology, whereby the bailiwick of astrology would no longer be purely the Hermetic seeker, but most sections of the general population, resulting in the famous astrological almanacs that appeared largely from the 16th century onwards.

Feirefiz & Prester John

The second unique aspect Wolfram's account is the presence of an epilogue, in which the story of the Grail under Feirefiz's rule as Grail king is explained. These passages are missing from the other accounts and are thus generally believed to have been inventions by Wolfram.

Like the Grail, Feirefiz is a "product" from the East: the child of Gahmuret's first marriage to the Moorish queen Belkane. But whether Titurel travelled in the East himself or whether somehow the Grail made its way from the East to him, is not stated in *Parzival*. However, Wolfram does state that Gahmuret, Perceval's father, did travel extensively in the East.

With Gahmuret's identification as Geoffrey II de Perche, we know that Geoffrey II was indeed "missing" from his homeland for an extensive period of time. Had Geoffrey, like Gahmuret, sought knightly adventures, abroad? Had he reached the country of the Queen Belkane, did he have a child with her, which would be named Feirefiz? In *Parzival,* Gahmuret abandoned her when she was twelve weeks pregnant. When Gahmuret was back in Europe, he married another woman, Herzeloyde, whom he almost immediately made pregnant. From this union, Perceval was born, who was Feirefiz's half-brother.

As mentioned, Geoffrey's II marriage to Beatrice did occurr upon his return to his ancestral home and his installation as ruler of his territories. Geoffrey's and Gahmuret's lifetime hence do overlap. Furthermore, as the historical record is blank as to Geoffrey's whereabouts for a decade, it does allow for the possibility that Rotrou II did have an older half-brother somewhere... in the East.

The name Feirefiz has been linked with the French "vaire fils", which means a son with a skin of different colours – "fair faced" – and it is stated that Feirefiz was indeed neither white nor black, but racially mixed. Queen Belkane, Feirefiz's mother, is described as being "black".[231] Children from racially mixed marriages are well-known in the 21st century, but in the 12th century, few Europeans had even seen the black people of Africa; interracial marriages were uncommon in Western Europe and sexual affairs between Western nobility and black foreign queens virtually non-existent. Only daredevils seeking fame, fortune or adventure on foreign continents would have been candidates... and both Geoffrey and Gahmuret were definitely such daredevils.

However, Belkane was not merely black, she was also a pagan, which allows for another interpretation of her name.[232] In Normand, "feirefiz" is close to "faerie fils", the "son of the fairies". Pagans, then and now, were deemed to be more in touch with the faeries than with the saints; witches were thought to have sexual intercourse with the denizens of the Otherworld, from which "strange" children were born: changelings. Like

Feirefiz, they had peculiar physical traits, but it is clear that this is where the comparison between Feirefiz and a changeling ends.

Feirefiz was a normal human being, who would make his way to Europe, make contact with the Grail court, where he married Repanse de Schoye, the woman who had been the Grail bearer. Their son was "Prester John". And though the Grail had been brought from the East, given to Titurel, handed down to Perceval, it would be his half-brother's son, Prester John, who would then take charge of the relic, and return it to his home countries, in the East. And thus, the Grail legend was complete: an object had apparently come to Europe for a short period of time, before it was taken back.

The story of Prester John as the guardian of the Grail is the topic of *The Younger Titurel*, a work that many scholars have linked with Wolfram. Presently, the author of *The Younger Titurel* is believed to have been Albrecht von Scharfenberg, who is thought to have written the text between 1270 and 1275, half a century after Wolfram's death. Still, it is believed that Albrecht based his story on fragment of Wolfram's own work.[233] Author Graham Hancock notes: "Albrecht's identification with 'his master' had been so complete that he had actually claimed to *be* Wolfram, 'adopting not just his name and subject matter but also his mannerisms as a narrator and even the details of his personal history.'"[234] We could wonder whether Albrecht merely used his imagination, or used the same source material that had been at the core of Wolfram's *Parzival*.

"Prester John" was a historical character – though some would prefer a "historical legend". The legends of Prester John (or Presbyter John) were popular in Europe from the 12th through the 17th centuries. They focused on a Christian patriarch and king said to rule over a Christian nation lost amidst the Muslims and pagans in the Orient.

At first, Prester John was imagined to be in India; tales of the

Nestorian Christians' evangelistic success there and of Thomas the Apostle's subcontinental travels as documented in works like the Acts of Thomas probably provided the first seeds of the legend. After the coming of the Mongols to the Western world, accounts placed the king in Central Asia, and eventually Portuguese explorers stated they had found him in Ethiopia. Throughout these centuries, Prester John's kingdom was the object of a quest, firing the imaginations of generations of adventurers, but apparently remaining out of reach – or so some want to believe.

In truth, the historical veracity is that there is an actual "Prester John", referred to in documents dating from the 12th century and thus at Wolfram's disposal when he wrote *Parzival* at the start of the 13th century. It is also known that Prester John had a magic stone, "of incredible medical virtue, which cures Christians or would-be Christians of whatever ailments afflict them".[235]

The first mention of a "Prester John" appears in 1145 – the timeframe when according to de Mandach Wolfram's renditions of the Grail story had just ended (1137) and thus indeed perfectly suited to be discussed in the story of *The Younger Titurel*, the sequel to Perceval's account; though some will no doubt see this as yet another coincidence. But rather than yet another coincidence, perhaps it is more evidence of a historical foundation?

The name of this "priest John" appears in the Chronicle of Bishop Otto of Freisingen. In a meeting with the Syrian prelate at Viterbo, in Pope Eugenius II's presence, the bishop learned about a John, both king and priest, a Christian living in the East, commanding vast armies, which he wished to put at the disposal of the defenders of Jerusalem. At a time when the Christian world was forever in need of armies to defend the Holy Land against Moorish rulers intent on regaining Jerusalem, such rumours had to be investigated. Not only could this Christian ruler reinforce the troops, if he indeed lived in the East, he could actually open a second front, directing those Muslim forces away from Jerusalem.

The Prester John mystery continued in 1165, when a letter allegedly from "Prester John", addressed to various kings and rulers of Western Europe, circulated widely in European courts. About a hundred manuscripts of the letter to Manuel of Constantinople are still extant (with many variants) and afford an interesting insight into this exceedingly complicated story.

The next milestone happened in 1177, when Pope Alexander III wrote a letter to Prester John. The Pope referred to a meeting between his physician-in-ordinary Philippus, who had spoken to some of Prester John's emissaries in Jerusalem, where the monarch had apparently requested a sanctuary in the Church of the Holy Sepulchre in Jerusalem. It is known that the Ethiopic Church did possess a chapel and altar in the Church of the Holy Sepulchre, granted to them in 1189, and this fact is therefore the first evidence that Prester John did indeed rule Ethiopia.[236] However, this chapel in the end was not granted by the Pope, so when the Muslim leader Saladin took control of the Holy City in 1187, Prester John himself directly appealed to Saladin, and was granted this chapel.

This series of events shows that the entire history of Prester John is indeed fact – not fiction. It is the story of a 12th century Ethiopian Christian monarch, making contact with the Christian west, at a time when Jerusalem is in Christian hands. He requests a chapel for his people inside the most holy church, but is apparently refused – or his request is at least not immediately granted.

The letters of "Prester John" and the connection with a Christian kingdom in Ethiopia fit well within the timeframe of the Grail – and even the life of Gahmuret's – Geoffrey II de Perche – life.

When we look at the information that is present in the Grail account, we learn that Feirefiz was said to have ruled a kingdom, known as Zazamanc. It was described in such splendid terms that "nothing can compare with his wealth, wherever it is spoken of, save that of the Baruch and the riches of Tribalibot".[237] The land was also said to be rich in precious stones, such as diamond and amethyst, ruby and emeralds.

One of his vassals is one Lidamus d'Agrippe and Wolfram's *Parzival* mentions two individuals named Lidamus, one being a Spanish noble. One of the fiefs of Feirefiz is listed as Azagouc (or Azagoch), a name that Wolfram seems to have taken from the *Collectanea rerum memorabilium* of Solin. If so, then this is the Ethiopian town of Azachaei, or Azuga, a town north of Beleguanze.[238] Wolfram thus provides us with a region, Zazamanc, a town, Azagouc, and the name of his mother, Belkane (sometimes spelled Belacane). And as a medieval map of the "domains of Prester John" lists a town as Beleguanze… could this be a reference to Belacane?

Author Graham Hancock argues that the town of Rohas that appears in Wolfram's account is Roha, situated "deep into Africa", and that this is the same as Lalibela, who was not only once known as Beleguanze, but also as "Roha".

If Belkane was indeed the Queen of Ethiopia, than she would have ruled from the capital, Lalibela, and that capital may thus have carried at one point her name: Beleguanze. Helen Adolf has argued that certain details of *Parzival* may indeed have their origin in Ethiopia: "Three features of the *Parzival,* all missing in Chrétien, force our eyes to look towards far-off Abyssinia: first, Indian and the Prester John; second, the Grail as a stone; third, Feirefiz, son of Belakane."[239]

The Ethiopian connection is strengthened when Wolfram identifies the son of Feirefiz as "Prester John", which is indeed the name of the priest-kings of Ethiopia. But, at the time of Wolfram's writing, as mentioned, the homeland of Prester John had not yet been identified. Only in 1328 did Friar Jordanus "Catalani" refer to the Emperor of Ethiopia as "Prestre Johan".[240] Further identification of the land of Prester John with Ethiopia came in 1352, when the Franciscan Giovanni de Marignolli spoke of "Ethiopia where the negroes are and which is called the land of Prester John." So, interestingly, though Wolfram could have introduced the popular legend of Prester John into his account, once again, it appears that Wolfram had certain information at his disposal, which showed that Prester John's homeland was Ethiopia – a connection that would not be made until more than a century after his death.

So, was Feirefiz an Ethiopian king? Beleguanze was the capital of Ethiopia during the Middle Ages; the town today is known as Lalibela. It is described as one of the wonders of the world, because of its rock-hewn churches that a king, Lalibela, constructed there in medieval times.

In *The Sign and the Seal*, Graham Hancock argued that the Grail is the Ark of the Covenant and that it resides in Ethiopia – a connection he made after having seen certain intriguing imagery in the cathedral of Chartres. Of course, in our analysis, the cathedral was built by the very family of Gahmuret and hence the notion that it would contain accurate information about that character, should not come as a surprise.

From ca. 1137 till 1270 AD, Ethiopia was ruled by a dynasty known as Zagwe. It is from this era that we have the first mention of the Ark's presence in Ethiopia.[241] Furthermore, all the Zagwe monarchs used the term "Jan" in their titles, itself derived from "Jano", a reddish-purple toga worn only be royalty. The word itself meant "King" or "Majesty", but would be easily confused with the word "John".[242] As such, "Prester John" literally was nothing more than "priest king" "of Ethiopia" – it was a title, not a name, and the "Prester John" of the Grail account (and the king who was in correspondence with various popes) could this have applied to an entire series of kings, not just one.

The timeframe – 1137 – coincides once again with the Grail story, when Feirefiz returns to his land, with the Grail. But that is not all: it is known that at some point, relatively shortly before 1152, something occurred in Ethiopia that the patriarch of Alexandria and his metropolitan in Ethiopia regarded as an usurpation. Later, Ethiopic legends hint that power changed hands because of a woman – though no further details are known. Could this be where the legendary Belkane needs to be slotted into the historical record?

In ca. 1140, Prince Lalibela was born in the town of Roha. Legend tells of rivalry between the young Prince Lalibela and his elder brother, King Harbay, following their mother's revelation that Lalibela would be king, despite his juniority. Was this the "usurpation"? As a consequence, Harbay attempted to murder his younger brother Lalibela; as a consequence, from 1160 till 1185, Lalibela had to go into exile, to the city of Jerusalem. It thus seems that he and his entourage were the people with whom the papal entourage had established contact. In 1185, Lalibela returned to Ethiopia, to depose his half-brother Harbay and proclaim himself king, a rule that lasted until 1211.

It is during the Lalibela's reign that we first hear of the presence of what could be the Ark of the Covenant in Ethiopia.[243] The source for this is an Armenian, Abu Salih, who lived in Egypt and wrote in Arabic during the late 12th and early 13th century. He stated that the Ark was in Lalibela, not in Aksum, where it is normally placed, including by the likes of Graham Hancock.[244]

The "tabutu al-'ahdi" contained two tables of stone, inscribed by the finger of God with the commandments that he ordained for the children of Israel. But this cannot possibly be *the* Ark, as Abu Salih states that the liturgy was celebrated upon the Ark. In the Bible, it is written that touching the Ark will result in instant death – a side effect of the power of God, it seems. Even if the Ark had somehow become "disabled", the top lid of the Ark is where the mercy seat of God is situated, located between two cherubim (angels), which means that the top of the Ark would not lend itself to any events held upon it.

With this Ark not being *the* Ark, is it possible that the real Ark was in Aksum, as Hancock and other suggest? Though the "Ark of Aksum" is never on public display, resting instead behind a veil, some people have seen it, and have spoken of their experiences. One of author Munro-Hay's informants stated that the tablet shines and inspires fears. The guardian at certain times offers it incense, but there are no other services.[245]

The "Ark of Aksum" is not our primary interest. But in Lalibela, it does appear that there are certain stones, inscribed by the finger of God, which was not the Ark, but which could easily be mistaken for it. But a stone (tablet), said to contain writing, revealing the writing of God is very much like the Grail. So could it be that the object in Lalibela was the Grail, which was returned from Europe to Ethiopia?

The next question then is whether Lalibela was the historical Prester John – or at least one of them? The answer seems to be yes. But was Lalibela the Prester John of the Grail accounts? The answer seems to be no.

There are definitely some parallels between Feirefiz and Perceval and the rulers of the Zagwe dynasty. Feirefiz and Perceval were half-brothers, from the same father, but different mothers. Perceval in the end confronted his brother, and was declared winner, though Feirefiz would have been the first in line for the throne. Harbay and Lalibela were half-brothers, from the same father, but with different mothers. Harbay was destined for the throne, but a prophecy favoured Lalibela. The Dutch author Klaas Van Urk has thus identified Lalibela with Perceval, and Harbay with Feirefiz.[246] It is definitely in the right direction, but in our opinion, not the total truth, if only because neither Lalibela nor Harbay would have been white skinned.

There are further problems with this identification. First of all, Ethiopia is not listed in the list of regions that Gahmuret visited. He visited Baghdad and Morocco, largely travelling throughout the region of Northern Africa and the Middle East – but it is not stated that he headed further south, into Ethiopia.

So where does this leave the story of Prester John and its incorporation in Wolfram's *Parzival*? The legend of Prester John furnished a wealth of material for the poets, writers and explorers of the Middle Ages. In England, Sir John Mandeville exploited it to excess. In Germany, it seems that Wolfram von Eschenbach was the first to use it. Some have speculated that Wolfram was inspired by the *Kebra Negast* itself, which is now the holy book of the Ethiopian church. But Munro-Hay has stated that at present, there is no evidence that the *Kebra Negast* existed at the time of Wolfram von Eschenbach.[247]

The central question is whether Wolfram linked the Grail with Prester John for narrative impact of his story – or whether there is indeed a connection between the two elements. It is an important question to ask, for in the concluding chapters of Wolfram's account, he writes that Feirefiz took the Grail with him to his homeland – which would place the Grail in Ethiopia. Before we are however able to answer these questions, we need to look into one other possibility.

A Libyan Feirifez?

Whether historically accurate or not, Wolfram had a very good reason to use the story of Prester John: once again, his desire to retell the *Corpus Hermeticum* had presented him with a "need": the need for a secondary myst: Feirefiz.

In the Hermetic treatises, the secondary myst is known as Hammon, who is, like Feirefiz, an African king.[248] In the *Corpus Hermeticum*, he makes his appearance in the 16th treatise, as well as in the *Asclepius*. As the secondary myst makes his appearances in the later chapters of the Hermetica, Wolfram apparently respected this sequence, by bringing Feirefiz on the scene in the last chapters of his narrative.

The name Hammon is most likely derived from the Egyptian god Ammon – Amun, who had a famous oracle in the Siwa oasis, in the land of the Garamantes. In Roman times, Ammon was referred to both as Garamanticus and Marmaricus Hammon.[249] The reference to Ammon and the Garamantes therefore does not take us to the south of Egypt, into Ethiopia, but instead to the west of Egypt, to the Siwa Oasis – a region that is within the realm visited by Gahmuret. Furthermore, S. Singer argued that Zazamanc, the land of Feirefiz, was a corruption of Garamantes, adding that the Marmarides were "speckled" blacks, like Feirefiz.[250]

The Siwa oasis would also resolve another problem: the Grail has a specific pagan – Hermetic – nature, whereas an Ethiopian connection would place it within a more Christian-African framework. Furthermore, though the Siwa oasis had remained outside of Egypt's political control for all of its history, a temple to the Egyptian supreme deity Amun had nevertheless been constructed in the oasis, underlining that the site was deemed to be a most important religious centre by the ancient Egyptians.

Later, the region was populated by the Garamantes, a people in the Sahara that used an elaborate underground irrigation system, enabling them to maintain a kingdom from 500 BC to 500 AD, the era in which the *Corpus Hermeticum* was composed. It is known that the Romans maintained close trade relations with these people, which has been substantiated by the archaeological discovery of a Roman bathhouse in Garama.

Still, little is known about the Garamantes, not even the name they used to call themselves. What is known is that one of their centres of power was the Siwa oasis, with its temple to Amun and it should therefore not come as a surprise that their religion was based on the Egyptian pantheon and that some of their dead were buried in small pyramids.[251]

Almost immediately after taking Egypt from the Persians and founding the city of Alexandria, the future home of the *Corpus*, Alexander the Great headed for the Siwa Oasis to consult the Oracle of Amun. On this voyage, he encountered many of the same problems in the desert that previous rulers had experienced; whole armies before him had been lost in the sands. Hence, it is not surprising to learn that Alexander's caravan got lost too, ran out of water and was even caught up in an unusual rainstorm. However, they were merely hinderances and nothing stopped him from arriving at the oasis and the Oracle of Amun, where Alexander was pronounced a god, an endorsement that was required to legitimise his rule of the country. It is, of course, highly interesting that Alexandar had to receive this endorsement in this oasis, and that, of course, this was the endorsement that he was indeed a sacred king, and hence fit to rule. One important question is therefore what specifically there was in this oasis that was so intimately linked with sacred kingship.

Though on a map the Siwa Oasis may seem a long way from Morocco, and hence far from Gahmuret's travels, in reality it is not. Gahmuret could have made the voyage, like so many others had before him. After the disappearance of the Garamantes, the history of the oasis relates that at a time of drought throughout the countries of northwestern Africa, the Amazigh people set off eastwards, searching for grass and water. When they reached the Siwa Oasis, with its natural springs and fields of olive, apricot and palm trees, all singing with life, they realised that they had found paradise – and would not leave it. The Amazigh people decided to make their home here and sent word back west to Algeria and Morocco for their families to come and join them to strengthen the tribe's power and claim on this fertile land.

Their first city was named Ami Misalum and built in the lowlands of the oasis. However, this left the Amazigh vulnerable both to attacks from hostile forces and to mosquitoes. In 1103 AD, they therefore built a strong citadel on the hilltop to protect themselves and their unique culture and made this their kingdom. New laws and rules were instituted which, along with the more secure location, allowed the tribal chiefs to govern Siwa as an independent state.

The above account is practically everything that is known about the oasis' history and any detailed identifications of kings and rulers is most likely impossible. Whether Gahmuret ever passed through and/or had a child with the local ruler will be difficult to establish. All we can argue is therefore that is possible… but may not have happened.

So, though it is clear that Wolfram had a need for an African "second myst", where does that leave us? There are three possibilities. Firstly, Wolfram may have used the story of Prester John merely as the historical basis to carve the second myst upon. Secondly, Wolfram may have thought that Prester John was indeed the half-brother of Perceval. If Wolfram had source material that Feirefez, a Christian king, had gone east, to his homeland, then Wolfram knew that there were not many foreign rulers in the East who claimed to be Christian; Prester John therefore fit the bill, and was the only historical account Wolfram will have known of that fit the Grail account. Thirdly, Wolfram may have had certain privileged information which did identify Prester John as Feirefiz. In the latter case, where does this leave us, and is it indeed possible that the Ark of the Covenant and the Grail are identical, as Graham Hancock has argued?

The Ark of the Covenant = the Grail?

The traditional story of the Ark in Ethiopia states that King Solomon was visited by the Queen of Sheba. Their son, Menelik, carried the Ark off with him, bringing it to Ethiopia, where it has remained for approximately 3000 years. The first to bring the story to a world-wide audience was Graham Hancock, in *The Sign and the Seal*. It took another decade before Stuart Munro-Hay would add to this material. Munro-Hay poured cold water on Hancock's theory, arguing that he had found no evidence for the old stories of the Ark's presence in Ethiopia before the Middle Ages, when certain Ethiopian rulers wanted to underline their relationship with Jerusalem, focusing on the story of Solomon and the Queen of Sheba. These rulers used the symbol of the Ark to forge that link – but it was not based on historical evidence.[252]

Still, though the Ark of the Covenant, it seems, was never in Ethiopia, the Tablets of Moses that were once inside, may have been. Furthermore, Grierson and Munro-Hay themselves suggest that even the Bible seems to indicate that there may have been more than one Ark – and hence it is a question of which Ark, not the Ark.[253] Though this has not diminished the importance of the object held inside the church of Aksum, it has placed it within a more complex framework than has previously been assumed.

Hancock was equally convinced that the Ark of the Covenant and the Grail was one and the same object. Though there are major discrepancies between the two relics, there are nevertheless some parallels. The Ark is renowned for its manna – food – and the Tablets of Moses, written by God himself. The Grail is known for its lush food that it provides to the Grail Brotherhood, and the names of those called to serve are written on it – it is implied that the writing is done by God. Like the Grail, the Ark had a procession and the miracles of the Ark are witnessed during this festival, which includes wood that begins to blossom and grows again in the presence of the Ark. The wooden poles used to carry the Ark continued to grow as well.

Like the Grail, the Ark offered a way by which men and women could escape from matter by rising into the spiritual world. Like the Grail, the Ark was a living mystical process.[254] It was a powerful device, which only the high priest was allowed to approach, once per year, and only then when protected by clothing and apparently by filling the entire room with incense. The Bible contains numerous stories of the danger of approaching let alone touching the Ark; the Ark kills.

And it is its lethal power that is the major discrepancy with the Grail, or the object in Lalibela. Though only those worthy of seeing the Grail will see the Grail, at no point does the Grail kill; the Grail maiden bears it on a simple green cloth, and no harm has ever come to her, or any of her predecessors. Whereas the Ark can kill those approaching it, the Grail is said to extend the life of those who live near its presence. If anything, it appears that both are divine, but that the Grail's effect are largely positive, whereas the Ark negative – somewhat in line with what the scriptwriters of Lara Croft's movie had in mind when tackling Pandora's Box: the cradle of life which in origin contained both all good, as well as all evil, but from which all good had been removed – by whom, it is not said – leaving only a Box that contained all evil – chaos.

So the parallels between the Ark and the Grail are there. But so are the discrepancies. It suggests that the Grail and Ark may be part of the same tradition. After all, the Ark may not have been a single artefact in the Biblical tradition – there were definitely Ark-like instruments elsewhere. The Austrian adventurer Carl Raswan spoke about a tribe gathering of the Ruala that he witnessed. A camel carried a large framework of acacia wood, known as the markab, or ship, which Raswan called the Ark of Ishmael.[255] The Ark was used as a standard to lead the tribe into battle. It was escorted by a young woman who had been chosen as the one to ride in the markab.

In this ritual, there are parallels both to the Ark and the Grail: the Grail was also used as a standard, and a young woman carried the Grail. Interestingly, another name for the markab was abu zhur, "Father of time", as it was believed that it would survive forever. It was also believed that those who possessed it, would have no problem in rallying other people to follow them in battle.

Confronted with the Arab "arks", we have a mixture of the box-like container that typifies the Ark of the Covenant and the sacred stones inside that seem to fit within the Grail tradition. The tradition of sacred stones, which can be found in most primitive cultures and which survived into the Middle Ages and in some regions is still alive today, is what lies at the origin of the Jewish Tablets of Moses.

But these stones were not the only sacred stones known to the Jewish kings: there was the shami, the stone of Solomon, which was said to have originated in Paradise – like the Grail. Like the Grail, it provided the power to rule over the kingdom; both could only be won by the person predestined to do so, both radiated light and both revealed the names in writing.

Returning to the container in which the tablets resided: another topic of debate is whether the Ark is typically Jewish or whether the design was copied – or the object stolen – from Egypt, at the time of the Exodus. Recently, the debate on the origins of the Ark has swung in favour of Egypt. For one, other box-shaped objects of a similar nature have been discovered there, including one from the tomb of Tutankhamun. Furthermore, knowing that the Israelites "came up" with the idea whilst leaving Egypt, the likelihood that they copied it from there seems more than likely. The Jews were fleeing Egypt and had to have a symbol, a sign of recognition of their unity, and power as a nation. It is clear that the Ark was exactly such a symbol, before in Egypt, and afterwards in other Arab countries. As to the debate whether the Israelites build the Ark, or stole an Egyptian one; in Roman times, Pompeius Trogus, a Celt from Narbonne, reported that Moses had secretly taken the sacred objects of the Egyptians.[256] We will leave it at that.

Moses is the key figure that links Egypt with the Ark. There are various sources stating that Moses was a priest of Heliopolis. One of these is Manetho, who himself was a high priest of Heliopolis and in our analysis was the creator of the *Corpus Hermeticum*. Could it therefore be that the "Ark" was a device connected to the cult of Heliopolis, and thus with the Hermetica? If so, it could explain the many parallels between the ancient Ark of the Covenant and the medieval Grail: both originated from the Hermetic tradition.

In Chapter 37 of the Exodus, Moses orders Bezaleel to build the Ark: "two and a half cubits long, one and a half cubits wide, one and a half cubits high. He plated it, inside and out, with pure gold." With one cubit measuring approximately 18 inches, the Ark measures 3 ft 9 ins long, 2 ft 3 ins wide and 2 ft 3 ins high.

In Egypt, the "Ark of Osiris" is a box of similar dimensions, which was said to contain the body of Osiris. Hence, the Ark of Osiris and the Ark of the Covenant are both boxes, of similar dimensions, and both are religious artefacts. The Ark was a sign of the bond between the nation and the god Jahweh, whereas the Ark of Osiris – a chest – was the centrepiece of the various rituals around the death and resurrection of Osiris.

The Egyptian origin of the Ark was also chanced upon by Graham Hancock during his visit to the Temple of Amun at Luxor (Thebes), the chief residence of the deity. There, Tutankhamun had ordered the depiction of the so-called Opet Festival, a festival that involved the two major temples of Thebes, Luxor and Karnak, whereby there was a procession between the two sites. Hancock was struck by how the object that was at the centre of this procession resembled the Ark of the Covenant: like the Ark, it was lifted on shoulder-high carrying poles. But, rather than a box or a casket, it appeared to be a miniature boat. As Hancock had just visited the Timkat festival in Aksum, he felt that the scenes of joyous procession, depicted on the temple wall, were identical to those he had witnessed in the Ethiopian town. And although there was a difference between a boat and a casket, Hancock explained that the word *tabot,* used in Ethiopia to designate the Ark, also meant "ship-like container".

Under the Ethiopian Zagwe Dynasty, which included Prince Lalibela, the word tabot was used for the box-like carved wooden altars. Some of the surviving tabotat actually mention King Lalibela. These older tabotat are legged cubic or box-like, whereas the present-day are flat tablets. The older ones are small enough to be portable and some have argued that this was one of their primary functions: a portable altar.[257] The Ark that Abu Salih saw, was in fact one of Lalibela's tabotat.[258] Even though the tabot and the Ark of Covenant are different, they once again share some characteristics. In essence, they should be seen as two different types of instruments, trying to achieve the same result – in different manners.

So, the Ark, the Grail and the tabotat all share a common characteristic: they were objects, instruments, that facilitated contact with God. In ancient Sumer, this instrument was labelled ME or MU. Mu is what in the Bible was called "shem". The word is normally translated as "name", which is once again intriguing as Wolfram specifically says that it are names that appear on the Grail.

Nevertheless, a century ago, G.M. Redslob pointed out that the translation of "shem" as "name", however widely accepted, was incorrect. The word was related to the word "shamaim", meaning "heaven". Both *shem* and *shamaim* stem from the word *shamah,* meaning "that which is highward". So it should not come as a surprise that the word *mu* means "that which rises straight". Once again, we are within the realm of the Grail, which is also said to be a stone that not only allows communication with God, but from which angels ascend and descend – no wonder therefore that author Zecharia Sitchin identified the shem as a space capsule, with which ancient extraterrestrial rulers of the world voyaged between their orbiting spaceships and Earth![259]

Though Sitchin pursued a somewhat too literal approach, the word *is* identical to the word "shaman", the pagan priests who "rise up" to the sky, and perform spirit flight and communicate with God. It was up to the shaman to enter Heaven and learn from the gods the rules as to how to live properly. The same applies to Moses, who sojourned on a mountain and returned to his people in the valley, with the Ten Commandments.

This also fits within the tradition of Solomon, who built a temple to house the Ark of the Covenant. God appeared to Solomon in a dream while sleeping at Gibeon and asked Solomon what he should give him. Solomon asked God for an "understanding mind" – nous. God said that he would grant this wish and when Solomon awoke, he went to the Ark in Jerusalem, stood in front of it, making burnt offerings and providing a feast for his servants. God then gave Solomon wisdom and understanding beyond measure, which included all wisdom ever accumulated by all nations, if not more. This was followed by a feast, in which "nous" was received by those who were in attendance.

This story is Egyptian in origin. It is now known that this knowledge of Solomon, written down in his proverbs, largely originated from Egypt, specifically the Teachings of Amenemope, written in the latter half of the 21st Dynasty.[260] But we equally note the clear parallels to the Grail story.

In the end, it is clear that Wolfram's Grail, a sacred stone, sits within the same tradition as the Arab stories of sacred stones. And this should not come as a surprise, as Titurel was said to have received it from the East – Arab countries. Equally, it is the homeland of those other "Prester Johns", the leaders of the Johannite Church that are believed to have made contact with the

Knights Templar, and which formed part of the Grail masterplan.

Though the Grail and the Ark of the Covenant are not the same, the Ethiopian tradition makes it clear that the worship of the tabot sits firmly within the worship of sacred stones, and thus sits well within the Wolfram's tradition. In fact, Munro-Hay's research has concluded that the Ark of Aksum is not Solomon's Ark, but instead a sacred stone:[261] a white stone that glows and shines – very much like the Grail, is it not?

Since the 17th century, this sacred stone of Aksum has likely been housed in a box or casket. It is perhaps as a result of this casket that people believed that this was the Ark of the Covenant, as the stone itself was linked with the Tablets of the Law of Moses, which the Bible states were held inside the Ark of the Covenant.[262]

It is here that we come to the crux of the matter. The "Ark of Aksum" is said to have been made by God at the time of creation. It was the habitation of God's glory upon Earth. Ethiopian texts state that it was brought down from heaven, so that Moses could make a copy of it: "Now the heavenly and spiritual [original] within it is of diverse colours, and the work therefore is marvellous, and it resembled jasper, and the sparkling stone, and the topaz, and the hyacinthine stone, and the crystal, and the light, and it catches the eye by force, and it astonishes the mind and stupefies it with wonder; it was made by the mind of God and not by the hand of the artificer, man, but He Himself created it for the habitation of His glory. And it is a spiritual thing and full of compassion; it is a heavenly thing and is full of light; it is a thing of freedom and a habitation of the Godhead, Whose habitation is in Heaven, and Whose place of movement is on the earth, and it dwells with men and with the angels, a city of salvation for men, and for the Holy Spirit a habitation."[263]

Here we see the Ark of Aksum as very similar, if not identical, to the Grail. It is a stone made in Heaven, but brought down to

Earth; it is perfect, and visited by angels, and represents God. It gives off light, and is a mechanism for spiritual salvation.

In the *Book of Aksum*, there is a description of this sacred stone in Aksum, which was known as the berot or the berota eben stone. The stone was located near the throne, was round like a shield; in the centre, it was red and round like a cup.[264] Though it may not have been *the* Grail, but it is clear that this was *a* Grail.

The Prester John of Wolfram may or may not have been the historical Prester John; Gahmuret may or may not have visited Lalibela. It is impossible to give a definitive answer; we can merely argue that it is entirely possible, but that there is no evidence for – or against – it.

But in the final analysis, we need to wonder whether it is important or not. What is important, is that we have uncovered a consistent framework, in which the tradition of sacred stones is of paramount importance; and it is now beyond any doubt that it was from this tradition that Wolfram had borrowed for his Grail account – and not from Christian iconography. It also underlines that Wolfram did have material at his disposal that was foreign – Eastern – in nature, and this should not surprise us at all, for largely, for Wolfram, the story of the Grail was that of a stone, that was taken from the East, remained in Europe for a few generations, before Prester John returned it East.

Alas, though we have come so far, we are now once again confronted with the fact that though the Grail is a stone, there are also several possible stones that could be *the* Grail; once again, it seems we are searching for the specific sacred stone that made it to the court of Aragon and which became known as the Grail.

To all intents and purposes, the "Ark of Aksum" could very well be *a* Grail. And hence, we are indeed confronted with a very bizarre situation: though there was only ever "the Grail", there were several sacred stones, each of which was apparently as powerful, and put oneself in contact with God, as the next. Indeed, nowhere is it mentioned that the Grail in the possession of the Grail Brotherhood was unique. If it was, would anyone have parted with it so easily, as seems to have happened? If the Grail was the only magical sacred stone in the entire world, would anyone have entrusted it into the safekeeping of an upcoming Spanish minor noble family? The answer has to be a definitive "no". Still, the question needs to be asked what this Grail stone was, and whether we can identify which, out of all possible stones, this sacred stone was.

Chapter 11: The identity of the Grail

In 2005, I found myself in the Mexican town of San Juan Chamula, outside of San Cristobal, in the state of Chiapas. In the mid 1990s, the region made headline news, as it was the stage for the Zapatista rebels, many of whom come from villages around Chamula. Today, the rebels are calm, but soldiers nevertheless remain close to tourists… just in case they need rescuing.

Chamula at first would appear to be just like any other mountain village, but Chamula has its own laws. And its own customs. It is considered sacrilege to enter the church with a hat on, to take photographs inside will earn you a trip to jail; but entering it with an opened can of beer in one hand and a lighted cigarette in the other is not offensive at all. If anything, the locals might appreciate you more…

From the outside, the church looks typical. It is dedicated to John the Baptist, but it is only very infrequently that a priest comes to do baptisms, the only sacrament observed in the church – which is perhaps properly, because of its dedication to the Baptist.

Once inside, you will find no pews; there is no altar. Instead, the walls are lined with glass cases, each containing a saint. These Catholic saints represent Mayan gods.

In a guidebook to the church, the people of Chamula explain that they worship the Father Creator – directly.

But the true importance of the Mayan origins of the town is easily overlooked: the stones at the bottom of the crosses that line the village square in front of the church. They might seem to be simple stones, but they represent something else: sacred stones. The local population worshipped sacred stones that were able to prophesise. They were the voice of the gods, who aided the local shamans in directing their people. The stones were said to have fallen from Heaven. When the Dominican friars came, they took the magical stones from the local shamans, which thus denied them the possibility to prophesise. The stones lining the square are the stones taken by the Dominican friars, but the locals know that their ancestors never gave the real sacred stones; they believe the stones lining the village square are replica, void of any magical charm; the real sacred stones are said to be guarded by families, who live in the hills surrounding the village. Everyone seems to know who they are, yet no-one will ever tell.

Hence, in Mexico, you find a religion that is based on a sacred stone, is linked with John the Baptist, is constructed around direct communication with the "Father Creator", the Creator God, whereby the sacred stone is now secreted away by families that are very much like a Grail brotherhood. Indeed, I could just as well be in San Juan Chamula, or in San Juan de la Peña, some centuries ago.

So, what is the Grail? In the sky, the Grail is represented by the constellation Crater. It is the symbol for the soul and the method of ascension to God. It fell to Earth, similar to Lucifer's Third Eye. Lucifer in the sky was linked with the planet Venus, the planet of the sunrise, dawn, the light bearer (literally, Lucifer), the beginning of a new era, which was equally identified with the Bennu bird – Venus and the bennu bird are linguistically close.[265]

Fallen on Earth, the Grail was also a physical object. Today, the Grail is believed by many to be the Cup of the Last Supper. It is the cup that modern tourists see a replica of when they visit San Juan de la Peña. If this is the Grail, then there is no longer any need for treasure hunters, as its whereabouts are known: the cathedral of Valencia.

Yet, when discussing the Grail as a Christian relic, Roger Sherman Loomis asked: "Would a holy relic or even a common paten or ciborium been placed in charge of a lovely damsel, not of a priest or a sacristan?" Answering his own question, he concluded: "No wonder the Church has never recognized the

Grail romances as authentic and has displayed a shrewd suspicion about their unorthodox background."[266] Indeed, if the Grail was indeed a Christian relic, why did Chrétien and Wolfram not identify it as Christian? Should the omission of a clear definition not side with the likelihood that the nature of the Grail is indeed pagan?

So, what is the Grail? At its first appearance, we are told that "this was a thing that was called the Grail, earth's perfection's transcendence." Richard Barber noted that "the Grail is a gateway to the spiritual world, a physical focus for the metaphysical."[267] Barber posits this in a largely literary way, but what if the stone was just that: a gateway? A stone that somehow was a gateway to the spiritual world – a communication device that enabled a person to communicate with God – the Creator Deity?

Let us immediately note that it is largely irrelevant whether God exists, or whether this stone was indeed able to accomplish this; what is important, is the question whether people *believed* they – through a sacred stone – were able to talk to God, or the gods. And the answer to that question, is a definitive yes.

Within the context of the *Corpus Hermeticum*, the central message of the Grail is not a treasure hunt, but a spiritual quest: a prize to be won. But despite this "spiritual prize", it is clear that Wolfram's Grail – and by extension the Hermetic Grail – is also a physical object, which aides the myst in his spiritual quest. Wolfram states the Grail was placed on Earth, and as angels descended and ascended to see it, it underlines its physical nature, as well as its unique nature, which is in line with the supernatural effects it is able to accomplish.

In the presence of angels, we are clearly in the presence of a "gateway". Wolfram stated that there were two groups of angels that visited the Grail. The first group returned to a heavenly region that is beyond the stars. This was the group that brought down the Grail to Earth. It is from that moment that baptized men have had the task of guarding it.[268] A second group of angels came to the Grail when the object was already on Earth. They are described as the neutral angels, "who took neither side when Lucifer and the Trinity fought – these angels, noble and worthy were compelled to descend to earth, to this same stone." In this explanation, Wolfram underlines that the Grail, though otherworldly in origin and somehow important for angels – "otherworldly beings" – nevertheless resides on Earth.

Its physical nature is also made clear when it is carried in the Grail procession in the Grail Castle. Yet even though an actual object, it is clear that it has otherworldy characteristics. When the unbaptised Feirefiz is present, he states that "I don't see anything but an emerald-green cloth" – the cloth on which Repanse de Schoye carries the Grail.[269] Later, it is said that "a barrier is raised around it" and that "lesser men" can thus not see it.[270] The appearance and disappearance of writing on the stone also suggest an otherworldly nature of the relic. The writing remains visible until a servant has been able to read the name of the person chosen to serve, and then it disappears.

The question is therefore what format the physical Grail assumes. Would it be a cup, to mimic its celestial counterpart, the constellation Crater? However tempting, specifically in light of its usual identification as the Cup of the Last Supper, Wolfram focuses on the nature, rather than the form of the object: it is a stone, not a stone in the shape of a cup… suggesting the Grail stone is in the form of an ordinary stone.

Wolfram stated that the Grail stone had fallen from heaven. Most often, the Graal is written as "lapsit exillis". Lapsit is not Latin, and hence early copyists often rendered it as "lapis exilis" or "iaspis exillis". Lapis means stone; exillis is a corruption and has been interpreted as "ex celis" – from heaven – or "exilii" – exile, i.e. the Stone of Exile, or "lapis exsulis", the Exile's Stone.

The correspondence is twofold, for there is the exile of Lucifer, who – if the jewel was once in his crown – lost it on expulsion from heaven, and there is the exile of humanity, which is the consequence of the fall of the angels.

Hence, though most have preferred to call it "stone from heaven", "the stone of exile" seems to be a more coherent translation, in light of the explanation given by Wolfram throughout his work, echoing the central doctrine of the Hermetica, that Man's soul had been exiled by God (the Fall, i.e. Lucifer), and its quest was to reunite itself over a series of incarnations; the return voyage, from exile to God, commenced when the myst had understood the Hermetic doctrine and joined "the Hermetic brotherhood", that body of awoken souls who had realised their spiritual mission.

Which Grail stone?

At the end of Indiana Jones' last crusade, he finds the Holy Grail – a cup – but its guardian has cleverly created an exhibit of dozens of chalices, amongst which the Grail is one. Of course, "Mr. Jones" is able to pick the right one.

The question we have to answer is whether, of all the possible Grails – sacred stones – we are able to identify *the* Grail stone.

The cult of sacred stones is both ancient and widespread, even in evidence with the Mayans in the Mexican heartland. We have seen how the cult object of the ancient Egyptians was the sacred benben stone. We can travel to the North of Europe, and 3000 year later, for another example. Here, the Saami (Lapss) tribe also worshipped sacred stones. Their "seidas", sacred stones, were usually situated on gentle rocky slopes and were quite similar to the megalithic monuments that are found in Western Europe. Some of the stones were natural rocks, others were shaped. The Saamis believed that the stones were the house in which spirits live. They were believed to help if animals (usually reindeer) were sacrificed. The sacrifice usually occurred near the seida, as the place where the stones laid was sacred. The sacrifice performed in or near the sacred stone is very similar to the regeneration of the phoenix that occurred on top of the benben stone.

This worship continued until at least the 10th century, very close in time to the Grail Court of Aragon. In Scotland, the worship of sacred stones even continued until the final decade of the 20th century. The Cailleach was the Celtic creator goddess. Deep inside Glen Lyon, a remote valley near Perth, an almost unique structure can be found to the creator goddess: the house of the Cailleach, or the Tigh Nam Bodach. This small stone structure, located high up the mountains at the head of Glen Lyon, is probably the only surviving shrine to the pagan Mother Goddess. Until his death some years ago, the last "servant" of the Mother Goddess was Bob Bissett, head stalker of the Invermeran estate.

The "house" was the home of the Cailleach (Mother Goddess), the Bodach (old Man) and the smaller Nighean (the Daughter), while two smaller children remained inside the house. The Cailleach and her family is symbolised by very heavy water-worn stones shaped like dumb-bells. The Cailleach herself is some 18 inches high, while her Daughter is only 3 inches tall.

The Cailleach resided past Loch Lyon, up Glen Cailleach, named after her. Fresh thatch was placed on the roof, and the stones were brought outside to watch over the herds during the summer. When the herds moved in October, the divine family were sealed up for the winter and the house was made weather tight. The ritual was said to have been performed for centuries until the pattern of farming changed, and as sheep replaced cattle, and the people moved away, the cult diminished – but Bob Bissett continued the custom.

Another well-known example of a sacred stone is the Stone of Scone, also known as the Coronation Stone or the Stone of

Destiny. Traditionally, the stone is believed to be that which Jacob used as a pillow when he had his dream of angels at Bethel. In Scotland, the stone had been kept at Scone Palace in Perthshire, where 34 successive Scottish kings had been crowned. According to tradition, the stone had been brought to Scotland from Ireland, where it had been used in the coronation ceremonies of the kings of Ireland on the Hill of Tara, their "primeval hill". The stone was brought to London by order of King Edward I in 1297, though Scottish legends state that the stone with which the English king ran off was a copy. Still, since the 13th century, every British king or queen (except for the first Mary) has been crowned monarch while seated in the chair over this stone.

The Stone of Scone thus shares aspects of the Grail stone: it is a gateway between Earth and Heaven, where angels ascend from and descend to, as witnessed by Jacob when he slept on it. It is linked with sacred kingship, the ancient tradition that the king was divinely appointed, which would grow into the image of Merlin and the magical sword; a sword which sits in a stone, whereby it seems that it is the stone who decides when to release the sword, thus identifying the future king. Like the Grail, the Stone of Scone possesses magical properties, though not in the form of writing: it is said that the stone could identify a rightful ruler of the country by emitting a loud cry, similar to the "release of the sword" of the Arthurian tradition.

The Greeks also had sacred stones at the centre of their religious experience. In the myth of Chronos, whom we have encountered in the Grail accounts as Titurel – the person who instigated the Grail Dynasty, Chronos – Time – had devoured his children, as he had been told that he would have been killed by one of them. When his wife Rhea gave birth to Zeus, she put *a stone* in the bands, rather than Zeus; Chronos swallowed a stone, without suspecting anything.

Archaeologists were able to retrieve the omphalos stone of

Delphi – or perhaps, as others have suggested, it was merely a copy. The stone was connected to Zeus and the recovered stone is made of a single piece of marble. The stone lay in the most important part of the temple of Apollo, near the Adyton, the seat of the Pythia. Here it helped her enter her trance – some believe that the high iron content of meteorite stones might have aided trance-like states, but as the omphalos of Delphi was possibly made of marble, this may not be a valid suggestion.

Like the Grail and the Stone of Scone, the Ka'aba which sits at the heart of Muslim religion was said to have been brought to Earth by an angel to record the deeds of the faithful, to be consulted on the Day of Judgement. The stone was the sole object from the pagan temple that the prophet Muhammed kept when he converted the shrine at Mecca into an Islamic temple. It underlines the power these sacred stones possessed.

The poet Ikbal Ali Shah stated that the Ka'aba was the heart of the body of the world: "And the stone that you call the Black Stone was itself a ball of dazzling light. In ages past, the Prophet said, it shone like the crescent moon, until at last the shadows, falling from the sinful hearts of those who gazed on it, turned its surface black. And since this amber gem, that came to earth from paradise with the holy ghost, has received such impressions upon itself, what should be the impressions which our hearts receive? Indeed, whoever shall touch it, being pure of conscience, is like him who has shaken hands with God."[271] Both the Grail and the Ka'aba are brought by an angel, placed as the centre of worship, on which names are written.

With so many stones to choose from, which one to pick? Obviously, some of these stones' history is well-documented; the stones of San Juan Chamula, nor those of the Cailleach, ever made it to Aragon. It is most unlikely that the Ka'aba stone, though being "in the East" from the perspective of Western Europe, was ever taken away. On the other hand, some important sacred stones disappeared from the annals of history, and chief amongst these, is the benben stone of ancient Egypt.

Commentators have noted that Wolfram cleverly mixed the imagery of the Grail as a container with that of a stone. It is a technique that was equally used in ancient Egypt, where the benben stone was both the container of the seed of Atum and a stone fallen from heaven, set at the centre of the world – on top of the pillar in Heliopolis. That one of the most important religious objects of the ancient Egyptian religion could simply disappear, is remarkable – but not unique, as the same fate befell the Ark of the Covenant. Still, it beggars belief that the ancient Egyptians – nor anyone else – ever noted the loss of the stone, and queried where it might have disappeared too. It disappeared from Heliopolis, but where, when, how, if not why, has never been questioned.

Speculating within this evidentiary void, it is possible that the benben stone was taken to the Siwa Oasis. The Grail came from the East, and we know that Gahmuret travelled in the East. Specifically, we know that Feirifez, in his role as the second myst, was identified with Hammon – Amun, who is the resident deity of the Siwa Oasis.

The Siwa Oasis plays an important role in the story of the *Corpus Hermeticum,* though in a somewhat circumstantial way. When the Greeks conquered Egypt, Alexander, for a reason that is not very clear, had to make his way to the Temple of Amun in the Siwa Oasis, where he was recognised as a divine ruler, which meant that he followed in the same tradition as all truly Egyptian rulers before him. Still, these Egyptian rulers had never travelled to the Siwa Oasis for that specific purpose. In fact, in the earliest history of ancient Egypt, it seems that the recognition of a Pharaoh as a divine ruler was the bailiwick of the priests of Heliopolis and we know that the benben stone played an important role in this. After all, the recognition of the "divine ruler" was the statement that the Pharaoh was the son of the Creator God; that he was therefore "of his seed". Again, we need to underline the parallel with the sacred stone of Arthurian tradition, whereby it is the stone that recognized who the true successor to King Arthur – the divine ruler – would be.

So, is it possible that the benben stone of Heliopolis, when it disappeared from its temple, was taken to the Siwa Oasis? Was this the reason why Alexander had to visit the oasis, where he could be recognised as the legitimate ruler?

It is a matter of record that the Siwa Oasis had a sacred stone. Perhaps the benben stone of Heliopolis was lost, and perhaps the sacred stone of the Siwa Oasis was therefore promoted as the "next best thing". Perhaps the sacred stone of Siwa was merely the benben stone under a new name.

Little remains of the Temple of the Oracle in the Siwa Oasis, though some hieroglyphic inscriptions can still be seen on the walls of the inner sanctum. The ruins of the Temple of the Oracle still exist, but for how long is questionable. The rock upon which it sits is cracking, and from time to time parts of it slide down. Fissures are seen on all side and we know that in ancient times, the rock was much larger. The temple is reached by climbing a path up the side of the rock it surmounts; a mini-rendition of a primeval hill. The temple does not occupy the entire area. Though the village was for the most part abandoned in 1926, after a heavy rainstorm, until very recently, at least some families actually lived in the temple.

The Greeks probably learned of the Oracle after they invaded the northern coast and established Cyrene (now Libya) in 637 BC. Afterwards, the Oracle was absorbed into Greek religion and associated with Zeus, whom the Greeks associated with the Egyptian Amun/Atum. The Oracle is reputed to have cursed Andromeda and she was tied to a rock to be devoured by a sea-

serpent. Perseus is said to have stopped off to visit the Oracle prior to beheading Medusa, and Hercules is though to have visited it before he fought Bursiris.

Cambyses, who ruled Egypt between 525 and 522 BC, wanted to destroy the Oracle, but he lost his army somewhere in the vast outreaches of the Western Desert. Pliny tells us that this was because the sacred stone at the temple was touched by sacrilegious hand, which caused a dreaded sand storm to rage. By the time that Strabo visited Siwa after the birth of Jesus Christ, he noted that the Oracle was no longer as powerful and was in decline. Though the Oracle eventually stopped uttering, the question once again remains where the stone of Siwa Oasis disappeared to.

The seed of the Creator God

J. Stuart Hay stated that "Elagabal [the sun-god of the Syrian city of Emesa] was worshipped under the symbol of a great black stone or meteorite, in the shape of a Phallus, which having fallen from the heavens represented a true portion of the Godhead, much after the style of those black stone images popularly venerated in Norway and other parts of Europe."[272]

The Egyptians were very clear and specific about what they considered the benben to be: the solidified seed of the Creator God. That the benben stone was a stone was not debated. But what type of stone? From the 1960s onwards, some Egyptologists have argued that the benben might have been a meteorite. Meteorites do fall from the sky and it would give these stones an otherworldly character. As the stars were linked with angels (and the constellation Crater with the Grail itself), perhaps meteorites were indeed seen as fallen gods – or messengers of the Gods, such as the Greek Hermes.

As the benben stone itself is missing for a chemical analysis, some scholars have based part of their argument upon descriptions of the Ka'aba, which "shone" when it was in the sky, but turned black when it fell upon the earth. For some authors, this is clear evidence that this stone turned black during its entry into the atmosphere and was originally seen as a shooting star. However logical it may appear, the "Black Stone" of the Ka'aba was originally white, but lost its brilliance because of the stain of the blood of the sacrifices that were performed in honour of the gods upon it. It has therefore nothing to do with burning meteorites. Still, meteorites are a logical choice for some of the other sacred stones, specifically when we note that the sacred stones were often known as sun or fire stones.

Meteorites have a known origin: the asteroid belt in our solar system. They are classified into three main groups: iron meteorites (usually 90 percent iron and ten percent nickel), stone/iron meteorites and stone meteorites. The largest group are the iron meteorites, which survive the impact with the ground more easily.

Meteorites come in all sizes: from the 25 metres meteor that created the wide Arizona crater to small fragments hardly distinguishable as such. One of the largest single known meteoritic mass is the 'Hoba' iron meteorite, found near Grootfontein farm in Southwest Africa. This meteorite is estimated to be a sixty ton chunk of iron. Several oriented iron meteorites weigh from five to fifteen tons.

If the benben stone was a meteorite, it would most likely sit in this category of magnitude. Intriguingly, when orientated meteorites hit the ground, they are found to be shaped like cones or pyramids, thus corresponding with the shape of the benben stone and enforcing the possibility that the benben was a meteorite.

Egyptologist Helmuth Jacobsohn of Marburg stated that the benben stone of Heliopolis was the archetype of the Philosopher's stone.[273] Some of the strange behaviour of the Grail stone could also be explained if it was a meteorite. Meteorites contain iron, and iron of course has magnetic properties. It is an intriguing coincidence that it is Guiot de Provins, one of the contenders for the role of Kyot, who speaks of a "la manete", the magnet, "une pierre laide et noirete", "an ugly and blackish stone".[274] It therefore suggests that the image of the Grail on Earth should be a stone – a loadstone.

References to iron and its relationship with the Grail – the Cup of Knowledge – can be found as far back as ancient Egypt. In the story of prince Naneferkaptah and his quest for the Egyptian grail, the "Sacred Text of All Knowledge" was kept in an iron box at the bottom of the river Nile. In the *Pyramid Texts,* we have references to the bones of the Gods being made from iron: "The king's bones are iron and the king's members are the imperishable stars..."[275] "I [the king] am pure, I take to myself my iron bones... my imperishable limbs are in the womb of Nut";[276] "my bones are iron and my limbs are the imperishable stars."[277] Graham Hancock even suggested that the Tablets on which the Ten Commandments were written and which were stored inside the Ark of the Covenant might be two pieces of meteorite.[278]

Iron was a novelty during the earliest history of ancient Egypt. Furthermore, British Egyptologist G.A. Wainwright has argued that the iron that was known in the Old Kingdom Period was mostly obtained from iron-meteorites. She added that ornamental beads made of iron date as far back as Pre-Dynastic times. Their analysis revealed high levels of nickel, which confirmed their meteoritic origin.[279] It should therefore not be a surprise to learn that the ancient Egyptian word "Bja" both meant "iron" as well as "material of which heaven was made". Black basalt was known as "Bja-Kam", meaning "black iron", suggesting that basalt and possibly granite were associated with meteorites. The capstones of monumental pyramids – benbenet – were probably made of granite, as is in evidence from the almost-black granite capstone of the pyramid of Amenemhet III, now in the Cairo Museum. It is this specific capstone that states that the benben is a doorway into another dimension, leading to God.

Though meteorites seem to be firm candidates, it is nevertheless difficult, apart from some magnetic qualities, to envision them as being capable of performing the magical feats the Grail is able to display. Why they should be linked with the seed of the Creator God is equally enigmatic. Still, some meteorites are believed to contain the building blocks of life and thus might have seeded life on this planet.

The theory that meteorites brought life to earth is known as panspermia. It is an an idea with ancient roots. The 5th century BC Greek philosopher Anaxagoras spoke of the "seeds of life" from which all organisms derive. The panspermia hypothesis was dormant until 1743, when it appeared posthumously in the writings of Benoît de Maillet, who suggested that germs from space had fallen into the oceans and grown into fish and later amphibians, reptiles and then mammals. In the 19th century it was again revived in modern form by several scientists, but panspermia began to assume a more scientific form through the proposals of scientific heavyweight such as Kelvin and Francis Crick, the co-discoverer of DNA's structure.

From 1903 onwards, the Swedish chemist Svante Arrhenius argued that life in the form of spores could survive in space and be spread from one planetary system to another by means of radiation pressure.[280] He generally avoided the problem of how life came about in the first place by suggesting that it might be eternal, though he did not exclude the possibility of living things generating from simpler substances somewhere in the universe.

More recently, scientists have been able to recreate the conditions of interstellar space in laboratory conditions. These experiments have taught them that life – specifically RNA, which is closely linked with DNA, which is at the core of life on Earth – originates "spontaneously" in the universe. That it could become attached to meteorites or asteroids and thus make its voyage to a planet like Earth, is a distinct possibility.

This would mean that the benben stone that carried the "seed of the Creator God Atum", his "seed", was a meteorite carrying the building blocks of life. This possibility creates new questions, such as how the ancient Egyptians would have known whether a stone had RNA or other genetic material attached to it, but to this complex question, I will merely provide two quick replies: "magic"; and that it is not important whether it actually had such material attached to it, but that it was important that they believed that a stone that had fallen from heaven had the seeds of life on it.

But, of course, it is never as simple as that. Some have argued that the correct rendering in Latin of Wolfram's Grail stone is "Iaspis exillis", which could indicate jasper. Albrecht, who continued Wolfram's story, called the stone "iaspis et silix" – jasper and flint. This identification would shift it from an iron-containing meteorite stone, but retain its aspect of being a precious stone.

It is known that the benben stone was present in Heliopolis by ca. 3000 BC, and could have been present even earlier. And some believe that rather than jasper, or meteorite, the benben stone was a real firestone: a stone that came from a volcano.

Though ancient Egypt did not experience volcanic activity firsthand, Egyptological investigations prove that obsidian found its way into Predynastic Egyptian craftsmanship. Alfred Lucas wrote that "So far as is known obsidian is not found naturally in Egypt, but it occurs in Abyssinia [Ethiopia], in the Sudan, in Arabia in the Aden Protectorate, in the Hadramaut and elsewhere, in Armenia, in Asia Minor and in various Mediterranean lands. Obsidian was used in Egypt in small amounts from predynastic times, at first in the form of flakes for use as implements, and as weapons, such as lance-heads. The subject of the use of obsidian in ancient Egypt, with particular reference to its place of origin, has been discussed at length by Wainwright, and shortly by Frankfort, the later of whom gives some physical constants of obsidian from various sources. Wainwright concludes that the obsidian used in Egypt was obtained from Armenia."[281]

There are both active and extinct volcanoes in the Middle East and it is, of course, the general region where Titurel found his Grail. But, largely, it seems an ill-fit, as obsidian seems to have been used in rather everyday objects, and does not seem to have been set aside any great religious reverence.

Still, Lucas believed that the greater part of the obsidian used in Egypt was brought to Egypt from Ethiopia, a view shared by W.F. von Bissing.[282] Predynastic trade with Ethiopia is further in evidence by the use of elephant ivory in Egypt.

This, of course, is of interest to us, as Ethiopia was the homeland of Prester John. Could it therefore be that the benben stone was of Ethiopian origins, was later returned to Ethiopia, the country of its origins, to be taken from there at some point to Aragon, from where it was, via Feirefiz and Prester John, once again returned to Ethiopia? It would make the movement of the Grail very much like a jojo-effect, but that in itself does give it an intriguing consistency.

In 1978, paleo-anthropologist Mary Leakey discovered sets of hominid footprints at Tanzania, Africa, which were hardened in volcanic ash. The footprints date to 3.6 million years ago. One can only wonder whether elsewhere, e.g. Ethiopia with its many volcanoes, our ancestors came upon these petrified footprints and began to dream away about the origins of Mankind.

Scholars in general hold that the earliest religions were closely associated with volcanoes because they contain fire. Historians believe that the first people to use fire collected it from trees ablaze from lightning strike and/or from spouting volcanoes, rather than learning to kindle it. Fire and Sun worship became closely associated, fire being seen as the earthly flesh of the Sun-god. And, as mentioned, the Egyptians, Greeks, and Romans tended sacred fires in their temples, and the "New Fire Ceremony" was an important event, linked with the New Year – which was also linked, in Egypt, with Heliopolis, the king and the benben stone.

The Oxford Old English Dictionary states that one suggestion for the etymology of the Greek word "pyramid" is fire. Some sources translate the word "pyramid" as meaning "fire in the middle." The imagery brings to mind an active volcano with its fiery interior. All of this would intimate that the Bennu bird or the Phoenix was originally a volcanic spirit rising from its ashes.

It is here that we need to tackle the hard question about how either meteorite or obsidian were able to induce visions, or actual contact, with the gods. What stone can apparently reveal the names of those who are called to serve? What stone seems to "ironise" the water that will be the initiation of the myst?

The benben stone of Amenemhet III, on display in the Cairo Museum, shows the deceased Pharaoh "as a small walking figure holding a sceptre in one hand and cupping a star in the other. This star or 'S'ba' to give it its Egyptian name has a dual meaning as a hieroglyphic. On the one hand it means 'star', but on the other it means 'gateway'."[283] Again, it underlines to role of the benben stone as a "stargate", an entrance into another dimension. Equally, the Grail stone was said to shine with an otherworldly light, and if the benben stone was ever to shine, it is clear that it must have been the light from the Otherworld – the sun at midnight that the initiate saw when he passed through the gateway of death.

The "sun at midnight" was at the core of many initiations, which conveyed to the initiate the certainty that death, the ultimate gateway, could be overcome. In scene 73 of the *Egyptian Book of Gates*, a variation of the famous *Book the Dead*, itself a variation on the *Pyramid Texts*, it is stated that the witness can gaze, without perishing, directly at the face of the sun.[284]

The "sun at midnight" is literally that: a sun that would shine in darkness; a brilliant light. As the initiation involves a symbolic death, it suggests that the mystery itself was a type of near death experience (NDE), a phenomenon that has been the subject of detailed studies since medical doctors and personnel began to observe the phenomenon in people that had been revived from the dead.

Whereas the Greeks considered this to be a secret revelation that one had to carry within oneself, Egyptian texts state that this glimpse was available to everyone, immediately upon crossing the threshold of death.[285] In NDEs, witnesses report a brilliant light at the end of a dark tunnel, which coincides with the image of the sun shining at midnight.

For the Greeks, to have this experience, either in the Eleusian Mysteries or the Pythia of Delphi, involved the presence of a cone-shaped rock, the omphalos, which was the Greek rendition of the benben stone. Both the omphalos and the benben stone were linked with birds (doves and the phoenix) and its cyclical return to the stone. It is here that we are match perfect with the Grail stone, carried by the Grail maiden (cf. the Delphic Pythia), who was able to mediate with the Otherworld and its deities through the sacred stone. What was in Heliopolis, was in Delphi, was in Eleusis, where, in the Eleusian Mysteries, just like the New Year rituals involving the Pharaoh at Heliopolis, we have further parallels with the Grail procession and the sacred meal held inside the Grail Castle.

Just as the Benben was Egypt's most sacred stone, the Omphalos was the most sacred stone of Delphi. Like the Benben, the Omphalos was considered the first matter to emerge from the receding waters of chaos. All of these match perfectly with the details given by Wolfram as to the nature of the Grail stone.

So, when we know that the Benben represented the foundation and centre of the world, the place where Atum alighted as the Bennu and set forth all of creation with a cry from his beak, so we know that this imagery was worked into Wolfram's *Parzival.*

Though we may never know whether the Grail stone is identical with, or similar to, the benben stone – until we either find the benben and/or Grail stone – we have identified beyond any doubt the nature of the Grail and discovered the framework in which it operated. The question remains what type of stone would be able to induce a near death experience, or shine with an otherworldly light. But we know that the ancient Greeks believed the omphalos was able to do this, and the ancient Egyptians believed similarly about the benben stone. We merely have to accept the Grail Brotherhoodd believed the same about the Grail stone.

Still, the magnetic qualities of the Grail and benben stone are persuasive. A specific reference can be found in the final phrase of Chapter 4 of the *Corpus Hermeticum*: "And now, O Tat, God's Image has been sketched for you, as far as it can be; and if you will attentively dwell on it and observe it with your heart's eyes, believe me, son, you'll find the Path that leads above; indeed, that Image shall become your Guide itself, because the Sight [Divine] has this peculiar [charm], it holds fast and draws unto it those who succeed in opening their eyes, just as, they say, the magnet [attracts] iron."[286]

It expresses the notion that for anyone who knows what the initiate now knows, that person will be drawn to God, like iron to a magnet… like the Servants of the Grail are attracted to the Grail… and through it, into the Otherworld, to God. But it is clear that in this instance, the magnetic properties of iron are used metaphorically: "To be capable of knowing God, and to wish and hope to know him, is the straight road which leads to the Good, and it is an easy road."[287]

Hermes' Stone

The connection between sacred stones and Hermes takes an interesting turn with the Greek author Pausanias. According to Pausanias,[288] "In olden times all the Greeks worshipped unwrought stones instead of images" and then described thirty square stones near a spring sacred to Hermes at Pharae in Greece. This is an important item of information, for it is of course Hermes that is at the centre of the *Corpus Hermeticum*. Pausanias thus links the cult of Hermes with the cult of sacred stones. Pausanias added that "in the gymnasium not far from the market-place [of Athens], called Ptolemy's from the founder, are stone Hermai well worth seeing."[289]

Thus, he actually labels certain sacred stones "Hermai", underlining the connection. Later, he adds: The Athenians are far more devoted to religion than other men ... they were the first to set up limbless Hermai."[290]

"Hermai" in Greek means "stone" and it is the root of "Hermes". Hermes in Greek is 'Ερμης' and means "pile of marker stones". It should therefore not come as a surprise that in Greek mythology, Hermes was also the god of boundaries – and doorways into other dimensions?

This identification smoothes out the final wrinkle in our argument: the connection between the *Corpus Hermeticum* and the Grail as a stone: the Grail was a sacred stone, dedicated to Hermes.

It was Hermes who called his servants to him, it was he who wrote the name on the Grail stone, as an invitation to become members of his Hermetic brotherhood. That Hermes was also the patron god of travellers is therefore very apt, for each myst in search of enlightenment is indeed a traveller, walking the path of life, on his voyage to enlightenment. The image of a gateway is equally appropriate: on our voyage, there will come a moment in which "things change". For a physical traveller, this is normally the moment when he sheds his fear of airplanes, delays, cancellations or mixed-up hotel and car bookings. For the spiritual traveller, it is the moment when he becomes convinced that he is on a sacred mission. For our spiritual voyager, the Grail is the gateway that transforms him from a stumbling, fearful being into a man with a clearly defined mission, having accepted the challenge; a man who has become a member of the Hermetic/Grail Brotherhood.

This man has "shed" his old skin. The phoenix is the symbol of the initiate, who would shed his old clothes and would be reborn a "new man". In *The Book Of The Dead* (Chapter 83), in the "Spell For Becoming The Phoenix (Bennu) Bird", the phoenix claims: "I am the seed corn of every god..."[291] Within the Hermetic framework, the seed of the Creator God is just that: the belief that within each person, there is a seed of the divine, of the Creator God. It is the task of the myst to nurture this innate divine seed of the Creator God into growth.

Descriptions of what the hermai stones looked like have survived; they were carved with the head and phallus of Hermes. The phallus is a reference to the seed of the Creator God, like the phallic pillar of Heliopolis carried the benben seed on its top – its head.

This image of a head and a phallus may explain the Baphomet of the Templars. Baphomet was after all a cipher for Sophia, the Goddess of Wisdom – an equivalent of Hermes. Baphomet was said to have been a detached head – and so was also a Hermai. We know that Hermes Trismegistus means "thrice great", but another title of Hermes was Trikephalos – three headed. He assumed this role when he became a teacher to travellers and instructed them into where the roads would lead them. This is the role of Hermes in the Hermetica, where the god instructs the initiate on the roads he can take in his life. The boundary stones along the path were markers of the initiate's voyage.

The Grail stone revealed its message through writing – similar to the tradition of the Ka'aba stone, which recorded the names of those who would be deemed worthy at the Day of Judgment. But the ancient gods also spoke and it is here that the role of the "head" of the Hermai takes on its full significance.

There are several examples of speaking statues: the Stone of Scone cried out when a king had to be selected; the Bennu bird equally cried out from its seat on the benben stone. Elsewhere in ancient Egypt, the Colossi of Memnon originally represented Amenhotep III and Rameses II. The statues flanked the entrance to the great temple of Amenhotep, now crumbled in the desert sands. From the first to third centuries AD, the colossus was famed for the eerie twanging sound it emitted at dawn, which was interpreted by the Greeks and Romans as the cry of the Ethiopian hero Memnon (who was killed at Troy) as he greeted his mother, Aurora, the goddess of the dawn – symbolising a new era, a new cycle.

The sonic phenomenon was, in fact, caused by the thermal strength of the rising sun, which, while warming and expanding the stone of the statue's base, came into contact with the cool channels of air running through the crevices of the statue's hollow interior, thus producing a mysterious sound effect. It is unlikely that the auditory phenomenon was intentional; nevertheless, it was not the only example of statues – the Gods – "speaking". And most of these incidents are far more otherworldly than the Colossi of Memnon.

The living spirit of the Sphinx had apparently spoken to one Pharaoh who was sleeping between its front paws, asking him to clear the statue from the desert sands. Bob Brier, in *Ancient Egyptian Magic,* states that "according to various ancient texts oracles could nod their heads and even talk. Since no talking oracle statue has ever been found, we are not certain how this was done. Perhaps the priests surreptitiously pulled strings to make the head nod or, divinely inspired, spoke for the god."

These stories may seem to belong only to the realms of ancient Egypt or Antiquity, but Pope Sylvester II (999-1003) was publicly accused by Cardinal Benno of sorcery, on account of his "Brazen Oracular Head." Albertus Magnus also allegedly made a talking head. The head was allegedly smashed to pieces by Thomas Aquinas, because it talked too much. We already came upon Magnus because of his known exposure to Hermetic literature. We can only wonder whether his talking head and his knowledge of the Hermetica are purely coincidental, or evidence that the Hermetic literature somehow allowed its student to create such a talking head.

Knowledge of the creation of talking heads seems to have survived in Muslim Spain. Pope Sylvester II, or to give him his real name, Gerbert, was a native of Aurillac, in the French Auvergne, who went to Spain in search of learning in the 960s. A French chronicler of the mid-11th century tells us that Gerbert went as far as Cordoba "in quest of wisdom", i.e. in search of Hermetic knowledge. Some indeed doubt that he went as far as Cordoba, though it is known that he spent some time at the monastery of Ripoll in Catalonia. Some argue that Gerbert studied in the Moorish schools in Spain and that he learned the skills of magic and creating an oracular head while in Spain. One allegation against this pope was that he would even have founded a "papal school of magic" in Rome!

Some years after his return to France, he wrote from Rheims to a certain Lobet of Barcelona asking for a copy of a work on astrology "translated by you". We know from other sources that Lobet was archdeacon of Barcelona, and although we cannot now identify the work which Gerbert wanted to borrow, we do know that Lobet translated another work from Arabic concerned with the use of the scientific instrument known as the astrolabe. Gerbert himself later composed a work on the astrolabe that seems to derive from a similar work (though probably not Lobet's) written in Catalonia in the late 10th century.[292]

Gerbert is evidence of the possibility – if not probability – that knowledge of making "talking Hermes heads" – stones that were able to predict the future and give divine guidance to its users, was present within Muslim Spain. That this knowledge would become known to the Aragon king, is not a great leap of faith – if anything, it is logical and to be expected. That it seems likely, is evidenced by the story of the Grail itself, where we are confronted with a magical stone, with oracular power, in the possession of the kings of Aragon, inside their Grail castle of San Juan de la Peña.

One contradiction does remain, and it is fundamental to the identity of the Grail: a Hermai stone does not resemble the conical shape of the benben. The two are largely mutually exclusive. So where does this leave us?

I argue that the Hermai stone was a representation of the actual benben or Grail stone. The Hermai stone shared many of its characteristics, but in essence, was a representation of the god – not the god itself. The Hermai stone was equipped with his symbols: it has a head, to symbolise its oracular power; it has a phallus, to symbolise the seed of the Creator God. But it is not the God – it *represents* the God; it is used by people who did not have the most powerful sacred relic themselves, but instead had a representation of it. The Knights Templar protected the Grail, but each house did not have a piece of it; it seems that each house did have a Baphomet – a Hermai, to symbolise their allegiance to the Grail. For any myst, the Hermai visualised the choices and boundaries of his journey, towards the Sacred Centre itself – the Grail.

The Aragon Grail

We know that the Aragon kings were and wanted to be buried in San Juan de la Peña, in the presence of the Grail. The tomb of

Alexander the Great has never been found, and whereas some people argue that it must be somewhere in Alexandria, the Siwa Oasis is another strong contender. What is certain is that Alexander himself expressed the desire to be buried in the Siwa Oasis. Marcus Junianus Justinus wrote that "... his body was to be transported, with all of the sombreness and ceremony due such an occasion, to the Temple of Ammon Ra, and Arridaios would be responsible for carrying out this task."[293] Diodorus Siculus wrote that "Arridaios was responsible for the construction of the funeral carriage and the transport of Alexander's body to [the oracle at] Ammon."[294]

To be the son of the creator-sun god Amun-Ra is a great privilege, reserved for the Pharaohs, similar to the Greek story of Phaeton, the son of the sun god Helios. When Phaeton ("the shining one") learned who his father was, he went East to meet him. He induced his father to allow him to drive the chariot of the sun across the heavens for one day. The horses, feeling their reins were held by an unsteadier hand, ran wildly out of their course and came close to Earth, threatening to burn it. Zeus noticed the danger and with a thunderbolt he destroyed Phaeton. He fell down into the legendary river Eridanus, where he was found by the river nymphs who mourned him and buried him. The tears of these nymphs turned into amber. For the Ethiopians, however, it was already too late: they were scorched by the heat and their skins had turned black.

It is a powerful myth, using all the characteristics that we have seen before. It is the story of the advent of a new age, in which the sun god may give rise to a successor. But the successor is weak, and as a consequence, the Earth is almost "baptised by fire". As punishment, Phaeton is struck down. Specifically, there is a reference to the black faces of the Ethiopians, who of course make an appearance in Wolfram's story, and hold a key position in the figure of Feirefiz, the second myst, whose identification just happens to be with the sun god Amun-Ra also.

There is one author, Pliny, who has made a connection between the story of Phaeton and the Siwa Oasis: "Chares vero Phaoethontem in Aethiopia."[295] The passage is the only authority for the existence of a shrine of Phaeton anywhere – *anywhere* – in the world. Specifically, it locates Phaeton's fall not in "Eridanus", but in Ethiopia, which he locates not in current Ethiopia, but in the Siwa Oasis.[296] Pliny quoted his source: he attributed it to Chares, who was a member of Alexander the Great's entourage and thus must have visited the famous temple of Amun at the Siwa Oasis.

Thus, in Alexander's time, the Siwa Oasis was believed to be the site where Phaeton had fallen to Earth; it was also Ethiopia. It may explain why Alexander had to go there, to be recognised as a divine ruler in the tradition of all sun kings before him. It also – almost miracously – smooths out our problems about identifying the realm as Prester John, and whether it was in Ethiopia or the Siwa Oasis.

The Oracle at the Siwa Oasis still existed in early Christian times. And even though the Oracle was in decline, there is no mention of the sacred stone of Siwa, which was at its core. Was the decline related to the loss of prophetic powers of the stone, or was the decline merely a sign of the new times? In the latter scenario, perhaps the stone was taken out of the temple, and hidden elsewhere, served and protected by a small group of people, most likely under the rule of local chieftains.

It is possible that Gahmuret – Geoffrey II de Perche – visited the Siwa Oasis. If the Siwa Oasis was the area where he found his beloved Belcane, then she may have told him of this one-time precious relic. If he married into the local royal bloodline, he would have been the protector of this sacred relic – if the relic was still in their possession.

Even though it was Titurel that is said to have received the stone from the East, there are no details as to how he got it.

Furthermore, why Perceval and later Feirefiz take on *such* an important role as the Grail king is slightly odd. Even though they were nephews of the Aragon king at a time when the bloodline was in peril, it seems that there is more to it than meets the eye – and that was written down by Wolfram's pen.

Could it be that in the middle of the 11th century, certain Europeans passed through the Siwa Oasis? This is more than likely. Is it possible that the local rulers gave their prized possession to these passing knights, ending up in the Grail castle of San Juan de la Peña? If Geoffrey II de Perche was indeed a ruler – if only in name – of the Siwa Oasis, like Feirefiz would be after him, then he had a claim to the Grail stone – just like his son, Rotrou II de Perche, had. Is this part of the reason why Gahmuret's son would go in search of the Grail? Was it perhaps part and parcel of his inheritance – an inheritance from his father, and his nephew, with whom the Grail was in residence?

Once Feirefiz was baptized, he witnessed the Grail. As soon as he had seen the Grail, writing on the Grail stated that any Templar whom God should bestow on a distant people for their lord must forbid them to ask his name or lineage, but must help them gain their rights: "The members of the Grail Company are now forever averse to questioning, they do not wish to be asked about themselves." Whereas the existence of the Grail Brotherhood at the court of the Aragon kings in San Juan de la Peña had not been a secret, the Grail had now commanded its servants to transform the sacred Brotherhood into a secret brotherhood – a secret society.

Feirefiz made his preparations to return to his homeland, together with Repanse de Schoye. He invited Anfortas, now his brother-in-law to join them, but he declined: "I do not wish my urge to serve God to come to nothing. The Grail Crown is of equal worth. Through arrogance I lost it. But now I have chosen humility. Possessions and love of women are far from my thoughts. [...] Never again shall I fight for love of woman."

As to Wolfram, he said that he intended "to speak no more of it than what the Master [Kyot] uttered over there. I have named Perceval's sons and his high lineage correctly, and have brought him to the goal which a happy dispensation intended for him, despite his setbacks. When a man's life ends in such a way that God is not robbed of his soul because of his body's sinning and who nevertheless succeeds in keeping his fellow's good will and respect, this is a useful toil."

As to the Grail? "Lohengrin [Perceval's son] grew to be a strong and valiant man in whom fear was never seen. When he was of an age to have mastered the art of chivalry, he distinguished himself in the service of the Grail." Lohengrin married, but he never told his wife anything of his secret alliance to the Grail – even though it seems that he once made a voyage to see it again.

And that, it seems, is all that Wolfram said... The Grail Brotherhood had become a secret brotherhood, operating within the royal dynasties of Europe, just like before it had worked within the bloodlines of the ancient Egyptian dynasties. Once again, the sacred task of the search for Hermes and his knowledge had become a secret mission. Since Alfonso I's failure and forfeiting of the Grail, it was the Grail – not the Brotherhood – who instructed its servants to become secret adherents.

Two centuries later, when the Knights Templar were disbanded, was the Grail still giving its commands, from somewhere in Europe? Or Ethiopia? Was it still trying to convert Europe into a Grail Kingdom? When they were abolished, were the Knights Templar still the henchmen, ruled by a secret inner core, who followed the commands of the secret Grail Brotherhood? Or were other people now the servants of the Grail – keepers of the Grail, keeping the secret...

As to the Grail? It seems to have remained under the control of the now secret Grail Brotherhood and the Aragon kings. But Wolfram's story ends in 1137… he did not want to say what happened afterwards; and we ourselves, though willing to trace the story of the Grail beyond Alfonso I's time, will leave that story for another time. We will end, where Wolfram ended…

Epilogue: The Grail Crusade?

In the final analysis, the "Grail Brotherhood" was a group of nobles with a common cause: to spread across Europe a new form of government, in which "enlightened rulers" would shepherd their countries. The masterplan of the Grail Brotherhood was a carefully constructed plan, in which existing family ties were used to forge ties with other family relationships, in an effort to extend the sphere of influence of the Brotherhood.

The scope of the project was extensive, but in theory virtually impossible to realise. It is one thing to inject a new way of thinking into Western society, it is another to seize control of the various powers in Europe. A millennium onwards, Europe is far less segmented than it was in the 12th century, but even in a time when there are clear directives for a "United Europe", the various nations can still not forge this alliance easily.

From the germination of the idea by Ramiro I until Rotrou's ascendancy as Grail King – a period of less than one century – the project was de-scoped. Originally, every noble who had heard about the plan, wanted to be part of this idea. But Perceval issued the warning that though many nobles thought they could join the Grail Brotherhood, in the end, it was up to the Grail to call them.

This change in scope is reflected in the popularity of the Knights Templar. At the organisation's official inception, in 1128, many nobles forsook all earthly possessions and allied themselves with the new order. In the following decades, this almost miraculous uptake slowed down; by the time of the order's abolition in 1312, hardly any serious nobility remained within the ranks of the order.

The message of the Grail has always been two-fold. Even though the Brotherhood in its native format was short-lived, the Hermetic aspect did lead to a "12th century Renaissance", which itself inspired the 15th century Florentine Renaissance.

At the core of the Renaissance and the Grail was the idea of a return to the type of divinely appointed rule that had existed in ancient Egypt. Though the idea of the Waste Land is more Arthurian in nature than Grail-related, the *Corpus Hermeticum* does contain the Lament. This treatise is a prophecy, speaking of a time when the gods of ancient Egypt will be "dead": no longer worshipped, Egypt has become a land of tombs and temples, where the presence of the gods is no longer felt. The hope of the Lament, the Grail and the Renaissance was to reawaken these ancient principles and reinstate a new form of divine rule: a theocracy, this time not ruling Egypt, but a unified Europe.

Ever since the 12th century, there have been sporadic attempts to create such a form of government. During the Renaissance, mystics wandered the streets of Florence, Venice and Rome, urging people to join them and build a new "Heliopolis", a new City of the Sun, in which divine rule would be established. Alas, what these mystics lacked, was worldly power and hence, they have gone down in the history books as "sects", rather than see them as offshoots of a more general social trend that was trying to emanate in Europe.

The late 11th and early 12th century court of Aragon was a court of the Grail – where the Hermetic principles reigned in the presence of a sacred stone. Despite the problems facing Alfonso I, his court was a Grail court, where divine rule existed. It is in evidence in San Juan de la Peña's mausoleum, where the layout is not so much of a cemetery, but of a carefully thought-out sanctuary, in which sacred water was canalised so that it would wash the bodies of the Aragon kings.

One century after Alfonso's rule, Wolfram von Eschenbach was writing about Perceval from his home in Germany, at a time when the region where he had learned about the Grail was in turmoil. In the area of the Pyrenees and Aragon, a new religion had arrived, which would become known as Catharism.

The tremendous popularity of the cult would eventually force the Pope to organise a Crusade against a Christian country – France – in an effort to stop its spread to other French counties and European nations – and reclaim the Pyrenean lands, and safeguard Europe, to the Christian cause.

The dualist Cathar religion has been both demonized and romanticized. At the peak of their existence in 13th century Europe, they were characterized as satanic demon worshippers. Today, the Cathars are most often portrayed as pacifist vegetarian feminists, medieval New Agers who were ruthlessly put down by a supposedly reactionary and corrupt Catholic Church. In fairness to both parties, the movement was neither.

The origin of Cathar beliefs has never been precisely identified, but there is a consensus that they derived from the dualist Bogomil sect in Byzantinium. Like the Bogomils, Cathars were dualists: they believed in the duality of the soul, which both had a divine spark, yet this divine spark had been subjected to the monstrous evil of the material world. This, of course, is also the very core of the Hermetic doctrine.

Whereas Christianity had classified Satan as being controlled by God, the Cathars believed that the material world was the reign of Satan, whereby God had little influence on this plane. Though God may have been more powerful, it meant that for man's task in life, both good and evil were balanced, presenting the challenge to Mankind, whose mission was to turn to God, and end his submission to materialism.

What is special about Catharism, is that it arrived on the scene at a time and in the sphere of influence when the Hermetica made its entrance in the Aragon kingdom. Is it a coincidence that the nearest countries to Aragon, specifically the County of Foix, was the heartland of the Cathar movement, and that it had the full support of the count himself?

One of the leading authors on Catharism, Yuri Stoyanov, has noted the parallel between the Cathar duality and the Egyptian doctrine, making specific references to the role of Heliopolis within the framework of Egyptian dualism.[297] He agrees that "the idea of the transformation of light into darkness" – the controversy of God vs. Satan – "as well as another Egyptian cosmogonic notion, which envisaged the primeval darkness as encircling the created universe, survived in some tracts of the Hermetic literature."[298] The Hermetica states that "they [the mysts] deem their sojourn here on earth a thing to be deplored; and having scorned all beings corporeal and incorporeal, they press on to reach the One and only."[299] Furthermore, "If you do not first hate you body, my son, you cannot love yourself"[300] maps perfectly on the hatred of the body the Cathars had. Cathars rejected sex as a continuation of the human soul's entrapment in earth-bound carnal evil. According to Cathars, marriage was a form of prostitution. Children were born as demons until they could be consciously lead to choose salvation in the Cathar path.

Furthermore, it has been suggested by the likes of Otto Rahn, E. Anitchkof and Julius Evola that some of the ideas provided to Wolfram by the mysterious Kyot originated with the Cathars. Though I believe that the true core of Wolfram's message is his exposure to a specific Hermetic treatise, rather than having had conversations with Cathar adherents, it is undeniable that the Languedoc at the time of Wolfram and Kyot was, in essence, a region where Catharism was the main religion.

The presence of Hermetic thinking within Cathars was profound. The Cathar priests were known as "perfecti", perfect man, which was the same name used for those who had received enlightenment in the Hermetic literature. The word Cathar itself comes from the Greek καθαϱοι, meaning "Pure Ones".

It would go too far to suggest that Catharism and Hermeticism were the same, but in general, they were based on the same core belief: that given Nous, a person could realise the truth and begin his ascent to God, discarding materialism and various earthly incarnations because of an overindulgence in affairs of the Earth.

The Pure Ones were strict vegetarians, abstaining from all animal products. They were celibate, although many of the ordinary believers were married. They believed that the world had been created by Lucifer and belonged to the devil. They believed that Lucifer had waged war against Heaven, as a result of which souls had been trapped in fleshly bodies.

Note therefore that one of the stories about the origin of the Grail states that it was a jewel that fell from Lucifer's crown. According to Wolfram, the Grail was a stone that was brought to Earth by the neutral angels, those who did not take sides in the warfare between God and Lucifer. Though to the unobserving eye there may be little to connect the story of Lucifer with the story of the Grail, when we note that the story of Phaeton is equally similar to Lucifer's fall from heaven, it forms an accumulation of evidence that suggests that an important stone plays an important role in the war in Heaven, between Lucifer and God, involving all the angels and wherein humanity is but a small aspect of. Yet those who were to possess this stone, would obviously be seen to play an important role in the future of Mankind, and politics. Again, whether such an object – the Grail – was genuinely placed on Earth by the neutral angels or not, is of secondary importance; what is important, is that some, or several people believed the Grail was a prized possession that was paramount in the religious salvation of Mankind.

Any path to salvation, and transformation of European society, will come with social transformations. And in 12th century Europe, one of the great discriminations was the inequality of the sexes. In Wolfram's Grail Brotherhood, we see the presence and equality of men and women, even though specific functions have been reserved either for men or for women: the carrying of the

Grail is a specific female privilege.

The Cathar Church also allowed for a higher than usual presence of women, who were even allowed to be "parfaits". Indeed, perhaps the biggest social nonconformity of Wolfram's account is that a woman is allowed to hold a religious office: the role of Grail bearer; it would have been unique, were it not for the fact that within the Cathar Church, women were also allowed to hold office.

Statistical analysis of Inquisition records show that of 719 identified active perfecti and perfectae, 318 were women, a little under 45 percent. This is a very high number, compared to how many women were nuns in the Catholic Church compared to all the priests, officials, monks, friars, clerks and other men engaged in official Church duty. It is therefore clear that the elite strata of the faith drew women. On the other hand, in analyzing 466 identified credenti followers or believers, only 125 were women, roughly 28 percent, indicating that Cathar beliefs were of less interest to the average medieval woman.

Still, the role of female perfectae and male perfecti was not identical. The perfectae were not allowed to perform the ritual of consolomentum, a type of Cathar baptism normally carried out in preparation for dying, as well as the raising of a credent to the rank of a perfect. Though some might see this as evidence that women were not totally equal, I would argue that the religion primarily endorsed that certain roles had to be performed by men, and others by women, like the Grail bearer not only had to be a woman, but also a virgin.

Some of the rituals of the Grail and those of the Cathars seem identical. Among the rituals at the Grail castle was a "showing" of the holy stone on Good Friday, which we know was linked with the spring equinox and the initiations of candidates into the Brotherhood, seen as confirmation that they had accepted their spiritual mission. The function of the Grail or "Cup" in such events was to symbolize the immersion of the soul in an experience bringing about union with the higher self.

During the siege of Montségur, beginning in 1243, we know that the papal troops gave special leniency to the people inside once the spring equinox in March 1244 approached: an extension of the deadline of surrender was given, which meant that the Cathars would come out after the spring equinox festival.

Some have labelled Montségur as the Grail Castle itself. Though it is not, that it sits on top of a mountain that looks like one giant conical primeval hill should perhaps not be seen as a coincidence, and might perhaps have been the reason why some believed it was the Grail Castle. Indeed, though it was not "the" Grail Castle, it obviously was chosen by the Cathars because the site itself was seen as an area of great religious significance. The "Seat" of their Church on top of the Pog of Montségur was religiously identical to the "Seat" of Atum on top of his Primeval Mound; Montségur was for the Cathars what Heliopolis was for its priesthood. And it is no doubt divine irony that like the Phoenix burnt upon his ashes to be reborn and announce a new era, the burning of so many Cathar priests after the siege of Montségur signalled a new era for that religion too.

The "Grail masterplan" never came about, but Catharism spread rapidly in Europe. In the Languedoc, it had virtually caused the collapse of the Catholic Church, which is why in 1208, Pope Innocent III launched the Crusade against them. Soon, the Catholic Church would create the Inquisition, initially with the purpose of eliminating all traces of the Cathar heresy from France, Spain and northern Italy.

The real danger of Catharism was twofold. On the one hand, it was popular with the general public. On the other hand, it was supported by the local lords, many of whom converted to Catharism. This meant that Catharism was both a political and a religious problem, which had in the Counts of Toulouse, one of the most powerful families in Europe, one most important ally. Though the Cathar Crusade is now often seen as a cruel act of the Catholic Church to suppress dissenting minorities within Europe, the fact is that Catharism was not a minority religion, and the Catholic Church – rightfully – felt it was fighting for its survival. Of course, the Catholic Church could have chosen for a "live and let die" approach to the problem, but instead decided to "act or die".

At the time of the outbreak of the Cathar Crusade, the Count of Toulouse was Ramon VI. He was linked to the King of England through one of his wives, Jeanne of England, and was also related to the King of France and the King of Aragon. Most of the lands he held under the feudal system were held as a vassal of the King of Aragon, but some (notably Provence) he held from the Holy Roman Emperor, with others from the King of France and the King of England.

The Counts of Toulouse were arguably the most enlightened rulers in Europe; they could be seen as the first wave of Hermeticism that the Grail Brotherhood was trying to seed across Europe. But the counts paid a high price: public flogging, dispossession and ultimately the extinction of their noble House. But despite the best efforts of the Roman Church to demonise their memory and of successive French governments to efface all vestiges of their rule, there are still powerful links in the Languedoc to a clearly remembered Golden Age, before the territories of the Counts of Toulouse were annexed to France… when this part of Europe was in the process of becoming a Grail Country. Let us also not forget that just east of this, the Knights Templar too were apparently trying to create an independent state; the plan, though it never materialised was obvious: the kingdom of Aragon and Catalonia, the Knights Templar new state, and the territories ruled by the Counts of Toulouse, could easily have become a new political entity – and a large, powerful player at that.

Chrétien's and Wolfram's account were written at the time when Catharism in the South was reaching its historical climax – when the pope ordered its total suppression, in order to safeguard the power of his Church, and the status quo of those nations allied to him. This new wave of literature must have worried the Church, as Wolfram's Hermetic message might have found a fertile plain in Northern Europe. That the Grail was therefore quickly "christianised" can be seen as a necessary step to guarantee that Hermetic thinking did not spread across Europe. The Grail *had* to become a Christian relic and what better Christian relic could there be than the Cup of the Last Supper?

And, as such, when the Cathar Crusade was being preached, and, as far as we can tell, Wolfram was laying the final hand on *Parzival*, it were not merely the Cathar perfects of Béziers that would fall victim to the destruction of the "Cathar heresy"; Wolfram's *Parzival*, to some extent, was a victim of that crusade too. In that respect, Otto Rahn was correct in titling his book *Crusade against the Grail*.

With the Cathar Crusade, the hope of turning the Wasteland fertile would have to wait – for its next cycle. During the Cathar Crusade, the Knights Templar remained neutral, very much like those neutral angels who had stood by when the War in Heaven was ravaging. But Peter II, King of Aragon and Barcelona, could not remain silent or neutral; he showed his alliance with the Cathar cause.

He was the son of Alfonso II of Aragon and Sancha of Castile. In 1205, he had acknowledged the feudal supremacy of the papacy and was the first king of Aragon to be crowned by the Pope. He had led the Christian forces to defeat the Moors at the Battle of Las Navas de Tolosa in 1212, but when he returned that autumn, he found that Simon de Montfort had conquered Toulouse, exiling Count Raymond VI of Toulouse, who was Peter's brother-in-law and vassal. This, he could not allow to happen.

Peter crossed the Pyrenees and arrived at Muret in September 1213 to confront Montfort's army. He was accompanied by Raymond of Toulouse, who tried to persuade Peter to avoid battle and instead starve out Montfort's forces. This suggestion was rejected as cowardly and unknightly. Like his ancestors, Alfonso I, Peter II would ride into battle.

The Battle of Muret began on 12 September 1213. The Aragonese forces were disorganized and disintegrated under the assault of Montfort's squadrons. Peter himself was caught in the thick of fighting, and being clad in ordinary armour, was mistaken for a common knight. He was thrown to the ground and killed. The Aragonese forces broke in panic when their king was slain and the crusaders of Montfort won the day. The question should be posed, is whether this was just another battle, or whether there was indeed much more at stake than Peter helping out his vassal and family member.

Driven by his deep interest in Catharism and Grail legends, Otto Rahn researched and travelled widely in France, Spain, Italy and Switzerland, from 1928 to 1932. Early in the summer of 1929, Rahn arrived in the Languedoc. He quickly settled in the village of Lavelanet and over the next three months systematically explored the ruined Cathar temple-fortress of Montségur, as well as the surrounding mountain grottoes. After several years of study, he believed with total conviction that the Cathars were the last owners of the Holy Grail and that the Holy Grail "perished" when they died at the hands of the "pope and the King of France" at the beginning of the 13th century. He felt that somehow, the Earth had split open in Montségur and the Earth had swallowed the Grail stone.

As many other men of his generations, Rahn often took things too literally, but it is clear that Catharism and the Grail tradition went hand in hand, and that the demise of the former, also signalled the death of the latter. But Rahn was also one of a series of pioneers, who would begin to restore the Cathar cause, which has now become one of the pillars of the New Age movement, in which the Grail is often used as the cement that holds the various portions of its belief together.

In retrospect, the "Grail Plan" as devised by the Aragon knights had some moderate success: the Knights Templar were its military arm, whereby the Brotherhood began to convert the people of the "homeland" towards the Cathar cause. When the Cathar preachers arrived, they were welcomed both by the people and the lords; if anything, the lords cherished the Cathar preachers more; in the Count of Toulouse's territories it was common for noblemen to bow to Cathar Parfaits of humble birth. It shows that the Hermetic doctrine, in which true spiritual devotion was valued more than just noble birth, and which was echoed in the Grail tradition, where noble birth or knightly prowess were insufficient in themselves to guarantee entry into the Grail Brotherhood, were factually in operation within these regions.

Set into motion, The Grail Plan nevertheless truly materialised and linguered for another 200 years. Its first and major defeat was the Cathar Crusade; a century later, its military arm would be hacked off by the King of France, working in co-operation with the Pope. But the message of the Grail seems to be that it cannot be conquered or defeated; its influence can merely be pushed aside for a while, which is nothing more than a period of regeneration. Like the phoenix, it revives time and again. In the end, it took "the Grail" just one century to surface again, this time in Italy, where it formed the foundation of the Renaissance.

It is clear that things were not as bleak as Rahn had imagined them, when the castle of Montségur surrendered to the papal troops. The Earth did not open up and swallow the Grail; the Grail had gone into hiding about a century before; Wolfram's story ends in ca. 1140 and Montségur surrendered in 1244. What is clear, is that the Grail Brotherhood in its new format of a secret society, had aimed too high too early; it was unable to properly fuel the Cathar cause. At the same time, the papal forces should have realised that the Grail cause could not be defeated by force. For as was written in *Parzival*: "The news spread to every land that it was not to be won by force, with the result that many abandoned the Quest of the Grail, and all that went with it, and that is why it is hidden to this day."[301]

The question, of course, is for how long it remained hidden. It was at the dawn of the 15th century that the enigmatic Grail of San Juan de la Peña would become identified as the Valencia Cup. A document dated 26 September 1399, from King Martin El Human, asked for the cup to be brought to the chapel of the Royal Palace at the Alfajeria in Zaragoza.[302] Ever since, the notion that the Grail was indeed the Cup of the Last Supper has gained ever more in popularity, becoming the most cherished explanation of what the Grail may have been. The true Grail, indeed, was hidden.

But historians have also observed an interesting anomaly that occurred in the 15th century, and which "coincidentally" involved a series of letters sent between the Kings of Aragon… and Prester John.

In 1427, King Alfonso was the object of diplomatic contacts from the empire of Ethiopia, receiving a letter from Yeshaq I of Ethiopia, borne by two dignitaries, which proposed an alliance against the Muslims and which would be sealed by a dual marriage that would require the Infante Don Pedro to bring a group of artisans to Ethiopia where he would marry Yeshaq's daughter. Indeed, the Kings of Ethiopia were proposing a double alliance – the medieval method to guarantee two families would be seen as bloodbrothers, largely becoming eternal allies – offering a racially mixed marriage. Echoes of Gahmuret's marriage to Queen Belkane?

Alfonso's reply is dated from Valencia, 15 May 1428, and begins: "Most eminent and most invincible monarch Lord Ysach son of David by teh Grace of God Prester John of the Indies lord of the tables of Mount Sinai and the throne of David and king of kings of Ethiopia." Alfonso sent a party of 13 craftsmen, all of whom perished on the way to Ethiopia. It meant that any potential (marriage) negotiations were interrupted, and soon died out.

But it was clear that the Ethiopians were vehement in remaining in close contact with Aragon. Yeshaq's successor Zara Yaqob sent a diplomatic mission to Europe in 1450, led by a Sicilian Pietro Rombulo who had previously been successful in a mission to India, specifically asking for skilled labour. Rombulo first visited Pope Nicholas V, but his ultimate goal was the court of Alfonso V of Aragon.

Alfonso replied, writing that he would be happy to send artisans to Ethiopia if their safe arrival could be guaranteed, but the letter probably never reached the Emperor. We can only wonder what type of "skilled labour" was so important that it required so many diplomatic missions? What type of "skilled labour" did Aragon possess that the Ethiopian Emperor could find nowhere – *nowhere* – else? The answer is as simple and as stunning as it can be: something which only the Ethiopians and the Aragons had any familiarity with: the care of the Grail; how to serve the Grail. That, for both dynasties, was the most skilled labour one could imagine.

Appendix A

The Cup or Monad (translated by G.R.S. Mead), fourth Hermetic treatise

1. Hermes: With Reason (Logos), not with hands, did the World-maker make the universal World; so that thou shouldst think of him as everywhere and ever-being, the Author of all things, and One and Only, who by His Will all beings hath created.

This Body of Him is a thing no man can touch, or see, or measure, a body inextensible, like to no other frame. 'Tis neither Fire nor Water, Air nor Breath; yet all of them come from it. Now being Good he willed to consecrate this [Body] to Himself alone, and set its Earth in order and adorn it.

2. So down [to Earth] He sent the Cosmos of this Frame Divine - man, a life that cannot die, and yet a life that dies. And o'er [all other] lives and over Cosmos [too], did man excel by reason of the Reason (Logos) and the Mind. For contemplator of God's works did man become; he marvelled and did strive to know their Author.

3. Reason (Logos) indeed, O Tat, among all men hath He distributed, but Mind not yet; not that He grudgeth any, for grudging cometh not from Him, but hath its place below, within the souls of men who have no Mind.

Tat: Why then did God, O father, not on all bestow a share of Mind?

H: He willed, my son, to have it set up in the midst for souls, just as it were a prize.

4. T: And where hath He set it up?

H: He filled a mighty Cup with it, and sent it down, joining a Herald [to it], to whom He gave command to make this proclamation to the hearts of men:

Baptize thyself with this Cup's baptism, what heart can do so, thou that hast faith thou canst ascend to him that hath sent down the Cup, thou that dost know for what thoudidst come into being!

As many then as understood the Herald's tidings and doused themselves in Mind, became partakers in the Gnosis; and when they had "received the Mind" they were made "perfect men".

But they who do not understand the tidings, these, since they possess the aid of Reason [only] and not Mind, are ignorant wherefor they have come into being and whereby.

5. The senses of such men are like irrational creatures'; and as their [whole] make-up is in their feelings and their impulses, they fail in all appreciation of <lit.: "they do not wonder at"> those things which really are worth contemplation. These center all their thought upon the pleasures of the body and its appetites, in the belief that for its sake man hath come into being.

But they who have received some portion of God's gift, these, Tat, if we judge by their deeds, have from Death's bonds won their release; for they embrace in their own Mind all things, things on the earth, things in the heaven, and things above the heaven - if there be aught. And having raised themselves so far they sight the Good; and having sighted it, they look upon their sojourn here as a mischance; and in disdain of all, both things in body and the bodiless, they speed their way unto that One and Only One.

6. This is, O Tat, the Gnosis of the Mind, Vision of things Divine; God-knowledge is it, for the Cup is God's.

T: Father, I, too, would be baptized.

H: Unless thou first shall hate thy Body, son, thou canst not love thy Self. But if thou lov'st thy Self thou shalt have Mind, and having Mind thou shalt share in the Gnosis.

T: Father, what dost thou mean?

H: It is not possible, my son, to give thyself to both - I mean to things that perish and to things divine. For seeing that existing things are twain, Body and Bodiless, in which the perishing and the divine are understood, the man who hath the will to choose is left the choice of one or the other; for it can never be the twain should meet. And in those souls to whom the choice is left, the waning of the one causes the other's growth to show itself.

7. Now the choosing of the Better not only proves a lot most fair for him who makes the choice, seeing it makes the man a God, but also shows his piety to God. Whereas the [choosing] of the Worse, although it doth destroy the "man", it doth only disturb God's harmony to this extent, that as processions pass by in the middle of the way, without being able to do anything but take the road from others, so do such men move in procession through the world led by their bodies' pleasures.

8. This being so, O Tat, what comes from God hath been and will be ours; but that which is dependent on ourselves, let this press onward and have no delay, for 'tis not God, 'tis we who are the cause of evil things, preferring them to good.

Thou see'st, son, how many are the bodies through which we

have to pass, how many are the choirs of daimones, how vast the system of the star-courses [through which our Path doth lie], to hasten to the One and Only God.

For to the Good there is no other shore; It hath no bounds; It is without an end; and for Itself It is without beginning, too, though unto us it seemeth to have one - the Gnosis.

9. Therefore to It Gnosis is no beginning; rather is it [that Gnosis doth afford] to us the first beginning of its being known.

Let us lay hold, therefore, of the beginning. and quickly speed through all [we have to pass].

`Tis very hard, to leave the things we have grown used to, which meet our gaze on every side, and turn ourselves back to the Old Old [Path].

Appearances delight us, whereas things which appear not make their believing hard.

Now evils are the more apparent things, whereas the Good can never show Itself unto the eyes, for It hath neither form nor figure.

Therefore the Good is like Itself alone, and unlike all things else; or `tis impossible that That which hath no body should make Itself apparent to a body.

10. The "Like's" superiority to the "Unlike" and the "Unlike's" inferiority unto the "Like" consists in this:

The Oneness being Source and Root of all, is in all things as Root and Source. Without [this] Source is naught; whereas the Source [Itself] is from naught but itself, since it is Source of all the rest. It is Itself Its Source, since It may have no other Source.

The Oneness then being Source, containeth every number, but is contained by none; engendereth every number, but is engendered by no other one.

11. Now all that is engendered is imperfect, it is divisible, to increase subject and to decrease; but with the Perfect [One] none of these things doth hold. Now that which is increasable increases from the Oneness, but succumbs through its own feebleness when it no longer can contain the One.

And now, O Tat, God's Image hath been sketched for thee, as far as it can be; and if thou wilt attentively dwell on it and observe it with thine heart's eyes, believe me, son, thou'lt find the Path that leads above; nay, that Image shall become thy Guide itself, because the Sight [Divine] hath this peculiar [charm], it holdeth fast and draweth unto it those who succeed in opening their eyes, just as, they say, the magnet [draweth] iron.

Appendix B

Apuleius, Metamorphoses, book XI

[1] About the first watch of the night I was awakened by a sudden fear and I saw the full orb of the moon rising from the waves of the sea with an excess of brilliant light. I immediately grasped the secrets hidden in the silence of the dark night. I recognized that the supreme Goddess exercises power with a unique authority and that the affairs of men are controlled by her providential care. Moreover, not only are the animals of the field and the wild nourished by the divine support of her light and power but so also are the objects of inanimate nature as well. Indeed the bodies of all creatures on earth, in heaven and on the sea grow with her waxing and obediently diminish as she wanes. Destiny, then, seemed to have dealt me my full share of misfortune and to be belatedly giving some ground for hope of rescue and I determined to turn in prayer to this manifestation of the Goddess.

With firmness I shook off my drowsiness and stood up. I immediately devoted myself to the the duty of the purifying washings by immersing my head seven times in the waves: the godlike Pythagoras has explained why this number is most appropriate in religious matters. Then hopefully and speedily I lifted my tearful face in prayer to the all-powerful Goddess, saying:

[2] "Queen of Heaven, whether you are Ceres the kindly creator of our food: she who because of the joyous return of your daughter replaced the savage fare of the ancient acorns and showed men a gentler diet and who now cherishes Eleusinian soil:

or Venus the heavenly one who at the first beginnings of life created Amor and brought together the separate sexes and are forever worshipped in the sea-girt temple of Paphos because of the creation of mankind:

or Phoebus' sister who have protected with soothing medicines so many from the pains of childbirth and are worshiped in the temples of Ephesus:

or Prosperina who are invoked in diverse rites as The Terrible One able to drive back the attacks of evil spirits with shrieking in the night and to close them up in the caverns of the earth even as you wander through the groves of the earth:

[O Queen] who shine with this feminine light on all the cities of mankind and nourish the glad seeds with your moist flames and give varying light in harmony with the changes of the sun:

By whatever name, with whatever rites, under whatever form it is proper to invoke you, [I pray:]

Help me now in my desperate sufferings, restore my ruined fortunes, grant me an end to and peace from these piled-up calamities. Let this be enough of trouble and enough of danger! Remove the vile appearance of a four-footed animal from me and give me back the shape of my own kind! Make me Lucius again! But if because of some offence a god is pursuing me with implacable cruelty, at least may I be allowed to die if I may not live as a man."

[3] In this way I poured out my prayers and laid them before the Goddess until at last sleep again surrounded and overwhelmed me in that same bed, exhausted as I was by my lamentations. I had not been asleep long when, behold, the divine form emerged and raised up from the middle of the sea those features revered by the gods themselves. Slowly an image, radiant throughout its whole body, seemed to take a position before me when the sea-

wreck had been shaken off. I shall try to describe to you its awesome appearance if the poverty of human speech gives me the skill to describe it or if the power of the Goddess affords me Her own lavish resource of eloquent oratory.

First Her long, very abundant hair curled lightly over her divine neck and, loosened, flowed gently down. A crown of many kinds and of many shapes of flowers surrounded Her sublime head: in the middle of the crown a flat disk like a mirror or, indeed like the moon, shed a clear light from over Her forehead while on the right and on the left it was enclosed by the coils of rising vipers. On the top it was decorated with upright stalks of grain (Cerialibus). She wore a many-coloured tunic of finally woven linen in some places shining with a white gleam, in others bright yellow with saffron dye, in yet others blazing with the redness of roses. Most striking of all in her appearance was a cloak of pitch black but shining with a black glossiness. This garment enveloped her, being wrapped under the left side to the right shoulder. Part of it hung down in the form of a knot and it flowed down to its edges with a tassled fringe.

[4] Along an embroidered edge and on the surface of the cloak shining stars gleamed randomly and in the middle of these a half moon breathed out fiery flames. Wherever the sweep of that magnificent mantle moved, a wreath garlanded of all manner of flowers and fruits was indivisibly joined to it. The things she carried were of quite varied kind. In Her right hand she carried a bronze rattle: in the middle of this there was bunch of sticks attached to a narrow sheet of metal shaped like a belt which gave out a sharp sound when shaken three times. In Her left hand she held suspended a golden jug: on its handle where it could be seen a snake arose with its head high and its neck puffed out. Her ambrosian feet were covered by sandals woven of leaves of victorious palm. Such was the Great Goddess who, breathing the

blessed fragrance of Arabia, deigned to address me with divine voice.

[5] "Behold, Lucius, moved by your prayers I am here, I Mother of the Nature of Things, Mistress of All The Elements, First Creature of The Ages, Greatest of The Deities, Queen of The Manes, First of The Heavenly Beings, Unitary Form of The Gods and Goddesses, I who administer with my commands the shining heights of the heavens, the healthy winds of the sea, the hopeless silences of those gone beneath the earth. My divinity alone in many forms, with different rites, with diverse names the whole world venerates. So it is that the Phrygians, the first of men call me Pessinuntia, Mother of The Gods, the autochthonous Athenians Cecropian Minerva, the island Cypriots Paphian Venus, the arrow-bearing Cretans Dictynnian Diana, the trilingual Sicilians Ortygian Prosperina, the Eleusinians, the Ancient Goddess, Ceres. To others I am Juno, to yet others Bellona, Hecate, Rhamnusia. The Ethiopians who are the first to be shone upon by the reborn god the Sun, the Africans and the Egyptians rich with the pristine teaching worship me with my proper rituals and call me by my true name, Queen Isis".

[8] Look, the parade which precedes the Great Procession is beginning with the participants decked out in costumes of personal choice. There was a man with a belt playing the part of a soldier, another with his cloak tucked up could be recognised as a hunter by his boots and his equipment while another tried to pass himself off as a woman dressed in gold shoes and lavish jewellery and a silk dress. On his head he had placed a wig and he walked with a provocative gait....

[9] Through the scattered mass of these popular entertainments the procession dedicated to the Goddess The Saviour was making its way. Women in gleaming white robes and dazzling jewellery

and floral crowns were strewing petals from their bosoms along the road on which the sacred company was proceeding. Some other women carried reversed mirrors behind their backs to show reverence to the Goddess coming after them. Others again carried ivory combs and acted out with gestures of the arms and bent fingers the dressing and combing of the hair of the Goddess. Another group sprinkled various perfumes and balm in drops along the streets. Then a large crowd of persons of both sexes came petitioning the Creatrix of The Heavenly Stars with emblems of light, lanterns, torches, wax candles and other kinds of artificial light. Then soft harmonies of sound were heard, pipes and flutes in the sweetest melodies. These were followed by a choir of select youths dressed in radiant snow-white tunics who sang an appealing hymn composed by a poet inspired by the Muses in which musical hints of the greater solemn rites were contained. The flute-players consecrated to the great Serapis next came and repeatedly played a theme peculiar to the Goddess and Her temple. A large crowd cried out for a passage to be cleared for the holy objects.

[10] Then came on the groups of those who had been initiated in the sacred mysteries, men and women, of all ranks and ages, shining in the pure radiance of their linen dress. The women had their damp hair wrapped round with a transparent veil and the heads of the men, completely shaven, gleamed brightly. A shrill tinkling sound spread around from the bronze, silver and even golden sistra which they were shaking.

Along with them were the noble priests of the sacred cult, the earth-bound stars of the great religion, in their white linen vestments bound around their chests and reaching to their feet. These carried the spectacular symbols of the greatest gods. The first carried a lantern giving out a clear light, not at all like those used to illumine our evening banquets but a golden cup giving out a flame broader than its central opening. A second priest, dressed in the same manner, carried the altar, that is, the auxilia, named because of the protective providence shown by the Goddess. A third walked carrying a palm-branch skilfully gilded and a staff of Mercury. A fourth displayed the symbol of justice, a deformed left hand with an open palm: this seemed more suitable than the right hand because of its natural sluggishness and its lack of cunning and versatility. The same man carried a small rounded vessel in the shape of a female breast from which he poured milk. A fifth carried a golden basket full of laurel twigs and a sixth an amphora.

[11] Without delay the gods then came forward, condescending to walk on human feet. First Anubis, gigantic in stature and holding aloft his dog's neck with his face on one side black, on the other golden, the dreaded go-between of the upper and the lower gods. In his left hand he carried his messenger's staff and in his right he shook a palm-branch still green. Immediately following in his steps came an image of a cow in a upright stance, pregnant symbol of the Goddess Parent of All Things, which one of the blessed priesthood bore on his shoulders with proud footsteps. Another carried a chest containing secret objects and concealing within itself the operta of the glorious religion. Another bore on his happy breast the adored image of the highest Deity. This was not like an ox nor a bird nor a wild beast nor even of a human being but it aroused awe by its artful inventiveness and uniqueness. It was an inexplicable statement of the higher religion which must be covered by a great silence. It was fashioned in the following manner: it was a small cup most skilfully hollowed out with a round base, decorated on the outside with marvellous Egyptian images. Its mouth was not very high but rose up to a channel ending in a long spout. The handle on the other side was twisted far back and joined to the cup by a long curve. On it was an asp which in a contorted knot held itself

up with its scaly neck in a streaked puff.

[16] ....[At the seashore] when the images of the gods had been set down, the chief priest named and dedicated the ship which had been skilfully built and decorated on the outside with marvellous Egyptian images. First he offered solemn prayers from his sinless mouth and then with a blazing torch, an egg and sulphur he purified it to the greatest purity. The gleaming sail of this fortunate ship had golden letters woven into it which proclaimed anew the prayers for prosperous trading in the new year's sailing. A rounded pine mast rose up magnificent in its splendour and with a magnificent mast-head. The stern had a curved beak and gleamed with a covering of gold plates and the whole hull shone with polished cedar wood. Then all the people of the religion along with the uninitiated struggled to put on board baskets laden with spices and similar offerings and offered to the waves cakes mixed with milk. At last the ship, laden with its lavish gifts and devout offerings, was released from its anchoring cables and given to the sea on the favourable breeze which was specially granted it. When the course of its movement took it from our sight the bearers of the sacred objects took up again what they had brought and returned eagerly to the temple in the same orderly procession.

23. I observed all these commands with devout restraint and at last came the day appointed for the divine encounter. As the curved sun was drawing on the evening, behold, a crowd of initiates gathered around from all sides and in accordance with the ancient rite each one honoured me with different gifts. Then, when all the uninitiated had been removed, I was dressed in a fresh linen robe and the priest took me by the hand and led me into inner sanctuary of the shrine itself.

You will perhaps ask me eagerly, avid reader, what was then said, what was done. I would tell you, if it was permitted to tell and you would learn if it were permitted to learn but both ears and tongue would pay an equal penalty for that rash curiosity. Since, however, you are perhaps moved by a religious need, I will not torment you with a long suspense. Listen, therefore, and believe, for this is the truth.

I reached the edge of death and crossed the threshold of Prosperina. I was driven through all the elements and I returned. In the middle of the night I saw the sun blazing with a clear light. I came close to the gods below and to the gods above and worshipped them in their presence.

Behold I have told you things which you must not understand, even though you have heard them.

References

[1] It holds a position in the top twenty of bestselling books ever, amongst the Harry Potter novels, the Bible, the Qur'an, the Book of Mormon, Don Quixote, and a select few others.

[2] Richard Barber, The Holy Grail, p. 1.

[3] Crusade Against the Grail: The Struggle between the Cathars, the Templars, and the Church of Rome (English Translation by Christopher Jones), 2006, from a 1933 original.

[4] "Revealed: Himmler's secret quest to locate the 'Aryan Holy Grail'", by Graham Keeley, The Independent (UK), 6 February 2007

[5] Joseph Goering, The Virgin and the Grail, p. 16 and 17.

[6] Aragon Crown Archives, Barcelona Collection Martin el Humano, Parchment, 136.

[7] Antonio Beltran, Estudio sobre el Santo Caliz de la Catedral de Valencia (4th ed.), Zaragoza, Octavio y Felez, 1984.

[8] "Kelch und Stein", Frankfurt and Bern, 1983.

[9] Richard Barber, The Holy Grail, p. 169.

[10] Richard Barber, The Holy Grail, p. 169.

[11] Cathedral Archives, volume 3.532, page 36 v - 37 v

[12] Vatican Reg. #2164/59

[13] Antonio Beltran, Estudio sobre el Santo Cáliz de la Catedral de Valencia, Instituto Diocesano Valentino « Roque Chabas », Valencia, 1984.

[14] Manuscript 136, Martin el Humano Collection

[15] Actually, the prophecy that "in 700 years, when the laurel grows green again" was unrelated to Montségur, though it is normally – erroneously – linked to Montségur. It was uttered by Guilhelm de Bélibaste, before he was burned alive in 1321 – suggesting the revival would occur in 2021.

[16] Guidebook to San Juan de la Peña, Ediciones Sicilia, Zaragoza, p. 6.

[17] Baptism is commonly associated with water, but in theory,

baptism could be with any of the four elements (air, water, earth, fire). The expression "baptism by fire" is a linguistic reference to such a baptism. In the Bible, people actually asked what the difference was between the baptisms of John the Baptist and Jesus Christ. Jesus answered that he himself baptised with fire.

[18] Andrew Sinclair, The Discovery of the Grail, p. 33.

[19] Richard Barber, The Holy Grail, p. 1.

[20] There is some confusion over dates. Some mention the entry of the relic into Bruges as 7 April 1150, others 3 March 1148.

[21] Richard Barber, The Holy Grail, p. 130-1.

[22] Mk 6:17-29 and Matt. 14:1-12

[23] RASHI, Maurice Liber Szold trans. (Jewish Publication Society, 1906), p. 68-69.

[24] Baigent, Leigh, and Lincoln, Holy Blood, Holy Grail, p. 312-3.

[25] Baigent, Leigh, and Lincoln, Holy Blood, Holy Grail, p. 313.

[26] Mircea Eliade. A History of Religious Ideas Volume 3: From Muhammad to the Age of Reforms, p. 105.

[27] Mircea Eliade. A History of Religious Ideas Volume 3: From Muhammad to the Age of Reforms, p. 107.

[28] Wolfram von Eschenbach, Parzival, translated by A.T. Hatto, p. 7.

[29] Joseph Goering, The Virgin and the Grail, p. 43.

[30] Wolfram von Eschenbach, Parzival, translated by A.T. Hatto, p. 11.

[31] Wolfram von Eschenbach, Parzival, translated by A.T. Hatto, p. 413.

[32] The Hidden Church of the Holy Graal, Arthur Edward Waite, 1909, p. 701-2.

[33] Richard Barber, The Holy Grail, p. 242.

[34] Jessie L. Weston, From Ritual to Romance, p. 3.

[35] Jessie L. Weston, From Ritual to Romance, p. 3.

[36] Erik Hornung, The Secret Lore of Egypt, p. 13.

[37] Richard Barber, The Holy Grail, p. 74.

[38] Richard Barber, The Holy Grail, p. 74.

[39] Wolfram von Eschenbach, Parzival, 454, 17.

[40] Kahane & Kahane, The Krater and the Grail, p. 121.

[41] Gilles Quispel, Hermetische Gnosis in de loop der eeuwen, p. 19.

[42] All Macrobius footnotes from The Selected Works of Porphyry, Translated by Thomas Taylor, Thomas Rod, London 1823, p. 186-189.

[43] Kahane & Kahane, The Krater and the Grail, p. 16.

[44] Tobias Churton, The Golden Builders. Alchemists, Rosicrucians and the first Free Masons, p. 33.

[45] Corpus Hermeticum, I, 18.

[46] Wolfram von Eschenbach, Parzival, 469, 14.

[47] Wolfram von Eschenbach, Parzival, 471, 10.

[48] Corpus Hermeticum, I, 26.

[49] Taylor, Thomas. Eleusinian and Bacchic Mysteries. Lighting Source Publishers, 1997, p. 49.

[50] Metamorphoses, XV, 393-406.

[51] The Book of Enoch, verse 2 and 7.

[52] Tobias Churton, The Golden Builders. Alchemists, Rosicrucians and the first Free Masons, p. 28.

[53] Wolfram von Eschenbach, Parzival, 465, 19.

[54] Kahane & Kahane, The Krater and the Grail, p. 3.

[55] Jacob Slavenburg, De Hermetische Schakel.

[56] Wolfram von Eschenbach, Parzival, 465, 19.

[57] Wolfram von Eschenbach, Parzival, 466, 19.

[58] Corpus Hermeticum, V, 2.

[59] Wolfram von Eschenbach, Parzival, 797, 28.

[60] Corpus Hermeticum, I, 6.

[61] Corpus Hermeticum, IV, 4

[62] Wolfram von Eschenbach, Parzival, 817, 4.

[63] Richard Barber, The Holy Grail, p. 80.

[64] Wolfram von Eschenbach, Parzival, 461, 28.

[65] Wolfram von Eschenbach, Parzival, 435, 10.

[66] Wolfram von Eschenbach, Parzival, 460, 28.
[67] Wolfram von Eschenbach, Parzival, 483, 19.
[68] Wolfram von Eschenbach, Parzival, 171, 17 & 239, 8.
[69] Wolfram von Eschenbach, Parzival, 329, 25.
[70] Wolfram von Eschenbach, Parzival, 124, 19.
[71] Wolfram von Eschenbach, Parzival, 827, 19.
[72] Wolfram von Eschenbach, Parzival, 452, 29.
[73] Kahane & Kahane, The Krater and the Grail, p. 57.
[74] Wolfram von Eschenbach, Parzival, 485, 10.
[75] Wolfram von Eschenbach, Parzival, 782, 29.
[76] Erik Hornung, The Secret Lore of Egypt, p. 53.
[77] Wolfram von Eschenbach, Parzival, 479, 8.
[78] Wolfram von Eschenbach, Parzival, 782, 29.
[79] Corpus Hermeticum, XIII, 3.
[80] Corpus Hermeticum, XIII, 13.
[81] Wolfram von Eschenbach, Parzival, 452, 29.
[82] Quispel, Hermetische Gnosis in de loop der eeuwen, p. 18-9.
[83] Wolfram von Eschenbach, Parzival, 438, 31-34.
[84] Wolfram von Eschenbach, Parzival, 235, 29.
[85] Wolfram von Eschenbach, Parzival, 809, 8.
[86] Wolfram von Eschenbach, Parzival, 235, 19-20.
[87] Kahane & Kahane, The Krater and the Grail, p. 101-2.
[88] Wolfram von Eschenbach, Parzival, 493, 16.
[89] Kahane & Kahane, The Krater and the Grail, p. 102-4.
[90] Wolfram von Eschenbach, Parzival, 236, 18.
[91] Kahane & Kahane, The Krater and the Grail, p. 105.
[92] Richard Barber, The Holy Grail, p. 10.
[93] Richard Barber, The Holy Grail, p. 91.
[94] Richard Barber, The Holy Grail, p. 92.
[95] Ulrich Ernst, Kyot und Flegetanis in Wolframs 'Parzival', WW 3/85, p. 176.
[96] Wolfram von Eschenbach, Parzival, 453, 11.
[97] Wolfram von Eschenbach, Parzival, 416, 17-30.
[98] Kahane & Kahane, The Krater and the Grail, p. 154.

[99] De Mandach, Le 'Roman du Graal' originaire: Sur les traces du modèle commun, p. 71-3.

[100] Kahane & Kahane, The Krater and the Grail, p. 2.

[101] Wolfram von Eschenbach, Parzival, 453, 5.

[102] Wolfram von Eschenbach, Parzival, 453, 15.

[103] Kahane & Kahane, The Krater and the Grail, p. 126.

[104] Kahane & Kahane, The Krater and the Grail, p. 151.

[105] De Mandach, Le 'Roman du Graal' originaire: Sur les traces du modèle commun, p. 60-61.

[106] Richard Barber, The Holy Grail, p. 175.

[107] Richard Barber, The Holy Grail, p. 175.

[108] A slightly updated edition of his work appeared in 1995. De Mandach, Le 'Roman du Graal' originaire: Sur les traces du modèle commun, p. 14.

[109] De Mandach, Le 'Roman du Graal' originaire: Sur les traces du modèle commun, p. 12.

[110] Kahane & Kahane, The Krater and the Grail, p. 2.

[111] De Mandach, Le 'Roman du Graal' originaire: Sur les traces du modèle commun, p. 19.

[112] De Mandach, Le 'Roman du Graal' originaire: Sur les traces du modèle commun, p. 20.

[113] He was later re-interred in the abbey of San Pedro el Viejo de Huesca.

[114] Ana Isabel Lapena Paul, San Juan de la Peña, a historical and artistic guide, p. 8-9.

[115] Ana Isabel Lapena Paul, San Juan de la Peña, a historical and artistic guide, p. 10.

[116] Wolfram von Eschenbach, Parzival, 286, 10-12

[117] De Mandach, Le 'Roman du Graal' originaire: Sur les traces du modèle commun, p. 23-25.

[118] Peter L. Hayes, The Limping Hero, p. 65-66.

[119] Wolfram von Eschenbach, Parzival, 657, 28.

[120] Zosimos, Commentaries on the Letter Omega, 7.

[121] Wolfram von Eschenbach, Parzival, 617, 11.

[122] De Mandach, Le 'Roman du Graal' originaire: Sur les traces du modèle commun, p. 113.

[123] The Virgin and the Grail.

[124] Joseph Goering, The Virgin and the Grial, p. 145.

[125] Wolfram von Eschenbach, 827, 1-18.

[126] Thompson, Kathleen. Power and Border lordship in medieval France. The county of the Perche, 1000-1226. Woodbridge/Rochester: The Royal Historical Society/The Boydell Press, 2002.

[127] Thompson, Power and Border lordship in medieval France, p. 4.

[128] Thompson, Power and Border lordship in medieval France, p. 4.

[129] Graham Hancock, The Sign and the Seal.

[130] All details of Rotrou II and his family come from Kathleen Thompson's historical research.

[131] Wolfram von Eschenbach, Parzival, 455, 12.

[132] Dowson, John (1820-1881). A classical dictionary of Hindu mythology and religion, geography, history, and literature. London: Trübner, 1879 [Reprint, London: Routledge, 1979].

[133] Kahane & Kahane, The Krater and the Grail, p. 113.

[134] The Cambridge History of English and American Literature in 18 Volumes (1907–21), Volume I. From the Beginnings to the Cycles of Romance (XII. The Arthurian Legend. § 9. Wace.)

[135] Chretien, de Troyes. Erec and Enide. Carleton W. Carroll, trans, ed. Garland Library of Medieval Literature; vol. 25. series A. (New York : Garland Publishing, 1987).

[136] Kahane & Kahane, The Krater and the Grail, p. 130-1.

[137] Kahane & Kahane, The Krater and the Grail, p. 130-1.

[138] Wolfram von Eschenbach, Parzival, 416, 25-30.

[139] Richard Barber, The Holy Grail, p. 80.

[140] Richard Barber, The Holy Grail, p. 175.

[141] Richard Barber, The Holy Grail, p. 177.

[142] Richard Barber, The Holy Grail, p. 177.

[143] Gilles Quispel, Hermetische Gnosis in de loop der eeuwen, p. 257.

[144] Frances Yates, Giordano Bruno and the Hermetic tradition, p. 16.

[145] Gilles Quispel, Hermetische Gnosis in de loop der eeuwen, p. 266-7.

[146] Jacob Slavenburg, De Hermetische Schakel, p. 206.

[147] Jacob Slavenburg, De Hermetische Schakel, p. 180.

[148] Corpus Hermeticum, IV, 4.

[149] Corpus Hermeticum, IV, 4.

[150] Richard Poe, Black Spark, White Fire, p. 109-10.

[151] Plutarch, On Isis and Osiris, sec 28.

[152] Plutarch, On Isis and Osiris, sec 28.

[153] Plutarch, On Isis and Osiris, sec 28.

[154] P.M. Fraser, Ptolemaic Alexandria, 1972, p. 253.

[155]John E. Stambaugh, Serapis under the Early Ptolemies, 1972, p. 10.

[156] John E. Stambaugh, Serapis under the Early Ptolemies, 1972, p. 43.

[157] Lynn Picknett, Mary Magdalene, p. 199.

[158] Lynn Picknett, Mary Magdalene, p. 199.

[159] Lynn Picknett & Clive, The Templar Revelation, p. 328. We note that though the Mandaeans hold John the Baptist as an important preacher, the Mandaeans themselves should not be considered to be descendents of the followers of John the Baptist.

[160] Shimon Gibson, The Cave of John the Baptist, p. 63.

[161] Shimon Gibson, The Cave of John the Baptist, p. 63.

[162] Shimon Gibson, The Cave of John the Baptist, p. 72.

[163] In De vita coelitus comparanda, Book III of Libri de Vita, 1489.

[164] Frances Yates, Giordano Bruno and the Hermetic tradition, p. 351-2.

[165] The Gnostics and Their Remains, by C.W. King, p. 161, quoting a letter by the historian Vopiscus in his work, the Life of the

Tyrant Saturninus.

166 Frances Yates, Giordano Bruno and the Hermetic tradition, p. 3, footnote.

167 Bruno Stricker, Het Corpus Hermeticum: Index op gecommentarieerde passages, 1993, p. 14.

168 De Mysteria, VIII 4

169 Frances Yates, Giordano Bruno and the Hermetic tradition, p. 16.

170 Erik Hornung, The Secret Lore of Egypt, p. 1.

171 Gary Greenberg, Osarseph and Exodus: Literary Reflections in an Egyptian Mirror

Delivered at the annual meeting of the International Society of Biblical Literature, Lausanne, Switzerland 1997.

172 Plutarch, The History of Isis and Osiris, VI.

173 Strabo xvii. cap. I. 27-28.

174 Alan Alford, The Midnight Sun, p. 36.

175 Alan Alford, The Midnight Sun, p. 67.

176 p. 160.

177 Richard Barber, The Holy Grail, p. 109.

178 Richard Barber, The Holy Grail, p. 109.

179 J.F. Borghouts, Ancient Egyptian Magical Texts, 2.

180 Robert Bauval, The Orion Mystery, p. 79.

181 a relative of the maple tree, both having five-pointed leaves.

182 Abdel-Aziz Saleh, Excavations at Heliopolis. Ancient Egyptian Ounu, Cairo University, 1981/3, p. 13.

183 Robert Bauval, The Orion Mystery, p. 222.

184 R.T. Rundle-Clarke, Myth and Symbol, p. 177.

185 Alan Alford, The Midnight Sun, p. 244.

186 Jacob Slavenburg, De Hermetische Schakel, p. 102.

187 Erik Hornung, The Secret Lore of Egypt, p. 48.

188 Jessie L. Weston, From Ritual to Romance, p. 16.

189 John Julius Norwich, The World Atlas of Architecture, p. 217.

190 Chapter II of Book Five.

191 Richard Barber, The Holy Grail, p. 305.

192 Wolfram von Eschenbach, Parzival, 468, 10.

193 Wolfram von Eschenbach, Parzival, 493, 22.

194 Wolfram von Eschenbach, Parzival, 472, 5.

195 Wolfram von Eschenbach, Parzival, 472, 5.

196 Wolfram von Eschenbach, Parzival, 454, 29.

197 Wolfram von Eschenbach, Parzival, 470, 21.

198 Wolfram von Eschenbach, Parzival, 470, 23.

199 Wolfram von Eschenbach, Parzival, 495, 1.

200 Wolfram von Eschenbach, Parzival, 818, 25; 819, 7.

201 Corpus Hermeticum, II, 17.

202 Wolfram von Eschenbach, Parzival, 495, 7.

203 Wolfram von Eschenbach, Parzival, 743, 21.

204 Wolfram von Eschenbach, Parzival, 478, 30.

205 Wolfram von Eschenbach, Parzival, 478, 13.

206 Wolfram von Eschenbach, Parzival, 478, 1.

207 Wolfram von Eschenbach, Parzival, 820, 13.

208 Wolfram von Eschenbach, Parzival, 494, 7.

209 Wolfram von Eschenbach, Parzival, 444, 23; 792, 21; 797, 13; 805, 22; 816, 18 and 818, 26.

210 De Mandach, Le 'Roman du Graal' originaire: Sur les traces du modèle commun, p. 19.

211 John Hutchinson, Their Kingdom Come, p. 33-4.

212 Idries Shah, The Sufis.

213 Lynn Picknett & Clive Prince, The Templar Revelation, p. 121.

214 Richard Barber, The Holy Grail, p. 308.

215 Lynn Picknett & Clive Prince, The Templar Revelation, p. 143-4.

216 Lynn Picknett & Clive Prince, The Templar Revelation, p. 144.

217 Lynn Picknett & Clive Prince, The Templar Revelation, p. 145.

218 John Matthews, The Grail: Quest for the Eternal, Thames & Hudson, London, 1987, p. 12.

219 Richard Barber, The Holy Grail, p. 94. Some sources mention 718 AD.

220 Richard Barber, The Holy Grail, p. 153-4.

[221] Richard Barber, The Holy Grail, p. 46.

[222] Richard Barber, The Holy Grail, p. 47.

[223] Wolfram von Eschenbach, Parzival, 501, 19.

[224] Wolfram von Eschenbach, Parzival, excerpts from 250, 22 to 253, 8.

[225] Die Parzivalfrage (Munich, 1928), p. 53-54.

[226] Corpus Hermeticum, X, 5.

[227] Wolfram von Eschenbach, Parzival, 501, 19.

[228] Kahane & Kahane, The Krater and the Grail, p. 36-7.

[229] Jacob Slavenburg, De Hermetische Schakel, p. 215.

[230] Kahane & Kahane, The Krater and the Grail, p. 85.

[231] Wolfram von Eschenbach, Parzival: 28, 11.

[232] Wolfram von Eschenbach, Parzival: 35, 21.

[233] Graham Hancock, The Sign and the Seal, p. 80.

[234] Graham Hancock, The Sign and the Seal, p. 80.

[235] Nicholas Jubber, The Prester Quest, p. 151.

[236] Graham Hancock, The Sign and the Seal, p. 85-6.

[237] Wolfram von Eschenbach, Parzival, 328, 11.

[238] De Mandach, Le 'Roman du Graal' originaire: Sur les traces du modèle commun, p. 108-9.

[239] Stuart Munro-Hay, The Quest for the Ark of the Covenant, p. 49.

[240] Graham Hancock, The Sign and the Seal, p. 84.

[241] Stuart Munro-Hay. The Quest for the Ark of the Covenant, p. 14.

[242] Graham Hancock, The Sign and the Seal, p. 111. Jan is actually a Dutch word, meaning John, similar to the French word Jean, all of these derived from the Latin Janus, himself linked with John the Baptist.

[243] Grierson & Munro-Hay, The Ark of the Covenant, p. 246-7.

[244] Stuart Munro-Hay, The Quest for the Ark of the Covenant, p. 76.

[245] Stuart Munro-Hay, The Quest for the Ark of the Covenant, p. 44-5.

[246] Klaas Van Urk, Zoektocht naar de Heilige Graal & de Ark. Mysterie van Rennes-le-Chateau ontrafeld, p. 164-5.

[247] Stuart Munro-Hay, The Quest for the Ark of the Covenant, p. 50.

[248] Kahane & Kahane, The Krater and the Grail, p. 88.

[249] Kahane & Kahane, The Krater and the Grail, p. 88.

[250] Kahane & Kahane, The Krater and the Grail, p. 89.

[251] Though Amun did not have a pyramid tradition, his northern Egyptian counterpart, Atum, whose chief seat was at Heliopolis, did.

[252] Stuart Munro-Hay, The Quest for the Ark of the Covenant.

[253] Grierson & Munro-Hay, The Ark of the Covenant, p. 7.

[254] Grierson & Munro-Hay, The Ark of the Covenant, p. 21.

[255] Grierson & Munro-Hay, The Ark of the Covenant, p. 176.

[256] Grierson & Munro-Hay, The Ark of the Covenant, p. 303.

[257] Stuart Munro-Hay, The Quest for the Ark of the Covenant, p. 31.

[258] Stuart Munro-Hay, The Quest for the Ark of the Covenant, p. 79.

[259] Zecharia Sitchin, The Twelfth Planet.

[260] Grierson & Munro-Hay, The Ark of the Covenant, p. 75.

[261] Stuart Munro-Hay, The Quest for the Ark of the Covenant, p. 195.

[262] Stuart Munro-Hay, The Quest for the Ark of the Covenant, p. 199.

[263] Kebra Negast 17.

[264] Stuart Munro-Hay, The Quest for the Ark of the Covenant, p. 103.

[265] Erik Hornung, The Secret Lore of Egypt, p. 28.

[266] Roger Sherman Loomis, Arthurian Tradition & Chrétien de Troyes, p. 272.

[267] Richard Barber, The Holy Grail, p. 112.

[268] Wolfram von Eschenbach, Parzival, 454, 27.

[269] Wolfram von Eschenbach, Parzival, 810, 9-11.

[270] Wolfram von Eschenbach, Parzival, 813, 17.

[271] Andrew Sinclair, Secret Scroll, p. 86.

[272] J. Stuart Hay, Life of Elagabalus, 1911.

[273] Erik Hornung, The Secret Lore of Egypt, p. 41.

[274] Kahane & Kahane, The Krater and the Grail, p. 110.

[275] Pyramid Texts, 2051.

[276] Pyramid Texts, 530.

[277] Pyramid Texts, 1454.

[278] Graham Hancock, The Sign and the Seal, p. 347.

[279] Robert G. Bauval, Investigation on the Origins of the Benben stone, Discussions in Egyptology, Volume 14, 1989

[280] Arrhenius, S. "The Propagation of Life in Space," Die Umschau, 7, 481 (1903) and Arrhenius, Svante. Worlds in the Making: The Evolution of the Universe. New York: Harper & Row (1908).

[281] Lucas, A., Ancient Egyptian Materials and Industries, Mineola, N.Y., Dover Publications (1999 1962), p. 415-416.

[282] Lucas, quoting F.W. von Bissing, Archiv fur Orientforschung, v (1928-9), p. 75, n. 2. See Lucas, A., Ancient Egyptian Materials and Industries, Mineola, N.Y, Dover Publications (1999 1962), p. 73.

[283] Adrian Gilbert

[284] Erik Hornung, The Secret Lore of Egypt, p. 14.

[285] Erik Hornung, The Secret Lore of Egypt, p. 15.

[286] Corpus Hermeticum, IV, 11.

[287] Corpus Hermeticum, XI, 21.

[288] Pausanias, VII, 24. 4.

[289] Pausanias, I.17.2.

[290] Pausanias, I.24.3.

[291] Robert G. Bauval, Investigation on the Origins of the Benben stone, Discussions in Egyptology, Volume 14, 1989

[292] Richard Fletcher, The Quest for El Cid.

[293] XII 15, 7.

[294] XVIII 3, 5.

[295] Pliny N.H. 37.2.33.

[296] Euripides: Phaeton, by James Diggle, p. 45-6.

[297] Yuri Stoyanov, The Other God, p. 6.

[298] Yuri Stoyanov, The Other God, p. 7.

[299] Corpus Hermeticum, IV, 5.

[300] Corpus Hermeticum, IV, 6.

[301] Wolfram von Eschenbach, Parzival, 786, 2.

[302] Aragon Crown Archives, Barcelona Collection Martin el Humano, Parchment, 136.

Chronology

Ca. 2300 BC	Appearance of the *Pyramid Texts* on the walls of the ancient Egyptian pyramids
Ca. 1200 BC	Egyptian quest stories about prince Naneferkaptah and Setne Khamwas, the Egyptian Percevals
Ca. 300 BC	The Greek conquest of Egypt and the installation of Ptolemaic Rule in Egypt, resulting in the codification of the ancient Egyptian religion into the *Corpus Hermeticum*
64-67 AD	St Peter dies in Rome as a victim of Neron's persecution against the early Christians.
258	Pope Sixtus II grants the Holy Grail to his deacon, St Lawrence, with the mission to put it in a safe place. Lawrence orders two Spanish soldiers to carry the Grail to his parents' farmhouse on the outskirts of Huesca.
Ca. 350-400	Edict against Gnostic Christianity, resulting in the destruction of e.g. the Library of Alexandria and the hiding of e.g.the Nag Hammadi Texts. The *Corpus Hermeticum* is forced to go underground.
553	The Cathedral of Huesca is built and, allegedly, the Holy Grail is placed inside it.
712	The Moorish invasion of Spain. The Holy Chalice was said to have been moved towards

	the Southern Pyrenees, passing through several chapels, churchs and monasteries.
1071	The Holy Chalice is said to have arrived at San Juan de la Peña
1104-1134	Rule of Alfonso I of Aragon, the Fisher King of the Grail legends
1118-1128	Creation and foundation of the Knights Templar, identified by Wolfram von Eschenbach as the protectors of the Grail
1134	The Holy Chalice is in San Juan de la Peña, according to a document by D. Carreras Ramirez, Canon of Zaragoza, dated 14 December 1134
1190	Chrétien de Troyes writes *Le Conte du Graal*
Ca. 1205-1210	Wolfram von Eschenbach writes *Parzival*
1209	Start of the Albigensian, or Cathar Crusade, with the total destruction and massacring of the city of Béziers occurring on July 22.
1243-4	Siege and destruction of Montségur, the last Cathar stronghold
1307-1312	Arrests and abolition of the Knights Templar
1322	Abulfat Mahomet, sultan of Egypt, claims have acquired from Jerusalem the cup used by Jesus Chist at the Last Supper. Jaime II, king of

Valencia and Aragon, buys the sultan from this chalice and places it in the Alfajeria Palace of Zaragoza.

1399 Martin 'el Humano', King of Aragon forces the Abbot of San Juan de la Peña to hand the Grail over to him

1416 King Alfonso V of Aragon sends the Holy Grail to Valencia. It is placed in the Palacio Real.

1427 King Alfonso receives letter from Yeshaq I of Ethiopia, proposing an alliance between the two nations

1437 Juan, king of Navarre, Alfonso's brother, places the Holy Grail in the Cathedral of Valencia.

1439 Council of Florence, in which Greek scholars reintroduce Hermetic thinking into the Western world.

1450 Ethiopian Emperor Yeshaq's successor Zara Yaqob sent a diplomatic mission to Alfonso V of Aragon, asking for "skilled labour"

1460 Latin translation of the *Corpus Hermeticum* by Marsilio Ficino.

Bibliography

Abdel-Aziz Saleh. Excavations at Heliopolis. Ancient Egyptian Ounu. Cairo: Cairo University, 1981/3.

Achad, Frater. The Chalice of Ecstacy, being a Magical and Qabbalistic Interpretation of the Drama of Parzival. Chicago, 1923.

Aelinus Sparticanus. The Life of Emperor Hadrian.

Albrecht (von Scharfenberg), Jüngerer Titurel.

Alford, Alan F. Pyramid of Secrets: The Architecture of the Great Pyramid Reconsidered in the Light of Creational Mythology. Walsall: Eridu Books, 2003.

Alford, Alan. The Phoenix Solution. Secrets of a Lost Civilisation. London: Hodder & Stoughton, 1998.

Alford, Alan. When the Gods came down. The Catastrophic Roots of Religion Revealed. London: Hodder & Stoughton, 2000.

Alford, Alan. The Midnight Sun. The death and rebirth of god in Ancient Egypt. Walsall: Eridu Books, 2004.

Allen, Richard Hinckley. Star-Names and their Meanings. London: G.E. Stechert, 1899.

Baigent, Michael, Leigh, Richard and Lincoln, Henry. The Holy Blood and the Holy Grail. London, 1982.

Barber, Malcolm. The New Knighthood: A History of the Order of the Temple. Cambridge/New York, 1994.

Barber, Richard. The Holy Grail. The History of a Legend. London: Penguin Books, 2004.

Bauval, Robert. Secret Chamber. The Quest for the Hall of Records. London: Century Books, 1999.

Bauval, Robert & Adrian Gilbert. The Orion Mystery. Unlocking the Secrets of the Pyramids. London: William Heinemann, 1994.

Beigg, Ean and Beigg, Deike. In Search of the Holy Grail and the Precious Blood – A travellers' Guide. London, 1995.

Bernadac, Christian. Le mystère Otto Rahn (Le Graal et Montsegur). Paris, 1978.

Birks, Walter and Gilbert, R.A. The Treasure of Montsegur. Wellingborough, 1987.

Bourre, Jean-Paul. La quête du Graal: du paganisme indo-européen à la chevalerie chrétienne. Paris, 1993.

Bouyer, Louis. Les liens magiques de la legende du Graal. Paris, 1986.

Budge, E.A. Wallis. From Fetish to God in Ancient Egypt. New York: Dover Publications, 1989.

Budge, E.A. Wallis. The Egyptian Heaven and Hell. Chicago: Open Court, 1925.

Budge, E.A. Wallis. Introduction to the Book of the Dead. New York: Dover Books.

Budge, E.A. Wallis. Osiris and the Egyptian Resurrection. New York: Dover Books, 1973.

Budge, E.A. Wallis. The Gods of the Egyptians, or Studies in Egyptian Mythology. London: Methuen and Co., 1904.

Campbell, Joseph. The Masks of Go: Creative Mythology. London, 1968.

Cavendish, Richard. King Arthur and the Grail. London, 1978.

Cazelles, Brigitte. The Unholy Grail: A Socisl Reading of Chrétien de Troyes' Conte du Graal. Stanford, 1966.

Chrétien de Troyes. Le Roman de Perceval ou le Conte du Graal.

Churton, Tobias. The Golden Builders. Alchemists, Rosicrucians and the first Free Masons. Lichfield, Signal Publishing: 2002.

Clark, R.T. Rundle. Myth and Symbol in Ancient Egypt. London: Thames & Hudson, 1959.

Clarke, Lindsay. Parzival and the Stone from Heaven. London, 2001.

Collins, Andrew. Gods of Eden. Egypt's Lost Legacy and the Genesis of Civilisation. London: Headline, 1998.

D'Arcy, Anne Marie. Wisdom and the Grail: The Image of the Vessel in the Queste del Saint Graal and Malory's Tale of the Sankgreall. Dublin, 2000.

Darlison, Bill. The Gospel and the Zodiac. The Secret Truth about Jesus. London: Duckworth Overlook, 2007.

Delcourt-Angélique, Janine. "Lapsit exillis": le nom du Graal chez Wolfram von Eschenbach (Parzival 4697). Marche romane, 27: 2-4 (1977), p. 55-126.

Devereux, Paul. Symbolic Landscapes. The Dreamtime Earth and Avebury's Open Secrets. Glastonbury: Gothic Image, 1992.

Duval, Paulette. La pensée alchimique et le Conte du Graal. Paris, 1979.

Eco, Umberto. Foucault's Pendulum. London, 1989.

Eco, Umberto. Baudolino. London, 2002.

Edwards, I.E.S. The Pyramids of Egypt (revised edition). London: Penguin Books, 1980.

Eliade, Mircea. A History of Religious Ideas Volume 3: From Muhammad to the Age of Reforms. Trans. Alf Hiltebeitel and Diane Apostolos-Cappadona. Chicago: The University of Chicago Press, 1985.

Ernst, Ulrich. "Kyot und Flegetanis in Wolframs Parzival." Fiktionaler Fundbericht und judisch-arabischer Kulturhintergrund. Wirkendes Wort, 35 (1985), p. 176-195.

Fanthorpe, Patricia and Fanthorpe, Lionel. The Holy Grail Revealed; The Real Secret of Rennes-le-Château. North Hollywood, 1982.

Faugère, Annie. Les origins orientales du Graal chez Wolfram von Eschenbach. Göppinger Arbeiten zur Germanistik 264. Göppingen, 1979.

Fideler, David R. The Path Toward the Grail: The Hermetic Sources of Wolfram von Eschenbach's Parzival. In: Alexandria (1991). Grand Rapids, MI: Phanes Press, 1991, p. 187-227.

Fourquet, Jean. Wolfram von Eschenbach et le Conte du Graal. Paris, 1966.

Frankfort, Henri. Archaeology and the Sumerian problem.

Frankfort, Henri. The Birth of Civilisation in the Near East. Ernest Benn.

Frappier, Jean. Chrétien de Troyes et le mythe du Graal. Paris, 1972.

Fraser, P.M. Ptolemaic Alexandria: Text, Notes, Indexes. 1972. Clarendon Press, Reissue edition, 1985.

Gallais, Pierre. Perceval et l'Initiation. Paris, 1972.

Gibson, Shimon. The Cave of John the Baptist. The first archaeological evidence of the historical reality of the Gospel story. London: Century Books, 2004.

Glencross, Michael. Reconstructing Camelot: French Romantic Medievalism and thre Arthurian Tradition. Cambridge/Rochester, 1995.

Godwin, Malcolm. The Holy Grail: its origins, secrets and meaning revealed. London, 1994.

Goering, Joseph. The Virgin and the Grail: Origins of a Legend. New Haven: Yale University Press, 2005.

Goetinck, Glenys. Peredur: A Study of Welsh Tradition in the Grail Legends. Cardiff, 1975.

Grierson, Roderick & Stuart Munro-Hay. The Ark of the Covenant. London: Phoenix, 1999.

Groos, Arthur. Romancing the Grail: Genre, Science and Quest in Wolfram's Parzival. Ithaca/London, 1995.

Grueb, Werner. Wolfram von Eschenbach und die Wirklichkeit des Grals. Dornach, 1974.

Hancock, Graham. The Sign and the Seal. The Quest for the Lost Ark of the Covenant. New York: Crown Publishers Inc, 1992.

Hein, Christoph. Die Ritter des Tafelrunde. Frankfurt, 1989.

Hesemann, Michael. Die entdeckung des heiligen Grals. Munich:

Pattloch, 2003.
Hornung, Erik. The Secret Lore of Egypt. Its Impact on the West. Ithaca & London: Cornell University Press, 2001.
Hüe, Denis. Polyphonie du Graal. Orleans, 1998.
Hunter, Jim. Perceval or the Presence of God. London/Boston, 1978.
Hutchison, Robert. Their Kingdom Come. Inside the Secret World of Opus Dei. London: Doubleday, 1997.

Jablonski, P.E. Pantheon Aegyptiorum. 1752.
James, Peter and Nick Thorpe. Ancient Mysteries. New York: Ballantine Books, 1999.
Jubber, Nicholas. The Prester Quest. London: Bantam Books, 2005.
Jung, Emma and Franx, Marie-Louise von. The Grail Legend. London, 1988.

Kahane, Henry & Renée. The Krater and the Grail: Hermetic Sources of the Parzival. Urbana: University of Illinois Press, 1965.
Kennedy, Elspeth. Lancelot and the Grail. Oxford, 1986.
Kienzle, Beverly. Cistercians, Heresy and Crusade. Woodbridge/Rochester, 2001.
Kolb, Karl. Vom Heiligen Blut. Würzberg, 1980.

Lacy, Norris J. (ed.) The New Arthurian Encyclopedia. Chicago/London, 1991.
Lacy, Norris J., Kelly, Douglas, and Busby, Keith (eds.). The Legacy of Chrétien de Troyes. Amsterdam, 1988.
Lawton, Ian & Chris Ogilvie-Herald. Gizeh: The Truth. The People, Politics & history behind the world's most famous archaeological site. London: Virgin books, 1999.
Le Goff, Jacques. The Medieval Imagination. Chicago/London, 1988.
Lehner, Mark. The Complete Pyramids. London: Thames &

Hudson, 1997.
Loomis, Roger Sherman. Arthurian Tradition & Chrétien de Troyes. New York: Columbia University Press, 1961.
Lutz, Henry L.F. Canopus, The City of "the chest of heaven".

Mahoney, Dhira B. The Grail: A Casebook. New York/London, 2000.
Mancoff, Debra. King Arthur's Modern Return. New York, 1998.
Mandach, André de. Le 'Roman du Graal' originaire: Sur les traces du modèle commun. Göppinger Arbeiten zur Germanistik 581. Göppingen, 1992.
Mandach, André de. Auf den Spuren des heiligen Gral. Göppinger Arbeiten zur Germanistik 596. Göppingen, 1995.
Markale, Jean. Le Graal. Paris, 1982.
Marlowe, John. The Golden Age of Alexandria. London: Trinity Press, 1971.
Matthews, John. The Grail: Quest for the Eternal. London/New York, 1981.
Matthews, John. At the Table of the Grail. London, 1987.
Matthews, John. King Arthur and the Grail Quest. London, 1995.
Matthews, John. Sources of the Grail. Edinburgh, 1996.
Munro-Hay, Stuart. The Quest for the Ark of the Covenant. The True History of the Tablets of Moses. London – New York: I.B. Taurus, 2005.
Muschg, Adolf. Der Rote Ritter: eine Geschichte von Parzival. Frankfurt, 1993.

Nelli, René (ed.). Lumière du Graal. Paris, 1951.
Neugebauer, Otto & Richard A. Parker. Egyptian Astronomical Texts I: The Early Decans. Brown University Press, 1960.

Parker, Richard A.. The Calendars of Ancient Egypt. 1950
Partner, Peter. The Murdered Magicians: The Templars and their Myth. Oxford/New York, 1982.

Phillips, Graham. The Search for the Grail. London, 1996.

Picknett, Lynn & Clive Prince. The Templar Revelation. Secret Guardians of the true identity of Christ. London: Bantam Press, 1997.

Picknett, Lynn & Clive Prince. The Stargate Conspiracy. Revealing the truth behind extraterrestrial contact, military intelligence and the mysteries of ancient Egypt. London: Little, Brown & Co, 1999.

Plutarch, The History of Isis and Osiris.

Poe, Richard. Black Spark, White Fire. Did African Explorers Civilize Ancient Europe? Rocklin: Prime Publishing, 1997.

Powell, Anthony. The Fisher King. London, 1986.

Pritchard J.B., ed.. 'ANET' ('Ancient Near Eastern Texts Relating to the Old Testament'). Princeton University Press, 3rd edition, 1969.

Rice, Michael. Egypt's Making. The Origins of Ancient Egypt 5000-2000 BC. London: Routledge, 1990.

Rivière, Patrick.Le Graal: histoire et symbols. Monaco, 1990.

Roquebert, Michel. Les Cathares et le Graal. Toulouse, 1994.

Sansonetti, Paul Georges. Graal et alchimie. Paris, 1982.

Sellers, Jane. The Death of the Gods in Ancient Egypt. An Essay on Egyptian Religion and the Frame of Time. London: Penguin, 1992.

Sinclair, Andrew. The Discovery of the Grail. London, 1998.

Sinclair, Andrew. The Sword and the Grail. London, 1993.

Sitchin, Zecharia. The 12th Planet. New York: Avon Books, 1976.

Slavenburg, Jacob. De Hermetische Schakel. Ankh-Hermes, 2003

Stambaugh, John E. Sarapis under the Early Ptolemies. 1972.

Stoyanov, Yuri. The Other God. Dualist Religions from Antiquity to The Cathar Heresy. New Haven/London: Yale University Press, 2000.

Strabo. The Geography of Strabo.

Stricker, Bruno. Het Corpus Hermeticum: Index op gecommentarieerde passages. Leiden: 1993.

Stricker, Bruno. De Brief van Aristas. Leiden: Leiden University, 1956.

Thompson, Kathleen. Power and Border lordship in medieval France. The county of the Perche, 1000-1226. Woodbridge/Rochester: The Royal Historical Society/The Boydell Press, 2002.

Vansittart, Peter. Parsifal. London, 1988.

Van Urk, Klaas. Zoektocht naar de Heilige Graal & de Ark. Mysterie van Rennes-le-Chateau ontrafeld. Amsterdam, 2004.

von Dechend, Hertha & Giorgio de Santillana. Hamlet's Mill. An Essay investigating the origins of human knowledge and its transmission through myth. Boston: Nonpareil, 1969.

Weston, Jessie L. From Ritual to Romance. Boston: IndyPublish.com, re-edition from 1920 original.

Williams, Andrea M.L. The Adventures of the Holy Grail: A Study of La Queste del Saint Grala. Bern, 2001.

Wolfram von Eschenbach. Parzival.

Yates, Frances A. Giardano Bruno and the Hermetic tradition. Chicago & London: The University of Chicago Press, 1964.

Zitman, Wim. Sterrenbeeld van Horus. Uniek kleitablet brengt bakermat van voorouders van de Egyptische beschaving in kaart. Baarn: Tirion, 2000.

BOOKS

O is a symbol of the world, of oneness and unity. In different cultures it also means the "eye", symbolizing knowledge and insight. We aim to publish books that are accessible, constructive and that challenge accepted opinion, both that of academia and the "moral majority".

Our books are available in all good English language bookstores worldwide. If you don't see the book on the shelves ask the bookstore to order it for you, quoting the ISBN number and title. Alternatively you can order online (all major online retail sites carry our titles) or contact the distributor in the relevant country, listed on the copyright page.

See our website **www.o-books.net** for a full list of over 400 titles, growing by 100 a year.

And tune in to myspiritradio.com for our book review radio show, hosted by June-Elleni Laine, where you can listen to the authors discussing their books.

9781846941559